LOVE IS THE KEY...
BETWEEN KNOWLEDGE AND DEVOTION...

Patrice Morchain

Manu Tahi Ori

LOVE IS THE KEY...

BETWEEN KNOWLEDGE AND DEVOTION...

An Autobiography

Translated from French by Patrice Morchain
And Edited and reread by Lee Pascoe
Director of The Silva Method in France

All rights of translation, reproduction
and adaptation reserved for all countries.
© Patrice MORCHAIN

ISBN :2951716877
Publisher : HELYOGOS
Date of publication : 18 août 2014

Notice

This book recounts the experiences and the personal path of the author.

The author and the editor can in no way be held responsible for the results of any self-treatment due do a misunderstanding of the contents of this book..

French law accords only medical doctors the right to diagnose and treat diseases. The elements contained in this book respect medical treatment and therefore, are meant to be a complement to any medical treatment in process.

SUMMARY

THANKS		11
NEW EDITION		13
FOREWORD		15
Ouverture...		20
CHAPTER 1	In the beginning...	23
CHAPTER 2	Transformation starts	31
CHAPTER 3	Nick...	35
CHAPTER 4	Vicky...	43
CHAPTER 5	From discovery to discovery...	49
CHAPTER 6	Group of Chakras...	59
CHAPTER 7	Memories come back...	63
CHAPTER 8	Martin...	73
CHAPTER 9	It works...	77
CHAPTER 10	And if I changed now…	83
CHAPTER 11	DO WHAT YOU FEEL LIKE DOING...	91
CHAPTER 12	An instructive journey...	97
CHAPTER 13	Welcome to the Club !	109
CHAPTER 14	What is AIDS ?	115
CHAPTER 15	En route to Healing...	133
CHAPTER 16	Accept the unacceptable...	143
CHAPTER 17	And now, what will I do ?...	149
CHAPTER 18	Around the world...	159
CHAPTER 19	I eat, therefore I am...	167
CHAPTER 20	Travels, Travels...	181
CHAPTER 21	A wonderful gift...	187
CHAPTER 22	Hervé...	199
CHAPTER 23	A new consciousness...	207
CHAPTER 24	The Levels of Consciousness...	217
CHAPTER 25	Amma...	241
CHAPTER 26	Acceleration...	261
CHAPTER 27	Something MUST change...	275
CHAPTER 28	The Dream...	289
CHAPTER 29	First trip to Saï Baba...	293
CHAPTER 30	Integration et Assimilation...	319
CHAPTER 31	An American Dream...	329
CHAPTER 32	My second stay with *Swami*...	345
CHAPTER 33	A new Departure...	351
FINAL		379
Love is the key...		379
And Since...		387

Love is the Key...

To Nick and to Vicky...

Love is the Key...

THANKS

I want to thank all those without whom I could not have lived all of the wonderful experiences I have been through and without whom this book would not have existed.

In particular, I thank my parents for having provided me with both my physical body vehicle and my first belief systems.

Thank-you to Jean-Marc for the years of therapy...

Thank-you to Vicky Wall, to Martin Brofman, to Lee Pascoe et Michael Dodson for the precious tools they provided me.

Thank-you to Louise Hay, to Eileen Caddy, to Richard Bach, to Neal Donald Walsch, Marianne Williamson, Deepack Chopra, Wayne Dyer for their wonderful books which were a marvellous source of inspiration...

Thank-you to Etienne Daho for such lovely words...

Thank-you to Alain, Nick, Myriam, Chris , Hervé, Patrick and Michel for the lessons learned together and that they still bring me.

Thank-you to Pierre, Claude Annie and Marc for everything you bring or teach me.

Thank-you to all my friends which I cannot cite here who participated in the creation of what I am now.

Thank-you to Annie, Evelyne, Eldon and Nathalie, for giving me confidence and pushing me into writing !

Thank-you to Agnès, Alain and Martine for providing the appropriate environment for writing this book...

Thank-you to Louise for her suggestions in the rereading of this book and to Anne for her refining of the corrections.

Thank-you to Michel for the different covers that he created for my books and different products.

Thank you to Marita, Danielle and to Chad for the inspiration source they represent.

Thank-you to Gina who helped me so much in the setting up of my company and in the naming of my books.

Thank-you to Lise for inviting me to Quebec.

Thank-you to Vania for helping with the lay out of this reediting.

Thank-you for all those who opened their doors to me in the last few years where I was without a fixed home...

Thank-you to all of you who followed my workshops for your discreet but undeniable help because as I was claiming to "teach" them something, I was actually constantly reminding myself of those things ...

THANK-YOU, whom I do not yet know, for giving me the desire to share my experiences, which I believe will be useful to you....

Thank-you to Amma and to Saï Baba for being like lighthouses illuminating the way, Living Manifestations of God's Love...

And THANK YOU, THANK YOU, THANK YOU to Life, to Love, and to this wonderful benevolent strength that some people call God, without whom I would not exist...

NEW EDITION

I think it is important that know that this book is a reediting of my first book « *A Path to God, between Knowledge and Devotion...* » that I wrote in 1998. This time it has the title that already appeared in the final chapter of the previous book. This chapter was called « Love is the Key »

You will soon understand that I do not believe in things happening « by chance » nor in « coincidences » in this perfect Universe, beyond my own perceptions at times...

In its « original » version, this book, (and here, « chance » brought things about perfectly, had a print-run of 1008 copies and you will see later, this number is highly symbolic for me !

In fact, this book, which at first was only a manuscript, was for purely material reasons, to be published in only 300 copies.

Nevertheless, as I did not have at that time, the necessary financing to produce it, I proposed to publish it in the form of a « subscription before printing » to my students.

It so happens that 80 of them wanted to purchase it before its publication !

My printer at the time then offered me another type of printing, more economical, and proposed to publish my book not in 300 copies, but 1000.

I therefore accepted his cheaper proposal. He then informed me that, as the machines functioned very quickly, he could not be sure to stop at exactly 1000 copies and offered to throw in the extra copies for free.

He afterwards told me that there were not 1007 nor 1009 copies but « 1008 copies » of this book, which for me was highly significant and symbolic. You will understand this too on reading this book.

In this reediting, I have added just a few pages to the « original » version to explain why I often use the past tense.

In fact, a book, famous since the dawn of time, starts with these words : « *In the beginning was the Word... and the Word was with God...and the Word was God* ».

Words are therefore for me extremely creative and we should thus « watch » and be « aware » of their power and their creative potential.

This is why I often talk of my experiences in the past.

I recall a very beautiful play on words : « Do you know why Angels Fly ? » and the magnificent answer is « Because they take things « Lightly ».

And « Light » is indeed « Light ».

Therefore, people who meet me can sometimes have a first impression that I take things « lightly and with a lot of humour »; which is for me **EXTREMELY** important if someone wishes to get rid of a pathology he no longer wants.

I therefore take them « lightly »…

I feel it is important that I express myself about this subject in future books.

I have also added some lines at the end to inform you on how I have evolved since, as some readers were curious to know more…

FOREWORD

Writing has never seemed easy to me but it is now important that I should tell you about myself... For you and for me...

A wonderful process is unfolding nowadays and I think that we all go through our lives for a reason which is both personal and collective ...

All the experiences that life presents us are opportunities which allow us to discover ourselves. They therefore have a great teaching value for ourselves and also for those around us. That is why I think it would be selfish of me to keep all these to myself as I deeply believe that they could be useful...

It so happens that life « presented » me with something I can now call a gift, even though at the time it seemed poisoned to me, in every sense of the word !

I received a great shock when, more than twelve years ago, I learned I had been HIV positive since the age of 19... Nevertheless, the wonderful transformations this triggered in me allow me to consider this in a totally different way and to know that it was actually perfect to me to go through this experience...

The personal choice that I made from the beginning, to take no medication, but instead to search for answers within, seems, after more than 20 years without medication, to have been beneficial...

But mostly, beyond the fact I now feel great, the wonderful experiences I was able to have and will continue to have because of this disruption seem now to be actually the <u>only reason</u> for which I had to go through being HIV positive. I am now filled with gratitude to God, whose reality appears to me more and more, for all the gifts He has given me, is giving to me, will give me.

I know that the word God, can sometimes be misunderstood and even seem shocking to some of you, because of associations and/or experiences you have had with this word, this concept. So, if this word shocks you, feel at ease to replace it by an other each time I use it.

It would be a shame to pass by experiences that could really revolutionize your life simply because of a three-letter word.

Don't we say the God is Love? Therefore, if this seems true to you, each time I use the word God, understand Love instead.

But may be, the word Life, or Universe, seem more appropriate to you. Know that in the end, this does not matter very much.

For me, the only word that it seems right to use is the word God even though I can understand it might be different for you. Every word being by nature limitative, it seems to me that "God" is the only word that can conceptualize the consciousness I am now in relation with.

Besides, if God is omnipresent, it is obvious that he is also in the deepest part of me, which means the essence of life animating me. Therefore, each time I use this word, know that I am referring to that part of me.

Finally, anyway, it does not <u>really</u> matter.

I hope my experience can inspire you too, being HIV positive or not, to help you transform your life, and why not, to become always closer to Him, to that consciousness, which is, I believe, the source, the cause and the solution of Everything.

I know that the knowledge or that the understanding of our nature can greatly help us to heal a pathology or a situation. I now know, through my own experiences, that the reality of God, of our Divine nature and of our confident surrender to this energy can accomplish the very same effects….

I can only tell you, that for me, (and may be for you, too), that the fact of having a new rational understanding of spiritual truths or of the functioning of my own consciousness helped me to built a bridge between the situation I was living and the one I wanted to live instead, between my reality and His.

Nevertheless, don't forget there are many bridges and do not be attached to any one of them.

I would like now to share with you my experience on a particular bridge which is situated somewhere between knowledge and devotion…

Go through this book as a testimony, but beyond the words, draw from it the strength that is necessary for transformation.

I know that is not by chance that you now have this testimony in your hands. Each moment, each experience we go through holds a gift of God.

May you, beyond the outer packaging, recognize the Sender of this gift and feel His Divine presence.

I pray Him now (although at the same time, I know it is not really necessary) , to fill you to overflowing with his grace, as He has always done, as He is doing right now, and will always do.

Having for more than ten years taught techniques for improvement of eyesight and vision, I could put this in a more precise way : May be it would be more appropriate to wish simply that He <u>open your eyes</u> so that you may see the real perfection in each of your experiences.

This is what I will try to share with you and to explain to you throughout this book.

But, may be for you, God does not exist, or he seems inaccessible to you, or the only thing that you believe in is simply yourself (which is a <u>very good thing</u>, by the way). In that case, you could now consciously choose to look in a new way …to see in a new way.

In fact, everything is already present, complete and perfect, here and now, waiting only for that little "click" in us to manifest in all its splendor

Did not Jesus tell us that we all have eyes to see [1] ?

Have we really used them ?

I know that a different way of looking can change many things and I hope to give you the desire to develop for yourself, this new way of looking that will allow you to see anew.

This consciousness we call God has always been beside us. Only we did not see it. So, open your eyes…

Wake up and open your eyes. You new way of looking will transform you.

I will simply share with you some of parts of my life, moments, realizations, and emotions which have led me to the wonderful realization that God exists, that He loves me, and that He is the Cause and Answer to Everything.

And even though I need to remind myself of it, I **KNOW** that beyond my perception of appearances, All is well.

All is well.

All is well.

All is well.

---

[1] « ... Having eyes, see ye not? and having ears, hear ye not? ». Marc 8:18

Important Reminder : *As I share with you some major experiences of my life, you should understand that, sometimes, several events or circumstances were happening simultaneously or were overlapping at any given moment or over several years. However, to make the story more precise, more structured or more clear, I chose to treat these experiences or realizations, separately, attempting to regroup them in one chapter whenever possible.*

Ouverture...

Il n'est pas de hasard
Il est des rendez-vous,
Pas de coïncidences...
Aller vers son Destin,
L'Amour au creux des mains,
La démarche paisible...
Porter au fond de Soi,
L'Intuition qui flamboie,
L'Aventure belle et pure...
Celle qui nous révèle
Superbes et Enfantins
Au plus profond de l'Âme...

Etienne Daho
Album « Corps et Armes »

Love is the Key...

Ouverture...

Nothing happens by chance,
There are rendez-vous,
not coïncidences...
Go to meet your Destiny
With Love held in your hands
Walking peacefully...
Carrying deep within,
Burning intuition
Adventure, pure and beautiful...
Which reveals to us
Superb and Childlike
the very depths of the Soul...

Etienne Daho
Album « Corps et Armes »

CHAPTER 1
In the beginning...

I was born October 9th, 1962, in the north of France.

And for those of you who like to define and label people, I was born Libra with Virgo rising.

Nothing in my childhood predisposed me, *a priori*, to live the experiences I am living now. I had a protected childhood, perhaps too protected, although I can now understand how it had to be that way.

When I was barely 3 years old, it seems that I was telling my mother:

-« When I grow up, I am going to be a cook. »

I had a so-called normal education until I was 14, when I started studying in the Catering school in Le Touquet.

I probably would have liked to go through an 'apprenticeship' but my parents encouraged me to sit for the exam to enter the catering school. They thought, and rightly so, that a training in catering would be an advantage in the job market.

Despite my natural apprehensions about exams, I passed the aptitude tests to start my diploma in cooking.. I was very happy to do this training. even if the rigour and the discipline of this establishment were sometimes difficult to bear.

In hindsight, I can nevertheless recognize that this relatively strict training was totally appropriate and necessary to create good professionals.

My happiness was sadly short-lived, as I soon became the scape-goat of certain students who took pleasure in degrading and humiliating me. I was an easy prey for these youngsters in need of recognition affirming their « superiority ». I felt very uncomfortable with myself, being much taller than other youngsters my age. I measured 6 feet 5 inches at only 14 years old and it was very difficult to live it.

Although the study itself was fascinating, the atmosphere in the boarding school was driving me into a chronic depression.

I didn't want to live anymore. The desire to die was stronger and stronger until one night, sitting on the ledge of the 10th floor window, I told myself there must be another solution, ..but I did not know what..

More over, I was very aware that this pseudo-attempt at « suicide » was actually only a call for help.

I was at the time barely 15 or 16 years old. This was also the time when I noticed a problem with my eyesight. I was becoming near-sighted. I can now understand why and we will be able to cover that subject later.

After about two years of hell in the boarding school, I passed the exam to be admitted into the advanced class.. Good news for me because I could now live outside the school and … at last … have some peace…

The situation was a little bit easier to me but I still felt lonely. Very lonely. So lonely that when I was barely 18, I remember clearly deciding to die once again..

This time, this decision was not followed by a physical act but it was nevertheless so deep that it totally shook my life. I can still see myself walking in the street, between the Le Touquet Casino and the catering school. I was feeling unhappy, abandoned, alone.

I looked around me, telling myself in a very intense, very deep way :

-« If life is like this, I **DO NOT WANT** to live more than 28 or 30 of age…. ».

I did not know it then, but I was programming the time bomb that was going to permit me to leave this world.

Nevertheless, everything was not completely black in my life. The universe is so made there are always two sides to the coin. I had a compensation, and not a small one... : Work.

I took great pleasure in getting even with my oppressors by getting way better grades that those who where humiliating me !

The Great Being <u>really</u> did a good job thinking out the Universe, always giving us some compensation in our apparent misery. It was only much later that I would see that clearly.

As the years passed by, my feeling of loneliness kept growing. My class-mates talked about their girlfriends but as for me, I remained alone.

Well, I had a small flirtation with a girlfriend, but I already felt at that stage that I was more attracted to boys. And that frightened me. Of course, like many boys I guess, I had been raised with all those unhealthy prejudices about the « disease » of homosexuality. And all that only aggravated my unhappiness..

I was torn between my desire to live a relationship with a boy and my fear of being myself "infected" by this " disease" or defect..

I was so shy and feeling so bad within that I had to wait until I was almost 18 before I had my first sexual experience and dared taking the step.

One has to take the leap one day, and after all, better late than never.

God helps those who help themselves... I told myself. I took the opportunity of a class trip to a Paris exhibition to discreetly slip away to go to a gay theatre of the capital.

I was entering into the lion's den...

You can well imagine that a « youngster » of 18, even though he is almost 7 feet tall, would arouse some interest in such a place.

I was picked up by the theatre cashier and what was meant to happen happened..., I had my first sexual experience.

Actually, it was sordid. Of course, I realise now with some hindsight that at that time, I could not attract any other quality of experience.

I had such a bad image of myself, such shame for feeling what I felt, that I could not attract a genuine warm relationship.

At the time, I had no idea, and certainly no experience, of the fact that we each are co-creators of what happens to us. It was only years later that I would have first the knowledge, then the experience. But we will be able to talk about that later...

And to crown it all and make my life more easy, (as if Life was out to get me !) this was the time when AIDS, better known in those years as «Gay Cancer » or as « the Homosexual Plague » was first appearing on the scene.

I remember the day when I learned, through a newspaper, of the death of the singer Klaus NOMI.

This news was a huge shock. I told myself :

-« With the luck you have, you can be sure that this disease is for you ! ».

This is how I again programmed the time bomb that could have killed me, if I had not, later, taken an other decision.

And the image of this disease haunted me. On the one hand, I was afraid of it and on the other, I knew that « it was meant for me »...

Years passed by during which I obtained my diplomas (BTH, and CAP) and 2 years later, having been admitted to the advanced class, my BTS diploma..

When I left the Catering School at the age of 21, I chose to work some months in London in a well known French restaurant.

I did not have a post at the same level as my training, but on the other hand, I discovered liberty and independence ! Hooray for London and the Good Life! By « chance », I no longer felt the need to wear glasses, since I left catering school. I know now why this was so ...

After four pleasant months spent enjoying the pleasures of London Life, finally being able in this tolerant city to live as a homosexual in the light of day, I decided to accept to work as a seasonal waiter/chef in Bavaria.

To say that the difference between London and Bavaria was a shock would be a euphemism.

As much as my stay in London was enjoyable, my stay in Bavaria was dreadful.

I have to say that the openness and tolerance of Londoners was very different from the hyper-conservative attitude of the Bavarians !

Gone were the Night Clubs, the Musicals, the easy life. I was often very depressed….

I would seek refuge in work and sporting activity, Ice Skating despite my relative bad luck, I had the good luck to be based in Oberstdorf, a charming Bavarian village which has very fine skating equipment. This was also the place where numerous international artistic and dance champions were training. I received there my first basics of Skating which allowed me some time later the great pleasure of practising dancing on ice..

When the season was over, I had a choice. Either go back to London to what was a very pleasant job but way beneath my abilities, or find a job that was more worthy of the level of my training..

Reason finally won out over the easy way, and I applied for a job in an important catering society where I had worked as an apprentice when I was finishing my BTS. diploma.

I manage to get an interview some days later and I was immediately hired as head chef of a restaurant for businessmen. Despite my first qualms about being in charge, I realised I liked this job very much…

I was head of a small unit serving about 120 meals a day and I had a team of 2 people.

At the time, I was both cooking and managing the establishment, moving from the stove to the office.

After about a year there, I was put in charge of the opening a small unit serving only about 70 meals a day.

It was at this time that I met Alain, with whom I finally moved in. It was the first time I had lived as a couple and I must say, the experience was very pleasant.. I was to realize, years later, that I had actually thrown myself into that relation to end a state of solitude that was so painful to me. He liked me and his company was pleasant. On top of that, he had probably also been experiencing a sense of solitude and this is how we got together. Nevertheless, a kind of routine quickly took over and I had to leave him after about one year.

After some months in the establishment where I was in charge, I was promoted as a Manager in a restaurant in rue de Sèvres, in the 6th arrondissement of Paris. This establishment was serving about 350 meals a day.

This time, it was goodbye to the stove. I was now properly Manager and the work became seriously interesting. I realized concretely how important a leader's dynamism can be in the development of a company.

Being of dynamic nature, I regularly organized special meals and events which would considerably increase the popularity of this establishment. Thus in a few years, the restaurant's number of clients went from 350 to almost 700 meals a day.

My experience showed that actually, relationships are the key to everything.; both for resolving in-house problems and with the clients. A smile, a small attention cost nothing but make people happy. Consequently, feeling happy and acknowledged, they enjoy coming to your establishment, which thus becomes more prosperous

Nevertheless, despite a pleasant job, my personal state was not optimal.

I always had the feeling something was not going the way it should. I was often very depressed, feeling ill at ease with myself.

I had to do something, but what ?

CHAPTER 2
Transformation starts

I was determined to feel better. I had the impression that all around me were people feeling good, but I somehow felt bad. What's more, though in London I did not have to wear my eyeglasses, I had to start wearing them again at work, from time to time... .Something deep within was telling me I had to feel better, that I had do something for me... this state of dis-ease could not last anymore.

For some time I searched unsuccessfully for a " traditional " psychotherapist who could help me. Yet it was at my work place that the Great Being finally served me up, on a platter, the means for getting out of my state and leading me to the path of healing, for myself and then others.

My first steps to the new life that was to lead me to teaching healing techniques and transformation actually started in my 24th year.

Acting lessons were being given at my work-place. In an attempt to improve my situation, I decided to enrol, feeling that this activity could be useful to help me develop a better self-image. During the lessons, we would practise regularly, before each session, a period of relaxation called « on the chair ». The principle consisted of sitting on a chair and slowly moving each part of the body.

I was very surprised to feel quite often, during these periods of practice, very strong and unpleasant spells of nausea. Our teacher would encourage us to then breathe out deeply and even to make sounds, or to cry out.

I can tell you that the character of these practices, was often very noisy.

Certain sessions were very intense and several times, during these experiences, I saw flashes from my past, disturbing images, often accompanied by powerful emotional releases.

One minute, everything was fine and the next, without knowing why, I would find myself in floods of tears.

I did not understand was happening to me. I just knew that it was happening to me. My instructor explained one day that the relaxation was allowing emotions and deeply hidden memories to come back up to the surface. Nevertheless, my experiences were sometimes so powerful that he proposed I see a therapist who could help me get rid of these burdens that were preventing me from experiencing fully all the happiness of this life.

He informed me that this therapist worked with a method of deep tissue massage and that it could be at times very physically painful, but according to him, very efficient.

At any rate, I was feeling so bad that I was ready to do anything to get over it.

And I realize now that it was what was needed to set off the beginning of my new life. I was about to be reborn, little by little.

I made an appointment with this therapist who, "by chance" had a waiting list of more than 3 months and could only see me on October 8th, the eve of my 24th birthday.

My birthday present was made to measure!!! And I have absolutely no regrets about the decision I made at that time. Actually, this therapist offered me a contract that I decided to accept as the best thing for me.

He said that sometimes he would have to cause me pain, even great pain, pushing deeply on certain areas of my body, but that if I wanted to work with him, I had to accept the contract and trust him.

He then explained that he was using certain *Reichien*[1] techniques and *Postural Integration*[2] which required powerful. deep massage of the muscles and body tissues.

He reassured me by telling me I could shout as loud as I wanted as his room was very well sound-proofed!!!

Nice program !

I accepted this « contract » with some misgivings.

The first session was memorable. Just imagine...

I lay down on the massage table after taking my clothes off, keeping on only my underpants.. Placing his hands for a few moments on my belly and chest, Jean Marc started to massage my belly, quite deeply, going under the ribs level with the solar plexus. Very quickly, I felt violently nauseous. But that did not make him stop!

On the contrary ! He had found my weakness and he was not going to let up !

He continued by working on my chest, applying himself conscientiously to pushing very strongly on my ribs as he traced around their shape..

The pain was extreme and I shouted with all my might as he impassively continued his work like a master torturer.

After what seemed an unending time, he deigned to stop this torment.

He then placed his hands on my forehead and in the centre of my chest and I had an astonishing experience. I really had the feeling I was being emptied through my head. Literally. Like a bathtub filled with troubled waters, I literally felt I was

---

[1] Techniques of work set by Wilhelm Reich on the muscles « cuirasses » by an in depth massage of the tissues.

[2] This technique set by Jack W. Painter is a deep massage on the *Fascias*. The *Fascias* represent the deep membranes surrounding all the muscles and organs of the body. A deep massage of the *Fascia* allows to free certain physical and chemical memories incrusted in the body.

emptying while at the same time a strange sense of "full emptiness " was filling me up. from it

I left him that evening floating on a cloud.

Nevertheless, once I was home, I noticed that I had bruises all over my chest. They lasted for about a fortnight!

But I was pleasantly surprised to discover that my bad habit of chewing my nails had stopped instantly, from one day to the next, even though I had suffered from it for many years.

I was obviously very happy and the painful memories of the session finally faded away, to give place to an increasing feeling of well being.

As the sessions went by, I started to notice changes, subtle at first but eventually more and more noticeable.

First, I noticed an increased sensitivity.

I just had to look at a romantic movie, listen to a word, have a thought, to start crying, without knowing why. It was only afterwards that I understood I was actually freeing myself of all those emotions that I had suppressed for so long.

And there were still quite a lot to free !

And I was nowhere near the end of my troubles….

CHAPTER 3
Nick...

It was at this time that I was to meet one of the people who most left a mark on my life.

I went to spend a long week-end in London with my older brother and my sister-in-law. It was in December 1986, and I was able to be a tourist guide for them, since I knew the city so well.

One evening, I decided to leave them some private time together and to go on my own to a gay bar in Earls Court, a well-known district in London.

As I was leaning on the bar, a charming young man accosted me and offered me a drink.

His name was Nick. And he was, without knowing it, to change my life for ever. And for that, I will be eternally grateful.

We stood there chatting a long time, sitting at the bar, then in a very natural way, he asked me to come back to his place for the night.

I will never forget nor regret that evening. Without knowing it, I was about to live one of the most important moments in my life.

He was tender and affectionate and I can say I had never had the chance to be with someone with whom I shared such a quality of experience. Although I had had several experiences in the past and had been with Alain for a year, I felt with Nick a quality, a sort of « intensity », that I had never felt before.

I felt really good in his arms, uninhibited and confident. It was a true relationship, beautiful in its sweetness and its simplicity.

That night, as I was lying on the bed, staring at my hand outlined on the ceiling, Nick told me :

-« You know, you have a beautiful green aura ».

This sentence, without me knowing, was about to totally change my life.

I had no idea what he was talking about, but he explained to me that if looked around my arm, and my hand, I too could see this « aura » which he described as a halo of milky white/green energy.

I must admit that, even though I looked intensely, I did not see anything at all !

Nevertheless, I trusted him and wanted to see what he was talking about..

After a while, I stopped trying and tenderly kissed him before falling asleep in his arms.

I spent the next morning with Nick, discovering, thanks to him, that sex between two men can be something else that a wild quenching of personal desires; instead, it can be a natural, tender, simple and spontaneous exchange.

I had to leave to meet my brother and sister-in-law, and then rejoined sweet Nick that same evening.

This was shortly before Christmas and we had planned that he would come to see me in Paris between Christmas and the New Year.

As I was returning towards Paris, sitting in the back of the car, I spent hours staring at the outlines of my arms and hands.

At last, I started to see « something » and, wanting to know more, I managed some days later to find a book about the aura. In this book, I discovered to my surprise that the color green was described as « The color of healers ». Some pages further on, I learned that healers had a « green aura ».

At the time, I said to myself :

-« Well, that's very interesting . »

Nick came to visit me, as planned, in Paris. I did not know it then but it was to be our last intimate moment together.

For my part, I continued reading books on the aura, which lead me to wondering and asking questions about myself. I wondered if it was possible that I, too, might have what appeared to me then to be a « gift », an ability to heal.

Of course, some time later I had the chance to know this for a fact.

We had planned, Nick and I, to see each other again as early as mid-January.

I remember calling him some days before our meeting but he told me that something had « cropped up » at the last minute which made our meeting that weekend impossible.

So we agreed to meet the following week. Unfortunately, that week too, something unexpected « cropped up » again to make our meeting impossible. And the same thing the next week.

I felt hurt, feeling vaguely that something was not clear, that perhaps he did not wish to see me anymore. I would not be satisfied by some explanation over the phone. I had to see him in person so that he could tell me clearly what was going on.

Then, I thought up a plan. Jean-Marc, my therapist, sometimes used certain colored oils to massage me. These oils were made by a lady called Vicky Wall[1], who he said was charming.. He had told me that certain specific colors could help people to feel better physically or mentally. Knowing that I used to go regularly to London, he had asked me to bring him back his « precious oils » on the next trip.

I called back Nick to inform him, that anyway, I <u>had</u> to go to London on 14th of February to buy these colored oils. I

---

[1] Vicky Wall created the Aura-Soma products. These wonderful products combine in an original way Chromo-therapy, (therapy trough Colors), Aromatherapy (therapy by the plants or their essential oils) and Cristal-Therapy (therapy by the Cristals). She wrote the book « *The Miracle of Colour Healing* »

'extracted' from him, thanks to this lie, an agreement to meet, so that we could at least talk face to face, be it only a few minutes.

A wonderful lie that was about to lead me to another person who would put me on the path of healing for good.

But before that, a significant event was to take place in my life.

I learned that my grand-father had been hospitalized for a fractured femur and decided to visit him.

As I entered the room, he had just had his operation and was still unconscious from the anesthesia. And in his sleep, he had a very bad breathing rhythm.

Being alone with him in that hospital room, I thought I could try this « healing thing ». After all, Nick had told me I had a green aura, and, according to the book I had read, green was the color of healers ! May be I was one of them.

Anyway, I had nothing to lose !

Intuitively, I decided to place my hand above his, without touching it. I closed my eyes and decided to pace my breathing with his. Then, after a while, I decided to consciously slow down my own breathing. What happened next really surprised me, because as if we were « connected » together, he started to slow down his own rhythm ! When finally I progressively came back to a peaceful rhythm, he too was totally at peace in his sleep. And, amazingly, as if we were again connected together, we both, at the same moment, hiccupped !

I did not understand what was happening, but the facts were there, they had happened.

It was only two or three days later that I had another disturbing experience related to healing.

When I was at my work place, one of the people in my team asked me if I had some aspirin to ease her head ache..

As the First-Aid box was empty, I timidly asked her if she would accept trying « an experiment » with me. As I remember telling her, *« I had done «something » to my grand father and I thought that I might be healer »*.

I managed to find somewhere to be alone with this courageous person and, laying my hands on her head, I imagined that they were « head-ache vacuums ».

As soon as I had this thought, I started to feel violent waves of nausea. They were so unpleasant that I immediately stopped the laying-on of hands.

The result was quite surprising. As far as the woman was concerned, the headache had somewhat faded away, although it was still there. On the other hand, where I was concerned, I felt terrible.

I started to feel a head ache, becoming stronger and stronger, as well as a very unpleasant feverish feeling.

I said to myself :

-«I have taken on this person's pain. ».

I did not know, at this time, that obviously one can not « take on anyone else pain » by laying hands on him. I know now, that because of this sense of empathy[1], it is quite possible for the healer to feel what the patient is feeling. Which of course does not mean he is « catching » his illness !

Nevertheless, at the time, I knew nothing about that and I was wondering :

-« What to do to get rid of it ? »

Then I had the idea to start our session again. Not that I was going to « exhale » through my hands to give her the headache

---

[1] Empathy is a sense of unity with the other. This sense is often very developed with a healer and this allows him (her) to feel what is patient is feeling. If there is lot of love between two beings, this sense of empathy can also manifest, each person feeling or his (her) partner feels or say as his (her) partner is about to say.

back, but I imagined I would continue to « suck » through my hands and direct this « pain » through my legs into the earth which, I thought, would know what to do with it.

At the very moment I had this thought, as I was restarting the session, I had a feeling of heaviness in my legs and all the unpleasant sensations left instantly. After some moments, I judged it was enough and asked this courageous person how she felt.

The result was that her headache had totally disappeared !

I myself was somewhat surprised. As for me, although I felt a little bit tired, all of the unpleasant sensations had totally left me.

Before this experience, probably like many of you, I had learned that, on this earth, there are, on the one hand, things that are real and, on the other hand, things that are imaginary, and that therefore, according to this model, everything that was imagined was therefore not real!

This experiment forced me to revise this concept and showed me that what is « imagined » is real. And this something <u>very important</u> which must not be forgotten. I am sure I will have the opportunity to come back to this as this book unfolds..

Anyway, because of this second encouraging experiment, I decided to do it again as soon as the opportunity arose.

But we were getting closer to February 14th and I had to go to Great Britain to meet Nick again.

As we had planned, I met him in a bar nearby Regent Street. I was truly very happy to see him again. Unfortunately, what he was to tell me was not so pleasant. He told me that it would be best not to continue our relationship. He explained that with him living in London and me in Paris, conditions were not ideal for developing the relationship any further.

What Nick was telling was of course very hard to hear and I felt abandoned.

Nevertheless, at least I had a clear and direct answer from him.

I just had to accept it.

CHAPTER 4
Vicky...

After Nick left me, I decided to go and see Vicky Wall, who made the colored oils used by my therapist.

He had told me that this woman « could see auras » and suggested I ask her for a « reading » that could prove very important to me.

So there I was, on the train to Windsor, not knowing at the time that I was about to go through something that would change my whole life for ever. I was much too unhappy about the end of my relationship with Nick.

When I arrived, I was very surprised to meet a charming old blind lady of about 70 !

I do not know why, but I had imagined she was only in her thirties.

The surprising thing for me was that, although blind, she was able to function like any one of us, perceiving people and objects through their energy fields, as she was to explain.

After the usual formalities and a few words about my therapist whom she apparently knew very well, Vicky said abruptly :

-« *Patrice, do you know that I can see auras ?* »

I mumbled a yes, that Jean Marc had told me. She then replied :

-«*I would like to give you a reading, because you need one... Do you have a tape with you, to record ?* »

I pulled out of my bag the portable tape recorder that I had brought along and set it down on the table in front of us. She then made me choose some bottles with wonderful colors that she was going to use as an aid during the « reading »

And as Vicky started gently to talk, I became more and more dazed!

This woman I had never seen before was talking about me as if she had always known me. In front of her, I felt as if stripped naked !

But most astonishing, considering my scepticism at the time about these « weird» things, was that she was not only talking of my future but also of my past !

At the time, it seemed actually « easy » to talk about someone's future...

But when a clairvoyant tells you about your past, and it is true, then you know that you can trust that person.

And as for Vicky, she was reading me like an open book.

She saw my inner struggle, my difficulty in accepting my homosexuality, the shock of the separation with Nick, and many other things.

It was as if I was transparent to her. I was deeply moved by what she said and, after some minutes, I felt a lump in my throat. I was on the verge of crying.

Then Vicky said to me, (although she was blind)

-« *There are tears within you,, Patrice , let them flow... »*

I burst into tears as she kept talking in her soft and reassuring voice.

Amongst other things she told me :

-« *Patrice, you are a healer and we have already worked together. Healing is your path for this life... »*

I was totally astonished. It's true I had done my first « healing » a few days ago and she was just confirming something I already knew... but with this was going a bit far !

« *We have already worked together »*...

This woman of more than 70 was charming, I must confess, but I had <u>never</u> met her in my life. (I must admit now that the memories about our past lives together came back to me only later.)

« Healing is your path for this life »... There again, she was going a bit far ! I had spend 6 years in a Catering school, passing every possible diploma imaginable in catering at the time and she was telling me I was destined to be a healer, whereas my future « career » in catering seemed to very good !

Nevertheless, what she was telling me touched me deeply and I was taken aback.

And as she was calmly talking to me, strange things were happening to me. I perceived colors around her. She explained then that it was her aura and that I too had the ability to see it. *(For my part, I had never had this experience with such intensity)*

After about an hour together, she left me for a while, and her companions offered me some tea. Indeed! This was 5 o'clock in the afternoon and I was in Great Britain. Tea Time was all important...

I was astounded and moved by everything I had just heard.

As Vicky was leaving the room to go and get some biscuits, a sense of panic gripped me. I turned quickly to her, thinking she was leaving « for good » and I asked her :

-*« Will I see you again ? »*

To which she replied with certainty :

-*« Oh yes !... You will see me again ... »*

and as she left, she turned around to tell me :

-*« Patrice, you have great teaching abilities and you will help many people... »*.

Then, she disappeared into the next room.

I did not know what to say. I was astounded.

Nevertheless, when I left her, on the train back to London, I had very strange visual perceptions.

I looked at the people sitting next to me, finding them beautiful, luminous and from time to time seeing colours around them. I did not really understand what was happening but I felt good.

Really good..

When I got back to my hotel bedroom, I listened again to the recording of my aura reading.

I was very moved as I listened again to what she had told me.

Just when the recording of Vicky's interview finished, there was a strange and magnificent phenomenon.

Now, since I do not believe anymore in Chance or Coincidence, I would be more likely to call it Synchronicity. In fact, the tape on which I had recorded the meeting with Vicky had been previously used. And at the moment the aura reading ended, the music on the original background continued : « *Qu'est-ce qu'on attend pour être heureux* » sung by Ray Ventura and his Collegiens...

> *Qu'est-ce qu'on attend pour être heureux ? la, la, la...*
> What are you waiting for to be happy ? la, la, la...
> *Qu'est-ce qu'on attend pour faire la fête ?...*
> What are you waiting for to celebrate?...
> *La vie est belle !... C'est merveilleux !...*
> Life is beautiful !... It's wonderful !...
> *Qu'est-ce qu'on attend pour être heureux ?...*
> What are you waiting for to be happy ?...

And as these fitting words filled my tiny hotel room, I burst into tears, overcome with gratitude for the perfection of the moment.

It was only three years after this experience, to the day, that I could really understand how that February 14th 1987 had been such an important and decisive point in my life. It is as if, before that date, my life was heading towards a catering career, and that, after this date, it was re-directed towards a different form of sustenance.

From nourishing the body, I was little by little going to nourish the Soul…

Anyway, after this meeting with Vicky, I decided to take part regularly in the workshops she gave on Color Therapy.

And it is thanks to this exceptional woman that I received the first « tools » of my transformation.

Without my knowing it, a wonderful process of opening up had started…

CHAPTER 5
From discovery to discovery...

At the same time as I was attending the Color Therapy workshops, I kept my activity of Manager in Company Restaurants where I was getting more used to laying on my hands when people told me about their aches and pains!

Sessions of therapy with Jean-Marc continued and I noticed definite changes were taking place within me, which at the time were quite incomprehensible.

The sessions were very often agonizing and the physical pain almost unbearable.

But I was about to discover something disturbing.

There was always a beautiful flower arrangement in Jean-Marc's rooms. These flowers were placed near the head of the massage table.

One day, as he was massaging me in a particularly « powerful » way and as I was struggling on the table, my hand happened to touch a flower.

At the moment that I made contact with the plant, I immediately felt the pain leave my body, going into the plant through my hand. It was as if I was being emptied of the pain as the plant was taking it. I did not understand the process... but I was living it... And what a help it was!

Of course, I did not talk about it to Jean-Marc that day, thinking he would take me for an idiot!

However, in the next session, when the pain started to become too intense, I managed to discreetly move my arm across *(thinking that Jean-Marc would not see it !),* and gently take hold of a flower or a leaf.

Silently, I asked the plant:

-« *Please, help me, take this suffering from me.* »

And it would take it away!

I did not understand the process then but what a help it was during several sessions ! How I loved these plants that were helping me in this way !

But it seems I was now ready to go on to the next step.

In fact, during the next session, I suddenly saw what seemed to be three beings floating on the ceiling. I decided to open up to Jean-Marc, telling him, in a rather worried voice :

> -« *Jean-Marc, there are beings on the ceiling !* »

To which he answered smiling :

> -« *Of course, there are often lots of people around here !* »

What was he talking about ? I must say he was not generally very talkative... On the other hand, I noticed as the sessions continued that if I asked him anything, he would answer me very precisely, seeming to know much more that he would generally say.

That is how he came to explain to me that, just as I, Patrice, am a spirit in a body, during the process we call Death, there is a separation of the spirit and the body which contains it.

He then explained that this spirit without a body still continues to exist, that it is possible to communicate with it and if necessary to ask it for help. He was explaining, little by little, the word of spirits out of their bodies. I was progressively discovering, thanks to him, a very different reality.

So I started, when the pain became too intense, to turn towards these « beings », asking for their help. And it worked ! Just as with the plants, I could feel the intensity of pain diminish when I invoked them !

Was it chance, coincidence or something else ?

An then, another surprising event took place.

I understand now that in fact, all this was part of the marvellous process, begun many years previously which, unrelentingly, was bringing me closer to what I to now perceive as being God.

I must say that although having been baptized Catholic, having politely followed my catechism and having obediently gone to mass on Sundays during my childhood, I had come to the conclusion that in the long run, « all that », was a beautiful tale for people who were a little weak-minded and needed to believe in this « twaddle » to cope with their sad lives !

However, I surprised myself one day looking at all these churches, and asking myself:

>   -« *There must be « something » in it for, all these buildings to have been built over the centuries.* »

Driven by curiosity and also by the need to get closer to this «force» called God, I dared from time to time go into these churches, mostly when they were empty.

One day, I had an experience which I can now call «formative», even though, at the time, it was rather «shocking».

It was a little before Easter and I had gone into this church which I had already visited several times before.

That day there was a «ceremony» which I did not know and which intrigued me.

There were priests all over the church, at regular intervals and I could see people queuing up to approach them one by one.

Curious about what it could be, I started to line up and waited for my turn.

When I reached a priest, I greeted him and remained silent.

>   -« *Well ?...* » he asked after a while.
>   -« *Well what ?...* » I answered.
>   -« *How long since you've confessed ?...* »

This was what this ceremony was about ! Confessions before Easter… I then mumbled :

> -« Oh...confessed ... it must be at least ten or fifteen years since I confessed... »

The priest looked discomfited, thought for a while, then told me almost sadly:

> -« Fifteen years... ? Well,... listen, ... , I can't do anything for you now... I advise you to go home, think about it and to make a list, then come back and ask for father So and So... »

I must say that I was a bit shaken when I left the church…

If **THIS** was the God that these priests represented, I did not feel like getting closer to Him ! I had to remember « sins » committed fifteen years ago for this God to forgive me ? I could not believe that, especially as my experience of that energy of love that filled me from time to time somehow made me sense that this gentle strength I vaguely felt to be Divine Love could not function that way.

Having felt this all powerful love within me, I could not conceive of God as presented by this priest.

Today, when I think again of what that priest said to me, I am grateful to him for having presented such a picture of God.

It was so far away from what I was starting to experience within that I could not accept it.

I had to find out for myself what this God was like Who seemed to be manifesting Himself to me from time to time.

On the other hand, what makes me sad sometimes, is to think that this priest and many others continue to present to the faithful an image of a vengeful God, accusing and punishing, Who has nothing else to do than observe me and punish me for the slightest mistake, unless I repent.

Nevertheless, beyond all that, and in the light of my current experiences, I recognize that once again, it had to be so.

I had to have this grotesque image presented to me so that I could make the decision to refuse it and discover through that another face of God, who, I now know, takes for me, for us, the form we think He has…

The universe in its perfection, sometimes gives us the opportunity to experience the opposite of something, to see if we give it life by our choices.

And if this is the case, we thus allow it to continue to exist for us. On the contrary, if we consciously choose not to accept this model as being really « real » so that we consciously choose an other one, this new model will become for us our new reality and our new experience.

This is what I believe one of the greats gifts of the universe. It allows us to determine It as we please and then accepts unconditionally to become for us what we believe It is…

It is finally an extremely simple process that we can only realise from « within », by living it and putting it into practice in our daily lives.

It is nevertheless important that you realize that this extremely simple process can, according to your experience, be perceived as a « blessing » or a « curse » …

That is where a certain control of your thoughts, words and actions will prove to be necessary in order to extricate you from an « apparently » infernal circle and then launch you into a beautifully « Divine » circle…

But, let us turn back now to the time when my transformation began.

I was starting at times to hear within me a small voice which, each time it spoke to me, filled me with joy.

I remember an event which occurred after a particularly painful session of therapy had been just completed. I came out of the subway, to find outside that it was raining in Paris, a fine, greasy rain. In the miserable state I was in, I remember looking at the bleak Parisian sky and saying:

> -« *And on top of that, it's raining ! That's all I needed! »*.

As if life was harassing me !

And as I looked at the uniformly grey sky, I saw a beautiful triangle of perfectly blue sky standing out against the greyness. At the same time, this voice in my head, both strong to put me back in my place and gentle to calm me, said :

> -« *Patrice, there is <u>always</u> a patch of blue sky somewhere. Only, you do sometimes have to search for it ! »*

This declaration instantly filled me with a joy which overflowed through every pore of my skin and I remember returning home, under the rain, totally wet and giving thanks to the sky for this beneficial rain.

And the changes continued...

Another time, as I was on my way to my little bed-sit, I saw a sad-looking woman passing by and filled with compassion, I seemed to know her whole life in an instant, and heard myself think spontaneously:

> -« *My God, please do something for this woman. May she get out of her situation ! »*

As the very instant I had that thought, I was overwhelmed by a wave of immense love I had never felt before.

When I talked about it to Jean-Marc, during the next session, he simply told me :

> -« *Of course, you just had an immediate return of Karma ! »*

What was that now ! Karma ? ...and what else next !...

He then explained to me the laws of cause and effect. An action brings about a reaction. You harvest what you sow, etc... etc... I am sure we will have the opportunity to talk about this further on.

I really wanted to know more because the events I had just lived were showing me through undeniable direct experience the validity of certain principles, which at the time, I did not believe at all. For Jean-Marc, of course, all of that seemed obvious.

I started to get more and more interested in « these things ».One day, I found a book on positive thinking. It seemed fascinating, even though a part of my mind was saying :

> -*« This is too beautiful to be true. Too easy for it to really work ! »*

This book explained, amongst other things, that if I would repeat positive sentences regularly and long enough, I could bring myself to believe in them.

This was new now !

I really was going from discovery to discovery...

But after all, looking at the state I was in at the time and telling myself I had nothing to lose, I started to repeat, purely and simply, without really believing in it, as I had a poor image of myself :

> -*« Patrice, you are brilliant ... Patrice, you are brilliant... »*

And again... And again...

And, in the tube, I used the period of travel to practise the affirmation techniques[1]. And after all, as I can now say, looking at my own experiences :

> -« *With the time and energy spent in reinforcing a limiting belief, we could just as well energise a belief that better reflects our TRUE unlimited nature.* »

And, believe it or not, but barely a week after I had started to practise this apparently simple little exercise, a female friend told me, word for word :

> -« *Patrice, you are brilliant !* »

What a surprise it was for me ! <u>Never</u> had anyone told me that before !

I did not really understand how it was functioning but I could only note one thing : it worked !

Little by little, my scepticism towards all of these things was disappearing to give way instead to more and more confidence in myself and the universe and I decided to take even more interest in the world of metaphysics[2].

I started to notice the effect of my more positive state of mind on my life. Whereas before, I expected problems on a regular basis since that had been my previous experience, now I found things became suddenly easier.

---

[1] An affirmation is a sentence, a belief you repeat at random until it becomes your new experience. The method of Emile COUÉ suggest this affirmation, for example :: « *Every day, in every way, I am getting better and better....* ». Nowadays the techniques using affirmation are sometimes called « *Techniques of mental reprogramming* », techniques with which we can change the nature of the beliefs whereby we used to function.

[2] Metaphysics explores the world which is beyond physics. (Meta means « beyond » in Greek). Physics tells us that an external cause brings about an external effect (a germ out there brings about a disease...) Metaphysics tells us that everything that happens out there is the effect of a cause which is within (in ourselves)... This vision of the world takes us out of the role of victim and allows us to take control our lives. In fact, if the cause is outside of me, I can not necessarily change it. On the other hand, if it (the cause) is inside me, by changing something in me I can free myself from the effect which that cause created.

In the book on positive thinking, I learned that, somehow, if I had a problem in my life, it was because I created it. In other words, if I got a slap in the face, I had created it...

This idea seemed unacceptable at first, but, as I had chosen to put these principles into action, I decided to accept them as being true, even though my own experience seemed to prove me the contrary. After all, I had nothing to lose...

So, little by little, I accepted the idea I was creating my reality.

A short while after, at my work, I received what I considered at the time a slap in the face. At the time, I did not feel very happy. Then I thought back to this idea :

> -« *Patrice, remember...* **YOU CREATE YOUR REALITY**. *This slap in the face, YOU created it yourself.* »

The effect was surprising. What I had just experienced as a problem <u>instantly</u> appeared not to be one... It became minor. The <u>simple fact</u> of having accepted my share of responsibility in the event was enough to make it acceptable to me. I was going from revelation to revelation.

I realized more and more, that thinking positive, makes you feel good. And as I had chosen to get better and better, I made sure to maintain, as often as possible, positive thoughts in my consciousness.

For example, when I travelled on the subway, I imagined that I was sending a gold rain on people present. I remember that it seemed difficult to me to imagine this gold rain falling simultaneously on each person present in my carriage. So, to make it easier, I imagined the rain falling and being retained by an immense cloth above the head of the passengers. Finally, the cloth would be filled with so much gold rain that it would break and all the people were then bathed by this beneficial rain.

And each time I did this, sitting back in a corner of the carriage, I felt marvellously well, whereas, I was « only » wishing happiness for my fellow passengers.

Thinking of the good of others made me feel good ! What a revelation it was for me at the time.

During one of my « gold showers », as I was imagining that beneficial rain falling on each of the passengers travelling with me, I was simultaneously overwhelmed by a real shower of liquid ecstasy, my heart overflowing with love of an incredible purity, as if it was exploding with love.

Then I heard that gentle inner voice tell me :

> -« *Through you, the Kingdom of Heaven will come on earth…*»

And at the same time, I understood that the true meaning of this message concerned not only my own physical person.

What it really was about, was the personal transformation of each person who will allow this « Kingdom of Heaven » to be established on earth.

This is, I am sure, our task here on earth.

I think that we are here, on earth, first, to realise our divine nature and then, to manifest it.

CHAPTER 6
Group of Chakras...

During the sessions with Jean-Marc, I continued my transformation, slowly but surely. One day he suggested, if I wished, that I take part in what he called a « Group of Chakras »[1].

Apparently, I was ripe to move up to the next step...

It consisted of evening workshops on the *Chakras*, these energy centres regulating the flow of energy in our bodies.

At that time, I had chosen to become vegetarian, thinking that a change in my eating habits could only be beneficial to me.

On top of that, having heard Jean-Marc talk about the benefits of fasting, I decided to prepare myself for this first « *Group of Chakras* » by fasting on water only during the three days before the evening.

Although a little trying, mostly because I was working in a business restaurant and could see hundreds of meals passing before my eyes each day, I discovered through this first fast that it was somehow strangely refining my perceptions.

I became extremely sensitive to smells, feeding on them. I could perceive my aura more precisely, mostly in a tactile way. When I brought my fingers close together, I very definitely felt this little « energy cloud » around my fingers.

Throughout this first « *Group of Chakras* » Jean-Marc guided us through a very interesting exercise, which could perhaps help you too.

The goal of this exercise was to free ourselves from subtle links which can prevent us from experiencing total freedom.

---

[1] *Chakra* is a Sanskrit word meaning either a wheel, a disk or a vortex of energy. *Chakras* are the energy centres situated along the spine. They are part of the human energy system and regulate the flow of energy in subtle energy channels, sometimes known under the Sanskrit word of *Nadi* or Meridians in acupuncture.

He proposed we should visualize these energy centres, informing us that it would be possible that in certain of these energy centres, we would feel or imagine some links or cords attached to them.

If this was the case, he asked us to imagine the person situated at the other end of that cord. Once the person or persons had been identified, we needed to recognize how that person had "vampirised" or controlled us. Once this was done, we were to thank that person for the interaction there had been between us in the past and to cut this cord mentally with golden scissors, without any aggressiveness towards that person.

We could then imagine that cord returning to the person who had attached himself to us and we mentally encouraged that person as well to take back their freedom and independence.

As Jean-Marc was guiding us and I was going through my own inner examination, I felt at the level of my two first *Chakras*, *(located at the level of the sacrum and the navel)* two cords connecting me to my mother.

As the exercise dictated, I mentally thanked my mother for past interactions explaining that, for her good as well as mine, it was now necessary that I take back my autonomy and that she should take back hers.

I explained to her that whatever energies she needed and had taken from me through these cords, she had now to find in herself or elsewhere.

I mentally informed her that from <u>that moment on</u>, I freed myself from her control or her mental pressures.

Taking mentally the golden scissors, I conscientiously cut these cords and returned them to her with much love.

What happened after that allowed me to validate the reality of the subjective work that had taken place.

At that time, having estimated how important a role the education I received from my parents had played in my state of misery, I went through, like many I guess, a period of rejection of my parents.

After all, if I was so unhappy, it was their fault, I thought…

It was only years later that I understood how I had myself chosen <u>these parents</u> for my own spiritual evolution.

Nevertheless, at that time, I seldom spoke to my parents because of this resentment. I would also see them very rarely.

And having left them without any news for a long time, the next morning after the process of freeing from the cords, I received a telephone call from my mother.

-*« Hello, it's Mum... »*

-*« Hello, how are you ? »*

-*« O. K.... Actually I had a weird dream last night... With your colours... »* (My parents knew about my interest in the symbolism of colours and the teaching I was receiving in Great Britain.)

I asked her :

-*« Oh yes ? Which colours ? »*

-*« Red... »*

I was speechless ! The synchronicity was too much. For your information, red is the colour associated, amongst other things, to the first Chakra, to vital energy and to the mother…

-*« Apart from that, anything else ?... »*

-*« Not really ... »* she replied... *« Actually yes... yesterday, a weird thing happened. I was washing some salad in the kitchen and without knowing why, suddenly, I started to cry. Daddy was with me in the kitchen and could not understand why... »*

Understanding what had happened, I asked her :

-*«Oh yes ? What time did this happen ? »*

-*« At about eight in the evening... »*

This was the **exact** time where I had cut the links ! I found that **very interesting**.

By the end of that conversation, my mother was telling me that they were going to come and visit that week-end.

Well, now that was REALLY something!

I had moved into my new bed-sit some months earlier, and, « by chance », my parents decided to come and visit after that work on the energy cords !

The picture was becoming clear !

My mother had been living partly on my vital energy. Having cut the cords that were allowing her to be nourished, she felt the lack and may be a form of rejection from me, therefore the flood of tears..

And, in order to reconnect the links I had cut the evening before, she decided to come and visit, just a few days later !

It was crystal clear ! This type of experience shows you clearly that there no such thing as chance or coincidence.

Being now aware of the real goal of her visit, beyond the fact of seeing my new apartment, I just had to make sure she did not connect up to me again.

CHAPTER 7
Memories come back...

Thanks to the training courses which I was following at the same time in the United Kingdom, I was starting to understand a little better how human beings functioned.

This new knowledge also helped me to understand better what was happening when I lay my hands on people.

Indeed, at the time, when I lay my hands on people asking me for help, I always had very violent waves of nausea, with the impression I was going to vomit.

I understood, thanks to these training courses, that I was behaving as a receptacle into which « negative » energies of the patient flowed before I gave them back to the earth. I could thus accept this process more easily, even if it was very unpleasant. Moreover, I suffered from GSC or « Good Samaritan Complex» at the time, and I accepted this suffering joyfully, knowing that at the time I felt it, it was leaving the person I was curing. It was as if I agreed to carry their bags for a while, since I knew I could let go of them at the end of the session.

Because of this, I warned each person at the beginning of the session :

> -« Don't worry if I have violent reactions while I am laying on my hands, it is simply a transfer of energies going on ... »

One day as I was treating someone's foot, who suffered a lot of pain, I was again shaken by this violent nausea. But this time, they were really VERY violent... To my surprise I saw my right hand spontaneously starting to do strange « passes » over the person's foot. And, surprisingly enough, as my hand was doing this strange « gesture », my nausea calmed down..

Great, I had discovered a trick that worked !

In the next session with someone else, as I started to feel the unpleasant nausea, I hastened to move my hand just as it had « done it » before.

And it worked ! The nausea eased.

It is only when I talked about it a few days later with Jean-Marc that he explained to me that these « gestures » of my hand were in fact « energy-releasing passes », used by healers to rid themselves of their patient's negative energies. I was dumbstruck because I had <u>never</u> learned that before.

So, my hands « remembered » what they knew how to do and what they had already done in the past !

I also realized why, before even the very first laying-on of hands on my grandfather, I had one day observed my hands, finding them suddenly very beautiful and saying to myself,

« I do not know what it is, but there is something to do with these hands... ». The wheel was turning full circle.

And as I continued to work in my staff canteen, I practised more and more laying-on of hands. Sometimes at the work place *(burns, cuts, headaches...)*, sometimes at home.

It was during a cure on an English friend that I was to have an experience which permanently shattered my beliefs about this energy commonly called God. She had asked me for help, explaining how she felt tired, depressed, at the end of her tether...

So I began the « work » which finally, was more a kind of prayer.

After asking her to lie down on the sofa, I began the session.

At the time, I did not dare touch people to heal them, so I put my hands over their bodies, a foot away. I worked intuitively and according to the following « ritual » : I placed my left hand, in the air, above the first *Chakra (that is, a little under of the sex area)* and my right hand above her second *Chakra (a little above her pubis).* Let us not forget that at that time, I knew that *Chakras* existed ! Before this time, a healing was mostly summarized by one prayer in which I simply and intensely asked the great Being to heal the person in question.

Well,... anyway, after having remained in contact with the first two *Chakras*, the ritual consisted in « sweeping » the first Chakra into the second, like sending « negative » energies with movements of my left hand, from the first Chakra into the second. Then, I placed my left hand above second Chakra and the right one above the third *Chakra*, on the level of the solar plexus. And again, after a time of harmonization, I again « swept » the negative energies of the first and second Chakra into the third... And so on. I had noticed that often, as I was at the level of the fifth *Chakra,* located at the throat level *(the one that is in charge of expression, among other things)*, people generally had very violent reactions. Often, as I did my « energy-releasing » passes on this *Chakra*, people started to cough or cry. The ritual generally finished, after working on the sixth and seventh *Chakra*, with a laying on of hands directly on the person's skull for a few minutes. After which, I asked the person to open their eyes again when they wished.

But let us return to this English friend. As soon as I was in harmony with her first and second *Chakra*, I was filled with a great sadness which I did not at first understand. Very quickly, I realised that I was in empathy with Rose. And as I « swept » her first Chakra into her second, she started to cough, then to cry. I reassured her, saying:

   -*«It is all right, stay open... »*

But as work progressed, I felt more and more unwell, crying with her, feeling her awful suffering.

Although the process was very painful, I accepted it nevertheless, knowing that while I was feeling bad, she was feeling better. I agreed « to carry her bags ». However, at the end of a certain time, I was feeling so bad, that I could only pray.

In a very intense way, in total empathy with Rose, I prayed to God to come to her aid. To myself, I said:

> *-« Oh God, help her please, may she feel well, may she be healed... Oh God, help her please, may she feel well, may she be healed ... My God, help her please, may she feel well, may she be healed ... »*

And when there was nothing more in me than this chant, a shower of an incredible love literally filled me in an instant.

It was of such an intensity that I had the impression of being instantly driven out of my body by this immense Love. And I could see myself laying my hands on this girl, whereas in fact I was on my right about 18 inches away. At the same time, I felt within me a presence or rather a gaze of an intensity and an incredible beauty which could only be that of Jesus.

I felt within me, His blessed eyes, incredibly clear, looking at this girl with such an intensity of Love and Compassion ! In this blessed moment there was only Love and Compassion within me.

Never before had I felt that. Love and Compassion. Love and Compassion. I loved this girl with all my Heart and I understood her suffering.

This sacred moment lasted a few minutes or a few seconds, I have no idea.

Anyway, after a while, I <u>knew</u> that the healing was completed.

Without any possible doubt, the miracle had happened, I knew it. There was around me such a transparency, such a purity that I felt unable to speak. I knew that, if I spoke, this kind of crystalline bubble of purity would break into pieces.

With my eyes full of Love, I looked at Rose, lying now peacefully beneath my hands and simply thought : *« It is over now, every thing is all right now, you can open your eyes when you are ready... »*.

To my great surprise, the moment I finished « simply » thinking this sentence, she opened her eyes. What she said to me then touched me deeply. She said to me:

-« *It is as if you smiled at me from within...* »

The most surprising thing is that, the following day, as she was staying at a mutual friend's place, this friend, who did not know what had happened, when she saw her next morning, found her so changed physically that she especially commented on it..

I found these phenomena fascinating.

However, at the same time, I was deeply disturbed by this experience. Indeed, I had started at the time to re-examine my beliefs in terms of God, but this experience of Jesus within me obliged me to re-think everything. Even though it had been relatively short, the experience had been so intense and so « real » that I could not deny its reality.

Not only did God exist but now, it was Jesus and his reality which I had to integrate into my belief systems.

In addition, other types of strange phenomena were happening to me. One thing particularly surprised me the first time it occurred.

I was in the subway one day when suddenly, I started to look in a strange way at a young woman sitting opposite me. She seemed cute, and, more surprising, attractive.

I started to desire her, imagining having a sexual relationship with her !

But what was happening to me ! ?

Previously, I had never had this kind of thought when I looked at women ! I obviously saw them around me but until then it made me neither hot or cold, leaving me rather indifferent and certainly not having a sexual desire for them.

And what had to happen, happened. I had become acquainted with a young woman when the *Chakras* groups were meeting.

When she learned that I practiced aura readings through the use of colored bottles, following the training courses I had done in the United Kingdom, she expressed her desire to know more about it.

So I invited her for a dinner one evening in my studio. After dinner and after presenting the colored bottles, when we were on the sofa, Myriam abruptly said to me:

-« *Patrice, I would like to know you more...* »

I freaked out... After all, I was homosexual... And I told her quickly :

-« *You know, I am gay...* »

-« *I know. That's no problem...* »

At once, panic gave place to amazement. I was well aware that I had had a particularly bad image of women because of the maternal model that I had had and I could conceive, at least intellectually speaking, that not all women could be « like my mother » or, to be more precise, the way I perceived her then....

I had had in the past a few rare sexual experiences with women, but they had seemed so frustrating that I had decided to stick to men.

At least, with them I thought, I can feel free to be what I am and moreover, with a man, sex is not a taboo experience but rather a true release experience of shared pleasures.

It is true that the few sexual experiences I had had with women had not been very exciting. In fact, these women, probably very embarrassed or ashamed of their bodies, insisted it happened in the dark.

I now understand that I could not at the time have created anything else. It was necessary for my evolution. Nevertheless, with men, I found sex much more fun, much more free, much more simple, and actually, much more natural and much more pleasant.

However, at the time I was with Myriam, I chose to put aside my prejudices about women and to live the experience which was offered to me in order to have a more objective idea of a relationship with a woman.

I definitely do not regret this choice. Actually, with her, it was very different from what I had lived in the past ! She was very tender and in no way inhibited like those I had known before. We settled together a short while after and spent more than a year together.

Thanks to the work that I continued with Jean-Marc, I had more and more confidence in myself and could see my life improving on many levels.

I was also having amazing encounters. I particularly remember Lili here.

This charming old lady, deceased today, was a regular at the restaurant which I managed at the time. Many customers nearby seemed not always to appreciate her. I must say, it is true, that she was accustomed to speaking rather loudly and that she wore very colourful clothes and hats, which I personally found « interesting ».

I found in her a dynamism and a « joie de vivre » unusual for a person of her age and she seemed to return the affection that I showed her. I took pleasure in serving her or chatting with her each time she came to have lunch.

One day, as she was paying her bill, she asked me what was my astrological sign. I knew that I was Libra but I was still very sceptical about all those things. Then she asked for the date, place and hour of my birth, to have my astrological chart done. After all, why not?

A few days later, she came back with a series of typed pages and a book that she offered to me.

As I went through my astrological chart, I was quite surprised by the correspondences that I saw there with my life. The most surprising, however, was the study of my chart through the book that she had offered to me. I realize now how this book was not here by chance. It was about "Karmic Astrology" by Dorothée Kœchlin de Bizemont[1].

This book, by studying the positions of the planets at an individual's birth, made it possible to understand the former lives of the incarnated soul and its path for this life with the strong and weak points that it brought to this life from its preceding incarnations.

And as, very simply, I analyzed my chart through that book, I discovered some very interesting things. According to the positions of the planets at my birth, this book explained that the Soul that I was had been a priest in former lives, had « strayed » in its last lives and that « wise or old women » *(this is because of the triple conjunction of the Moon - Saturn – and of the southern Node in Aquarius)* would put me back on my path and that Healing was very important on this path.

Until then, I had never really believed in astrology but here, I could not deny that there was « something real » behind all of this.

Indeed, at the time of my meeting with Vicky Wall, I remember being surprised to discover an old woman and it was clear also that this meeting had been important for my life…

In addition, what Vicky had told me while reading my aura was now confirmed to me by this chart. And I can honestly say today that my meeting with Lili belongs to the meetings that I consider played a major part in my process of transformation. It is thanks to her that I started to study astrology seriously, first learning how to create an astral chart, then starting on the interpretation of planets, etc…

It was by studying my chart that I realized more and more the perfection of the experiences that I had already lived. I understood that my meeting with Jean-Marc, an extremely important meeting, had taken place exactly at the time when the

---

[1] Published by Robert Laffont.

sun passed over my sun sign. In the same way, exceptional astrological configurations in resonance with my astral chart occurred on February 14, 1987, the day I first met Vicky Wall in Great Britain.

It was fascinating !...

And as I understood the planets' influence more and more, I started to wonder. Like some of you who are perhaps somewhat interested in astrology, I very quickly learned about the famous « Saturn return ».

It is generally accepted that the return of this slow planet to its position at birth *(it takes it 28 years to go through all of the zodiac !)* often brings major changes for the individual.

These « Saturn returns » thus occur at the ages of 28, 56, and 84. My life had improved so much between 24 and 26 that it was difficult for me to imagine how I was going to be affected by « my » own Saturn return. I had been so wretched and I already felt so good. I was often filled with gratitude for what I was living lived and often wondered:

-« But what is going to happen on my 28th birthday?... ».

I now realize how this positive state of expectancy maintained for nearly two years allowed me to create the splendid transformation which was to happen at this date.

CHAPTER 8
Martin...

It is thanks to Myriam with whom I lived that in May 1988, I met a man who was going to change my life drastically.

One day, she told me she wanted to attend a conference presented by an American healer named Martin Brofman[1]

He said that he had healed himself of a cancer as well as eyesight problems and proposed to teach people to do the same. He presented a tool of self-knowledge and of healing.

The governing idea of this conference was that our body is a mirror of our consciousness and that, consequently, if we have a problem in a specific part of our body, that reflects a specific tension in a very precise part of our consciousness.

As I heard these ideas for the first time, I was fascinated both by the simplicity of the system and by the width of its potential.

To know more about it, I decided to take part in meetings where people who had followed the training courses met to share their experiences.

Thus I met the person who at that time translated Martin Brofman's training courses. During these informal evenings, it sometimes happened that I helped this translator when a word escaped him since I spoke English correctly.

After several meetings, he approached me one day. He wished to cease working with this healer and asked me whether I would agree to replace him.

I was delighted. Indeed, I really wanted to take part in the training courses but the relatively high price made it inaccessible. The translator told me that Martin wished to meet with me before the conference in order to know more about me.

That is how I met this fascinating man. I discovered a precise man, rigorous, demanding and deeply respectful of people who

---

[1] Martin Brofman has written two books : «Better Eyesight without Glasses » and « Anything can be Healed »

came to see him. He explained to me that each word that he used had a specific goal and that it was very important to him that the translation be as exact as possible.

Although panicked by the idea of facing dozens of people in a few minutes, Martin knew how to put me at ease. To work with him that evening was an enriching experiment and to notice his presence with each person a great lesson.

The next morning a training course began called « A Vision Workshop » which I will always remember.

It was somewhat as if my eyes opened to another reality, already existing, but that I had not yet perceived.

I should explain that I had been short-sighted since the age of 15 or 16, when I had been sent to boarding school. And as I heard for the first time these ideas explaining why somebody can develop myopia because of certain experiences, I understood how, considering what I was going through at the time, the aggressions and the repeated humiliations had brought me the perception that it was best for me to stay hidden inside myself.

I had to protect myself from the external world which I perceived as threatening. I also understood that the difficulty of accepting my homosexuality had accentuated this process of turning inwards. And to my great surprise, I realized that it was « normal » that I developed this symptom.

Martin had such a clear manner of explaining the process of somatisation, which means how our body develops symptoms because of tensions held in our consciousness. It all seemed so simple.

I understood also, thanks to this method, that I had the possibility of getting rid of this vision problem. It was enough for me to choose to see clearly, believe that it was possible for me to see clearly without glasses and to see myself henceforth as being able to see clearly. I should also choose to look at myself, as well as the world, in a completely different way.

When I returned home to see Myriam after this first training course, I remember that I was in a state which I really perceived as « extra-ordinary ». My body was filled with an energy which I felt vibrating and sparkling on my hands, my arms, my face…

I had the impression everything was becoming possible again.

And indeed, my experiences proved this as time went by.

I was like a blind man who had recovered his sight. Thanks to the understanding this course had given me, I became really aware of the creative capacity laying more or less dormant within me. I also understood how I was going to be able to transform my life radically.

And whereas a few weeks earlier, I wondered how some of the people could stop their therapy and « leave » Jean-Marc, because of the extent of the improvements I had obtained in my life, I realized that I too had to stop this therapy as quickly as possible.

After the course in which I had just taken part *(although simply as a translator)*, I realised that to go and see a therapist, I had to <u>perceive</u> myself as being « sick ». If I really wanted to be well, I would have to, one day or another, <u>perceive</u> myself as being well.

But when ?

I had understood thanks to Martin, that it was just a decision to make and to maintain.

I was feeling so well following this course that I decided that the moment had come for me to stop my therapy.

Which I did with Jean-Marc's blessing at the following session which had been fixed for a few days later.

A new life was beginning for me…

CHAPTER 9
It works...

After this first course on vision improvement, the next weekend I had to translate a course more specifically directed towards healing.

During this course, I went again from discovery to discovery. I understood now what I had been doing for more than two years in a completely intuitive way when laying on my hands.

I discovered with this course the potential of the method that Martin had developed and said to myself: *« But It's true, Everything can **really** be healed.».* And because of my sensitivity towards homosexuals, I also thought: *« Later, I will be a specialist in H.I.V. and AIDS ».*

Surprisingly enough, one or two weeks later, I had to have a medical check-up. I arrived with my glasses on, saying to myself, when I was about to be tested for my sight :

> *-« Patrice, you have just taken part in a vision improvement course, you know that you can see clearly..., **you KNOW that you can see clearly** !»*

Taking a deep breath and closing my eyes for a second to concentrate, I began the tests. I read everything I was supposed to without any problem ! The doctor concluded the test with :

> *-« Perfect, everything is fine... » .*

I remember saying to the doctor :

> *-« But Doctor, it was not like that last test, I think. I had an eyesight problem, didn't I ? ».*

Studying my file, she then said :

-« In fact, you had 5 and 7 out of 10 last year.. »

I then explained to her that I had just done a vision improvement course, that everything was in fact in our consciousness and that it was there we should seek the solution to our problems. She showed a certain interest in what I was telling her but, however, she quickly sent me about my business.

At the time, I was nevertheless surprised. Of course, I had « participated » in a vision improvement course, but as a **TRANSLATOR** ! I had not even been able to do all the exercises that Martin Brofman suggested, I had only translated them or heard them ! Nevertheless, I can understand now what had happened.

I believe that everything starts in our consciousness and that everything is only a state of consciousness

You can understand that the difference between somebody who is happy and somebody who is unhappy, is a state of consciousness.

Well, I think that the difference between somebody who is « lucky » or not, is also a state of consciousness. The difference between somebody in good health or not…, again a state of consciousness. The difference between somebody who sees clearly or not…, yet again a state of consciousness.

A state of consciousness can be reached in one second. You just need to change your consciousness. It is simple, isn't it ?

Of course, it is simple. On the other hand, though the process is certainly simple, is it always easy?

Not necessarily. However, what is certain, is that it is possible. And that is the most important thing.

Always remember **that there is nothing you cannot do, there are only things you have *not yet learned* how to do.**

And, no matter what you want to do, you also now will be able to *choose* to do it, then learn how to do it.

I was realizing with hindsight what had happened to me and my sight.

As I was translating this training course and hearing in English for the first time how one can become short-sighted, as I understood in a better way the functioning of my consciousness, I went from major awakenings to sublime discoveries ... and from sublime discoveries to illuminations... Everything was so simple actually...

Within, it was a series of realisations such as :

-« *Of course, it is all clear now !* ».

I understood it had been « normal » , given my past experiences, to have developed this myopia.

At the same time, I also understood that it was <u>necessary</u> that I change, that it was <u>necessary</u> that I choose to look at these past situations differently and that it was <u>necessary</u> that I choose to perceive my future in another way. In fact, it was the only thing necessary to my healing. While healing, my body had only thereafter to « align himself » with my new decision, with my new consciousness.

Many people believe that healing is a physical state, but for me, it is not really the case. Healing is initially, before everything else, a state of consciousness. It is the base of the training courses which I present regularly and it is what allows me, sometimes, to see apparently miraculous things occur during these courses.

Having seen this same process thereafter occurring for other people, I always explain at the beginning of these courses that Healing is not a physical state but rather a state of consciousness and therefore can be very fast.

I must however recognize that it is true that sometimes, it takes time. This is then due to the degree to which the person lets himself or herself change or **choose** to let go of his or her limiting beliefs in order to **choose** instead to develop new attitudes and new habits.

It is true nevertheless that even if Healing can be very fast, many people often prefer a slower process, more « reassuring ».

To me finally, the important thing is not the speed with which a person heals but simply, that she/he heals. I like to say that if it took God himself six days to make up the world, if our healing takes a little more time, it is not really so important.

What is important however, is to <u>remember where we come from</u> *(for example : disease, blurred eyesight, disharmony, sadness...)* then to <u>know where we are going</u> *(health, clear eyesight, harmony, joy)* and then to <u>notice where we are</u> **now** relative to these two points. This allows us to become aware of the movement and transformation we have initiated. Once this progress is noticed, we just have to **accept** that state as being **natural** for us.

For myself, even if I now realize how my life could greatly improve, because I know now what my potential is, I am aware of where I was when I was 20. I also know where I am now. And even though I am not yet arrived where I know I'm going, I know that where I am now is nevertheless <u>MUCH BETTER</u> than where I found myself at the time.

And this is what drives me to continue transforming myself.

The important thing is not necessarily a fast transformation (although it can be the case).

The important thing is to be aware that we are moving.

The important thing is to become aware **that in this very moment**, we are already closer to where we want to be, even if we recognize at the same time that we are not there yet.

A slow and permanent transformation is much more interesting than a fast but fleeting one. Because you must understand that if everything is just a state of consciousness, then to achieve healing is not a question of « simply » developing a new state of consciousness.

It is in fact about developing a new state of consciousness and <u>MAINTAINING</u> it... This is where a certain conscious mastery of your thoughts can prove to be necessary.

Is it easy ? Not necessarily ...

Is it possible ? **YES**, you can be sure of it.

What is sure is that that is **REALLY** worth it.

The only question to ask yourself now is:

« *When am I going to choose to do it ?* »

Will I choose to change **now**, for the simple pleasure of experiencing and expressing **now** a more magnificent version of what I can be ? Or, will I wait until life forces me to change, due to an illness or having to go through hard and/or unpleasant events, as in fact I did myself at the time?

I know now that it is not necessary to wait for such intense events in order to change.

I know now that before attracting to me and manifesting an event or an intense illness, the Universe gives me « signs » drawing my attention to the fact that something in me must change... Something which is not right for which I am...

However, do I perceive these signs? Do I see them ?

And even though I see them, do I choose to take notice of them and change ?

Real change, transformation is finally only a deep, sincere and determined choice.

And I think that it is good that it is NOW that I decide to change.

You too can decide to change **NOW**...

CHAPTER 10
And if I changed now...

The « side » effects of the training courses in which I had taken part were not long in being felt. I had, during these training courses, sincerely asked for changes in my life. Martin had warned me that, although the external form of « work » used was very gentle, the effects were nevertheless very powerful. However, I did not suspect at the time how right he was!

As if by « chance », in the two months following my first training courses, some dramatic positive changes took place in my life. From one day to the next, I stopped the therapy begun two years earlier with Jean-Marc. I got a promotion and wage-increase in the catering company for which I worked and I moved with Myriam into a small house that we were buying together.

And all this was only a beginning.

During the first courses with Martin, I heard him present an idea about money which seemed revolutionary. In fact, it really was, because it transformed my life forever.

The process which I will now explain to you in fact happened over a period of approximately 18 months.

Martin explained that we should **NEVER** agree to do something only for money, unless we would accept to do it for free. He said that to do a thing simply because we were going to be paid for it was not a sufficiently valid reason for doing it. We should do things because we wanted to do them and then only, we could agree to be paid for it.

And when I heard this idea for the very first time, I was deeply moved.

It is true that I really liked my work in the catering company but I realized that this job of translator filled me with joy and made me feel really useful. What's more, I was being paid to do it! It was such a pleasant activity for me that I would even have agreed to pay to do it! However, I was being paid one thousand francs a day (about 150 €) at the time for this « work » which was a real pleasure !

Having understood, thanks to the courses I had taken, that I could create what I wanted in my life, I understood that, in life, I had the choice.

I had the choice to : either do something which I did not really like and to agree to be paid for it, or I had the choice to do something which I really liked doing and to agree to be paid for it.

I must say that my choice was quickly made ! I decided to create a change in my life.

I sat down to do a small series of calculations : at that time Martin was teaching courses of two days, sometimes four days, mainly in the Paris area, in Switzerland, in the South of France and in Belgium. There were at the time three interpreters translating his courses. One of them worked on the Paris area *(it was me)*, another, Yves, translated the courses held in Switzerland and in the south of France and a third, Pierre, dealt with the courses in Belgium.

My small calculations brought me to a quite simple conclusion. I adored translating these courses *(as I already said, I would have done it for free)*, **therefore**, according to the principles suggested, it was an activity that I could choose to do, while agreeing to be paid to do it. On the other hand, there were only a few courses in the Paris area and that would not have been sufficient to live on ! However, if I were Martin Brofman's only interpreter, this activity could be sufficient to gain a living.

So I decided, without Martin knowing, since according to him, everything was possible, to become his « one and only » interpreter .

I was sure that the principles he taught us were right and I just had to demonstrate them…

However, a small problem of conscience arose : If I became the Martin's only interpreter, that would mean that Yves and Pierre would find themselves « unemployed » and I felt uncomfortable with this idea.

So I decided, since everything was possible, that both of them were going to find another activity, more pleasant and better paid and that because of this, they would ask me to replace them.

I think that when you want to create a change in a situation in your life which implies changes for other people, it is always judicious to wish that this change be also to their advantage. Now, of course, I know that this is not really necessary, but when you realize that EVERYTHING that you think, say or do comes back to you sooner or later, I think that very quickly, you also will wish positive changes for others.

In any situation, there is always a solution in which all the protagonists can gain something. Personally , it is that which it seems preferable to choose.

When I received a phone call from Yves barely one or two months later, I was astounded...

He telephoned to tell me that he had met a charming young woman, that he wanted to be able to spend more time with her and asked to me whether I could henceforth take his place translating the courses into Switzerland !

You can bet I agreed ! So it was really working!

The good news was that the courses in Switzerland took place over four days, which meant double pay for me...

This is how, gradually, I started to earn more and more money doing what I really liked. Of course, at the beginning, these small « extras » represented barely a quarter of my incomes in the catering business, but little by little, the ratios changed.

I noticed that, following the courses in which I took part, the people whom I took in private sessions would give me more and more money whereas I left them free to give what they wanted. At the very beginning, before I met Martin, people generally gave me between 50 and 100 francs for a healing (about 7,50 to 15 €).

Then, gradually, people started to give me between 200 and 400 francs. Then, one day, three people whom I saw successively made the same remark. It was clear that this was a sign that I had to pay attention to ! They were feeling uncomfortable because I left them the freedom to give me what they wanted and they asked me to fix a price. So I explained to them that people generally gave me between 200 and 400 francs (about 30 to 60 €) and that, if they wanted, 300 francs could be a base (about 45 €), even if I left them the possibility of giving what they wanted or what they could. After that I saw people gave me much more than I asked them…, and that really surprised me.

In fact, this is how I learned that, as I really did not feel at ease being paid for these individual sessions, because of the obvious pleasure it gave me, I was thus not recognizing either the value of the service I gave, nor my own value.

On the other hand, people coming to see me recognized the value of my « work » and symbolized it by the money that they gave me, thus obliging me to recognize for myself my own value.

This process was wonderful to discover…

When you start to see how the Universe functions, you can only marvel at the means It uses to make you evolve !

As time passed by, the sums which I earned either while doing Healings, or for the translations, took an increasingly important proportion of my total income. Whereas at the beginning they represented barely a quarter of my monthly income, gradually, this ratio became a third, then a half, then two-thirds, finally reaching three-quarters of my monthly income.

It is the moment when I <u>knew</u> that I could stop my paid activity to live henceforth from what made me fully happy. But we will speak again about this later.

Nevertheless, thanks to these experiences, I learned something very important about money.

The majority of us have been raised with the following idea :

> -« *You shall earn your bread by the sweat of your brow* »[1].

This idea, even if I am aware that it can be perceived as being true for many of you, implies that work must be something painful, or unpleasant. But I now realize that other realities exist which are just as true.

Very different realities.

Realities which, in my opinion, reflect more what I believe to be the <u>true</u> spiritual values.

Did not Jesus tell us :

> -« *Behold the fowls of the air: for they sow not, neither do they reap, nor gather into barns; yet your heavenly Father feedeth them. Are ye not much better than they? Which of you by taking thought can add one cubit unto his stature? And why take ye thought for raiment? Consider the lilies of the field, how they grow; they toil not, neither do they spin: And yet I say unto you, That even Solomon in all his glory was not arrayed like one of these. Wherefore, if God so clothe the grass of the field, which today is, and tomorrow is cast into the oven, shall he not much more clothe you, O ye of little faith? Therefore take no thought, saying, What shall we eat? or, What shall we drink? or, Wherewithal shall we be clothed? (For after all these things do the Gentiles seek:) for your heavenly Father knoweth that ye have need of all these things. But seek ye first the kingdom of*

---

[1] Genesis 3:17-19, the exact formulation is : « ... In the sweat of thy face shalt thou eat bread, till thou return unto the ground ; for out of it wast thou taken. »

God, and his righteousness; and all these things shall be added unto you. Take therefore no thought for the morrow: for the morrow shall take thought for the things of itself. Sufficient unto the day is the evil thereof.» [1].

He also said:

-« for the labourer is worthy of his hire... » [2].

It is true that often, in our society, we think that working must be something painful and unpleasant but I sincerely think that this is false.

It is only one <u>perception</u> which obviously, through the creative process of the words we use, will become our experience thereafter.

However, we are, each one of us, <u>free</u> to change our perceptions and thus to change our experiences. And when you choose to do this, a whole new world is offered to you.

A world in which you can do what you like to do and to live from it. A world which enables you to be the most beautiful expression of what you can be.

The only difficulty which arises then is to accept to be paid for doing what you like to do.

Indeed, many people have trouble accepting money for something they enjoy. It does not seem « normal » for them to be paid for being happy. But I believe that the Great Being did not place us on Earth to suffer.

I think that He placed us on Earth so that we could choose to become what we want to become, using the creative capacity which He placed in each one of us. And thus we define each day, through the words, thoughts or actions which we project outwards like many signals determining us in the Universe, like many messages that we send to the Universe while we keep on telling it through our thoughts, words and actions :

---

[1] Matthew 6:26-34 ; Luke 12:22-31
[2] Luke 10:7 ; Matthew 10:10

-« Here is what I am and what I choose to be. »

For my part, I believe that if what I do is useful and « organic » within the « organism », of this society, it will always work. I am « condemned » to success. On the other hand, if what I do threatens the balance of the « organism », of society, my action is by its nature doomed to fail.

In fact, in nature, an « organic » process, which supports the survival of the organism, will always be encouraged; whereas a « non-organic » process, which threatens the survival of the organism, will always be discouraged, the entire organism then mobilizing to fight against this non-organic process.

It is true that the relationship with money can be to study, but it is not the object of this book.

Just understand that if you yourself do not realize and accept your own value, the Universe itself will reflect that to you.

And you have all a great value…

Realise it, all as soon as possible… and start to manifest it… Choose to manifest it !

Choose to become **more** that you thought you were !

And get out of the mental prison in which you either trapped yourself or let yourself be trapped.

Take up again the reins of your life in your own hands and see yourself as greater, more powerful, happier, more loving, more patient, in better health and **ALLOW YOURSELF** to become it !

CHAPTER 11
DO WHAT YOU FEEL LIKE DOING...

After nearly six months working for Martin, I realized more and more that the « model » of healing which he had set up was really marvellously well thought out.

Although Martin did not really invent anything new, he was inspired, in developing his workshops, by techniques that existed already and that he combined in an original way. He also put together existing knowledge of Eastern philosophies, studied the human energetic system and compiled them into a very complete synthesis. This synthesis was simple and easy to understand for Westerners who had little familiarity with Eastern concepts.

For example, to develop his « Vision Workshop », he had judiciously combined tools directly inspired from the Silva Mind Control Method[1], for which he had been an instructor, and others which found their inspiration in the Bates Method[2]

This original way of combining both physical and mental tools made his own so called « method » a more comprehensive one.

By adding some of the tools referring t7o the human energy system (the energy centres or *Chakras*) he made of it a very complete tool, simultaneously working on the three principal aspects our being: body, mind and spirit.

With simple words, he could render comprehensible spiritual concepts that were generally very esoteric.

---

[1] Silva Mind Control is a method of mind control in which participants learn to use their mind as a tool to change situations in their bodies or lives. This method was put together by Jose Silva, an American with Mexican roots, after nearly 20 years of research. It was first presented in 1966 and was inspired, among other things, by the work of Emile COUÉ. There are many books on this method, notably The Silva Method, by Jose Silva and Philippe Miele, prefaced by Lee Pascoe and published by Editions Helios (French edition) and by Simon & Schuster (English edition).

[2] The Bates Method, put together by Doctor William Bates, proposes different types of physical exercises to stimulate and re-energise eye functioning. This method was partly inspired by exercises taken directly from Hatha-Yoga. These exercises are commonly called« Eye Mobility Exercises » and have been adopted by Optometrists.

As I started to understand more and more the principles of healing and transformation, I thought that one day, it would be very useful to adapt these tools specifically to help people who where H.I.V. positive or who had AIDS, a subject about which I naturally felt concerned.

I did not know yet how concerned I was with this subject ! I was to discover this only later on.

At that time, I obviously continued to work in the catering company during the week, periodically translating workshops at weekends.

As Martin and I finished presenting the first day of a two-day workshop, we had just recommended that the participants have a good time that evening.

It seems now obvious to me that it is really of <u>CAPITAL importance</u> that each of us do what we know we have to do in order to remain happy and in good health as long as possible. Indeed, I sincerely believe that if we are not happy, we cannot hope to remain in good health a very long time.

The recipe for happiness is after all so simple.

In order to be happy, just do what makes you happy and stop doing what makes you unhappy.

Once again, it's simple, isn't it ?

But it's true it is not always easy to put into practice !

It is all a matter of motivation. But I can tell you that if you put it into practice, you will never regret it, because it is worth it !

Anyway, that evening I really wanted to have another a sexual experience with a man. I had been living with Myriam for already more than a year, without really during this period having any desire for a man. However, that particular evening, the desire was very present and I decided to indulge myself in an « extra ».

When the workshop was over, I went to a meeting-place « reserved for men who like men ». There I met a charming boy with whom I had a very pleasant time, very « safe sex »[1].

I felt in fine form, happy, fulfilled, when I returned to be with Myriam at home.

Being so close to Martin for several months had taught me that clarity is something of paramount importance. Clarity in terms of yourself, clarity in terms of others.

I thus decided not to hide anything from Myriam and to tell her quite simply, as I came home :

> -« *Myriam, I just spent some time with a man.* »

To which, Myriam answered :

> -« *Listen Patrice, you can do what you want. On the other hand, if you'd like to do it again, I'd rather not know...* »

And although with these words, she proved her love and acceptance to me, it was not at all what I felt.

What I felt, was that I had done something wrong, since she preferred not to know. As Jacques Salome[2] says so well :

> -« *It is not the person talking who is making the communication but the one who is receiving it..* »

I decided not to say anymore at the moment. However, a certain feeling of guilt started to fill me. I kept telling myself

> - « *You shouldn't have..., You shouldn't have...*».

I realize now that this continued guilt maintained the unpleasant feeling, but, moreover, it was constantly reminding me of the good time I had had with this charming young man.

---

[1] « Safe-sex » means literally « Sex without risk », corresponding to sexual practices « without risk of contamination» or, as doctors today prefer to say, « with less risk of contamination » (Safer-Sex).

[2] Jacques Salomé is the author of numerous books on communication and relationships.

With the result that the desire to relive the experience imposed itself more and more

Guilt is an interesting emotion to study. It seems to come from within, whereas in fact, it comes initially from outside. It comes from our parents, and from our society which projects to us an image « known as » good. If what we wish or feel in the deepest part of us is not in agreement with this « good model », then, we feel this Guilt.

It is one of the problems that our Judeo-Christian society often has towards sexuality, be it heterosexual or homosexual. For a long time, sexuality was more or less presented as a taboo, even dirty, degrading or « bad ». And it is clear that for homosexuality, it is unfortunately still worse. Hence the conflict which can often emerge when a person discovers his or her sexuality.

How can something « bad » make me feel « good » ? There follow the processions of guilt which can then attack one, if, of course, one lets them enter.

I spent the following fortnight torn between, on the one hand, my desire to be with a man again, and on the other hand, this guilt feeling which I had accepted and created, I must now admit.

Finally, I decided to indulge myself this again in this agreeable little « extra ».

However, I must say that this « damn » guilt made the experience completely uninteresting. It undermined me.

I felt it before I met this man, while I was with him and obviously afterwards.

Because of this, just as the experience two weeks before had seemed to me rich and fulfilling, so this second experience seemed to be empty and meaningless.

Of course, I did not tell Myriam that I had had this new « extra-marital » adventure, keeping all this guilt to myself alone, unable to unburden myself to her and thus allowing it, unwittingly, to undermine me even more…

CHAPTER 12
An instructive journey...

It was only a few days later that I went to the United Kingdom for a weekend which would prove extremely instructive.

In fact, there was a Body-Mind-Spirit[1] exhibition in London where Vicky Wall had a stand presenting her Aura-Soma products. At the time I used to help her regularly during such exhibitions, where all volunteers were welcome.

I remember that this trip posed a problem for me. In fact, on the very same date, three possibilities were available to me.

I could go to Belgium for a exhibition of the same type as that in the United Kingdom to do Healings with other healer friends, I could go « to give moral support » to a friend who was going to give her very first workshop on Healing in the South of France, or I could go and see Vicky in London.

The three options were equally tempting, and I didn't know what to do.

It was Thursday evening and the next morning, I was supposed to take my luggage ready to leave work at the end of the day, to one of these three destinations. What was I to do ?

Thanks to Martin Brofman, I had met just shortly before some charming people, Lee Pascoe and Michael Dodson, directors and teachers of the Silva Method about which we spoke previously.

They had at the time invited me to take part in their courses for free so I could be trained in this method.

---

[1] This is an annual exhibition presenting an alternative, holistic approach to health. Different exhibitors present their methods and products. In France, similar exhibitions are Marjolaine, Rentrez Zen, Medecine Douce, Vivre et Travailler Autrement, Santé Autrement etc...

In fact, they thought they might need my services as interpreter in the future and preferred that I know the Method in order to be more skilled in the translating.

It was during these classes that I discovered how much Martin had been inspired by them to develop his own workshops. He had never hidden the fact, having been himself a Silva Method instructor in the past, and thanks to which he had healed himself of terminal cancer.

As I took part in these classes, I discovered wonderful transformational tools. Moreover, these tools were simple, practical, concrete and easy for anybody to practise.

Having this conflicted choice to make between London, Brussels and the South of France, I thought of a very simple problem-solving technique which I had learned in the Silva class : « The glass of water technique ».

This technique is used when you do not know what decision to make at a given time in your life. Perhaps it will help you too.

Here is how it works. This technique in two steps is generally practised in the evening before going to bed. If you have a choice to make, or a problem to solve, take a glass and fill it with water. Then, just before going to sleep, relax by taking at least three slow, deep breaths, feeling yourself relax more and more with each breath out. Normally, after three deep breaths of this kind, ,you are at the «ideal »level to practise this exercise.

Take your glass of water and close your eyes. Raise them upward as you drink half of the water, saying to yourself mentally:

> -« *This is all I need to do to find the solution to my problem which is:... here, you mentally formulate your problem... ».*

Open your eyes again and leave your glass on the night table.

You can then fall asleep.

The next morning, as soon as you awake, you can again take three deep breaths although, generally, you will be naturally calm upon awakening, and can directly go to the second phase of this technique.

Again take your water glass left on the night table, and, again, close your eyes, raise them upward and drink the rest of the water, while saying to yourself mentally: .

> -« *This is all I need to do to find the solution of my problem which is:... here, you mentally formulate your problem again...* ».

With this exercise, in the 24 hours following the beginning of the technique, you should obtain the answer to your question. This answer can have come to you during the night via a dream, or it can appear to you in the day in the form of an idea which comes to you, a message you hear, a word read on a billboard or in a magazine, a question which strikes you and which gives you simultaneously the answer, or all sorts of other possibilities ...

I was to leave Friday evening for one the three destinations. Not knowing what I was going to do that weekend, I practised this technique Thursday evening, telling myself mentally while I drank half the glass of water :

> -« *This is all I have to do to find the solution to my problem which is to know where to go this week-end, Brussels, London or the South of France...* ».

When I woke up next morning, I still did not know what to do..

So I drank the rest of the water, repeating my « magic » little sentence.

I prepared my bag and loaded it into my car, still not knowing if, that same evening, I was going to go to London, Brussels or the South.

During that morning, while I was busy with my work, a powerful idea crossed my mind :

-« Patrice, if you were to die after this weekend, what you would have rather done of these three options, ... before dying ? »

I was filled with wonder to see how the glass of water technique brought me the solution to my problem ...

Suddenly, it all became extremely simple.

It seemed obvious to me, that if this weekend was to be my last one on earth, I wanted to see again Vicky at least one last time before leaving. She had brought me so much !

So I said to myself :

-« OK, Patrice, you're going to London tonight... »

As soon as I had formulated that thought, I said to myself :

-« But you can't go to London, it will be too expensive and you don't have enough money; you need to take the boat, it is expensive, and then you will need a hotel, more expenses etc... etc... »

Fortunately, I already had within me all these tools. I again had a problem, so I said to myself:

-« Do the glass of water technique again !».

Since it was the middle of the day and I needed a very fast answer, I adapted the method by drinking the glass of water this time in only one session, unable to wait till the evening to practise it.

And mentally, I told myself :

-« This is all I need to do to find the solution of my problem which is to know how to get to London without money... ».

Reassured and trusting the technique, I carried on with my activities.

At the beginning of the afternoon, a flash went trough my mind. I was being told :

> -« *Patrice, it simple to go to London without money ! Here is what you're going to do : you just need to get to Calais with your car. Then at the port, where the vehicles for Great Britain gather, you will hitch hike. A truck driver will take you on board and take you to London.* »

It was so simple ! How did I not think about it before ! Thank you glass of water !

That is how I went the same evening to Calais. Once there, as I had been told, I hitch-hiked and a truck-driver took to me in his truck onto the boat. I even had my meal offered, the truck-drivers having a room for their meals reserved ! And as I had been told, this truck-driver drove me to an underground station on the way into London. I easily found a small hotel and Saturday morning , I was at the exhibition « Body, Mind and Spirit », joyfully meeting this astonishing woman that was Vicky Wall.

I settled down at her booth, explaining to people the principles of colour therapy and of the Aura-Soma products, sometimes doing aura readings for the people passing the booth.

After a very full day, I was invited to lodge with a friend working on the booth and I thought, again, that I had been wrong to worry about the expenses of the hotel, etc…

The Universe was looking after me again .

Marvellous Universe...

The following day, I managed to find a bit of time to visit the exhibition because the day before, I had been so busy with the booth that I had not been able to see anything.

As I walked along the rows, I discovered a booth which presented Kirlian photography. I had of course already heard about the aura and this process of electro-photography allowing it to be represented on paper, but until then I had never seen this machine.

So I decided to treat myself to a photo of my aura. Especially since that day at Vicky's booth there was a woman specialising in the interpretation of these photos. She was even conducting workshops on Kirlian photos and their interpretation.

So it was very proudly that I returned to the Aura-Soma booth and that I showed this friend the photo of my Aura.

As she was looking at it attentively, she said :

> -« *Well, Patrice, you look tired right now,... and... oh..., you do not have much energy,... and there is something strange about your blood... and your immunity... it seems very low...* »

You can imagine what was going on in me at that time.

Ok, I had had homosexual relationships.

Ok, I had taken risks, but it didn't happen often, and it was a particularly long time ago.

Ok, I was sometimes very tired. But still !

I had the impression she was announcing I had AIDS... I was devastated.

I stayed on the booth until 3 or 4 in the afternoon, then I took my leave of Vicky. I had to return to Calais hitch hiking after all. I had to be at my work in Paris Monday morning...

I did not feel great, I must say. The idea of AIDS haunted me.

I got on a bus supposed to take me out of London to Greenwich, where I could hitch hike for Dover and catch a boat.

After a long detour in the London suburbs, I started to worry. Obviously, I was not going towards Greenwich, I was sure of it, knowing London and its suburbs very well.

After having received confirmation from the driver, I got off the bus and found myself in a small suburb, without any indication how to get to Greenwich, in a little backwater where there were hardly three men and a dog.

After asking around in vain, I felt very uncomfortable.

Time was passing, I was going to miss the boat, how would I get back to Paris... In fact, everything was going wrong.

Then, suddenly, in a fit of rage-prayer, I invoked what I call the « higher powers ».

I told them :

> -« *Listen, I really need a hand <u>now</u>. Send me **now** someone to show me the road to Greenwich.* »

I had barely finished this thought when someone turning the corner of the street came straight towards me. Inside, I told myself:

> -« *It works !* »

I questioned him and he said :

> -« *I don't know, but go and see that man over there, he'll know.* »

Again, I said to myself,

> -« *It's all just bullshit after all... You see, you ask « them » for help and they send you someone useless....* »

Actually, I repented quickly, because the person they showed me gave my all the necessary information to get quickly to Greenwich ! !

It goes to show, you sometimes have to turn your tongue seven times in your mouth, or more accurately, in your mind, before you **THINK** something...

And so it was that I found myself hitch-hiking again, and very quickly, as the second car passed by actually, I found a driver.

Unfortunately, this gentleman did not go all the way to Dover and he left me by the road, with still 15 or 20 miles to go.

So there I was again, waving my thumb.

And in front of me the cars passed by, one after another.

And inside of me, negative thoughts came up, one after another...

> -« But how do you expect a car to see you, they drive way too fast here !..., There's no place for them to stop !... At this hour, you will not get a boat anymore !... You lost too much time with the wrong bus !... etc... etc... »

I was very upset because I must have been hanging around for more than an hour in the same place and time was passing, reducing my chances to get a boat on time.

Until the time came, when it was REALLY necessary I get my head in order.

I had learned to be an observer of my thoughts in order to control them if I realized they were not helping me.

And, at that stage, it was **more than necessary** I put them back in order !

I started to wonder :

> -« Patrice, why did you create this situation ? »

I realized first that the mental confusion I was in could be the cause. Also, I became aware of all the limiting beliefs I had about the fact that it was impossible for a car to see me and pick me up.

And as I was doing my analysis, I especially noticed that I **TOTALLY REFUSED** the situation as it was.

Now, I had learned that it is useless to resist circumstances. After all, it is true, like it or not, this circumstance exists, here and now.

I knew what I had to do.

After having taken a slow, deep breath, I started to converse again with my friends « up there».

It was like this :

> *-« Well, it's true, I recognize that I have not accepted, in fact, I've even resisted the experience you sent me. So, OK, I am willing to stay here an hour or two if needed, but I would REALLY like to have one car NOW so that I can get a boat before it is too late. »*

Barely had I finished my sentence than a car stopped and picked me up. Not only did the driver go to Dover, but on top of that, he was a ship captain and he left me right in front of the ferry departure gates!

Coincidence, you may say ? Perhaps... but quite honestly, I doubt it, even though, at the time, I was often asking myself this question.

Nevertheless, today, I have lived so many of these chance happenings or coincidences, that I KNOW they <u>cannot</u> be.

And as I like to say in my workshops :

> *-« Some day, you will finally have to OPEN your eyes and realize that Mister Chance and Miss Coincidence cannot have such broad shoulders to bear everything you put on them... Wake up... The sooner the better.. »*

Once in the departure hall, I rushed to the boarding office, noticing that a boat was leaving in less than half an hour. I was telling myself : *« At that hour, I've no time to hitch hike for a truck, I need to be in Paris the fastest possible. »*, especially as the following boat left two hours later.

As I was ordering my ticket, she told me that the boat was full and I would have to take the next one. And in no way could I get her to change her mind.

Obviously, when I went back to sit in the lounge, I was angry with HER personally, SHE had made me miss <u>MY</u> boat !

Instantly, after a brief moment of anger / panic / refusal of this situation, I suddenly realized that all this, was just a « test ».

Of course, it is a test !...

A test that my friends from « up there » were putting me through. They wanted to know again, if I resisted or accepted what is.

Instantly, I closed my eyes, filled myself with love and talked to them like this :

> -« Ok guys..., I understand your little game. It is true I refused having to take the next boat... It is true I refused to have to stay two hours longer, so OK, **I ACCEPT**, I am willing to stay here two more hours if needed, but I would <u>**REALLY**</u> like to be able to board the first boat which would allow to return earlier into Paris. »

Once my « conversation » finished, I felt calm, peaceful and confident as I reopened my eyes.

I stood up calmly, filled with love, and went up to the cashier lady who had turned me away some minutes earlier, as I imagined sending her lots of love :

> -« *Hello, you told me the boat leaving now was full... (and inside, I was thinking : Love, Love, Love...) but may be could you recheck... (Love, Love, Love...). May be you could phone on board... (Love, Love, Love...) as there may be a last minute cancellation... (Love, Love, Love...)*»

She took her telephone, and I heard her say a few words as I kept repeating, like an unending chant:

> -« *It's all right,... It's all right,... It's all right,... It's all right,.... It's all right,... It's all right,... It's all right,... It's all right,... It's all right,... It's all right,...* »

And then, without saying a word, continuing her telephone conversation, she handed me a boarding card, waving her hand to show me where to go. ...

I thanked her and rushed to the boat, exploding with joy, hoping I would never forget this wonderful lesson of acceptance...

The Universe was really wonderful, so wonderful...

CHAPTER 13
Welcome to the Club !

Once returned to Paris, I got on with my job and my routine.

The relationship with Myriam had greatly changed. I found that we were more distant than before.

On the other hand, I was worried about what that friend had told me when she interpreted the photo of my aura. Fear of AIDS was haunting me and the words she pronounced game repeated themselves in my head.

> -« *Well, Patrice, you look tired right now,... and... oh..., you do not have much energy,... and there is something strange about your blood... and your immunity... it seems very low...* »

Over and over again...

Finally, unable to stand it anymore, I decided to go for a test in a free and anonymous clinic in the 20th arrondissement of Paris.

I needed to know, not knowing was becoming unbearable.

I found myself there, in the waiting room, filling in a questionnaire, while people there looked at each other from the corner of their eyes.

I saw a woman, who had probably come for the results of her test, coming out of the doctor's office, her eyes red from tears.

The atmosphere was heavy and dismal.

When my turn came, I gave my questionnaire to a smiling nurse who took a sample of blood.

> -« *So far, so good...* » I thought, like an optimistic person falling from a building...

She then taped some stickers on the bottles and another one on a card she handed me, telling me I should come back in a fortnight to get the results. With this card, she insisted ! It was actually my « password» which gave me the right to have my results !

It is true that at that time, May 1989, labs were very slow to deliver the results. Luckily, great progress has been made since, thus shortening this very painful period of waiting and doubts.

That fortnight seemed to be long, very long, too long.

Fourteen days to keep thinking:

> -« Am I or Am I not ?... But, yes, of course you are... but no, it is not possible, it cannot happen to you... But no, you are not... stop freaking out for nothing, Patrice,... What she saw on your aura was just temporary... It's all right... Yes but still you are gay, you took risks in the past... But yes, but I was barely 18 or 19 at the time, it was too early to be contaminated...No, no, NO, you're creating these ideas,... It's all right... It's all right, ... But if you had it anyway... Oh yes, it's sure with the luck I have, I am, it's sure, But no, no, no...I am not, it is not possible... not me... I'm too young... ! »

Fourteen days of facing the clientele, with a smile please :

> -« Hello madam, how are you today ? ... Yes, Yes... I am all right... And what will you have today... a little steak as usual... with fries and green beans ? Ok... Enjoy your meal...Hello sir, how are you?... Yes, yes... I'm fine... »

And inside, I was thinking. wanting to shout at them all :

> -« It's all right, It's all right, It's all right... no !... It's not all right !..., It's not all right !..., It's not all right ! !... I'm afraid !... I'm afraid !... I'm afraid !... Afraid of having AIDS may be...afraid of being sick... afraid of croaking, ... afraid of dying alone in a hospital room... afraid of being rejected by Myriam... by my parents,... by my friends,... by my brother and sister... by my colleagues... by my boss... by you !... I am afraid of finding myself alone, rejected, sick...
>
> Afraid of suffering,... afraid of getting thin and rotting from within,... afraid of having may be contaminated

someone,... I'm afraid ! So Shit! I'm not all right !... No, I'm not all right !...»

But what could they do about it ? Nothing.

They could not know... and probably not understand.

So I had to wait... wait...wait before receiving the final verdict.

Finally D-Day arrived. I went to the clinic, my « password» in my hands.

I was received quite rapidly by a female doctor who sat me down, and after going through my file, announced the terrible news.

She said that, for safety's sake, they had to take some blood again which would be analysed so that we can have a confirmation.

It was a bit as if the ground gave way beneath my feet.

She talked, talked, talked... but it was as if I did not really hear her... She seemed so far away... so far...

Inside, I was saying to myself: *« Well, there you are, you wanted to help people by specialising in H.I.V. and AIDS, well, Welcome to the club ! »*.

I did not realize at that time the perfection of that moment.

In the state of torpor in which I found myself, I went like a zombie to have some blood samples taken and then went out onto the street.

I went into a phone box to call a friend and after a few words, I burst into tears as I was telling her the news.

She had been to classes and knew how to find comforting words

After all, it is true, in my apparent « bad luck », I had luck. I was not alone, I had at my disposal very powerful understanding and tools for transformation.

I just had to use them.

When Myriam came back that night, I told her the news.

She took it calmly, with her natural wisdom. For my part, waves of tears kept engulfing me, as it seemed to me, everything was over...

And then, as usual, time had its effect.

The Universe is so made that there are always two openings to a tunnel. You go in one time, but anyway, you come out some other time.

Very quickly, I gathered myself together, realizing that all of the experiences I had had up until now had been to give me the tools and the strength to get out of this situation..

When I told Martin about my being H.I.V. positive, he reacted in a great way because he said immediately :

> -« *Listen Patrice, I invite you to take part in my next workshop. You were supposed to translate it, I know, but don't worry,... I will ask Yves to translate it instead and you will have these four days to work on your healing.* »

When I returned to the clinic some time later to get the new results, I must say I felt much stronger..

The doctor who had received me two weeks earlier told me that, unfortunately, the test was confirmed. She then commented on the analysis they had done.

It seemed, according to her, that I was already in an advanced stage of the disease, my T4 cells being low, according to the medical norms because I had only 180. She explained that there were defined stages of development and that I was in stage 3 or 4 of « pre-AIDS » She then announced that at this stage, it was very important that I started a treatment and she started to write out a prescription so that I could go to a Parisian hospital and get some AZT. *(This was the only « treatment » proposed at the time.)*

I calmly explain her then it was not worth it. That I would not go and get this medication.

As I knew nothing happened by chance and that everything starts in my consciousness, I asked her if it was possible to know roughly when I was contaminated. After a little sigh, she said :

> -« *You know, it is rather difficult to evaluate with precision but seeing the few T4 cells that you have... (Thank you Ma'm, that is reassuring) I would say it was probably at least six or eight years ago ... »*

I started to explain her some principles of healing, the approach through positive thinking that I was willing to put into place to achieve my healing, and she had a beautiful reaction.

It was as if she was reassuring me, telling me how she was sure that this approach could help me. She explained how some people she had been following for years could have wonderful changes and progress as soon as they had a passion driving them.

She told me :

> -« *Even if it is growing peas, I can see it helps the patients stabilize their progress whereas others collapse after a few months, ... ».*

She told me the story of H.I.V. discordant[1] homosexual or heterosexual couples not using condoms after they talked about it together and in which the « healthy » partner had never been contaminated.

In terms of that, Myriam had not, thank God, been contaminated.

I can obviously understand why now. She had simply not decided to die. But we will talk of all that later.

This lady doctor was explaining me that she noticed in her practice that positive attitudes played an important factor in the advance or otherwise of the disease..

---

[1] One of the partner is H.I.V. positive and the other is not.

She then showed me a medical magazine, in which a surprising story was reported.

It was the story of a young man having developed a Kaposi Sarcoma[1]. The article explained how he one day « decided » that the horrible stains on his skin were actually ink spots and, each time he washed, he imagined they were progressively disappearing . After some time, they had disappeared ! Sadly enough, this article concluded with an ironic note « Colourful, isn't it ? »

It seems nowadays, things have changed a little and that researchers are starting to get really interested in what they call « long-term H.I.V. survivors » ant what they call « co-factors »[2].

So it was with her encouragement that I left her that day.

She advised me nevertheless to go regularly for tests in order to follow the progress of the disease.

All I had to do was to roll up my sleeves and get to work !

---

[1] It is one of the diseases associated with AIDS, sometimes described as a kind of « cancer » of the skin. It is a proliferation of malignant cells in the area of the skin, mucous membranes or inner organs. It manifests through the appearance of purple painless spots.

[2] A co-factor can be, for example a particular food, stresses, practising relaxation or meditation, smoking, drinking a lot of coffee,... Actually, any factor that could explain the advance or otherwise of the pathology.

CHAPTER 14
What is AIDS ?

It seems important to me to pause here in order to explain H.I.V. seropositivity and AIDS as well as the different approaches to health I could have used.

These approaches are based on my different experiences, on different readings and on the knowledge I have gained throughout time.

You may feel I use a light tone sometimes towards this disease.

It is not by chance.

I believe that words are very creative creatures. Some words are filled with fears and a whole set of projected images. I know that it is in that case <u>necessary</u> to use an other word, less charged, or to de-dramatize everything that has been associated or « put » around that word.

You should understand that something can only have power over me if I give it that power. If I see something as « serious, serious, serious » to that extent, it will be difficult for me to detach from it.

I had made the choice, from the very beginning, to see H.I.V. positivity or AIDS as a little unimportant illness, like a kind of flu coming one day and leaving another, as easily as it came.

One thing was sure for me : **There is neither chance, nor coincidence in the Universe**. On the other hand, all my experiences since the beginning of my transformation confirmed one thing **« I create my reality »**.

It is therefore in the light of these ideas that I will now get to the subject of H.I.V. positivity or AIDS. Nevertheless, this book not being intended to be a thorough explanation of the process of healing, I will just try to be relatively brief and focussed on H.I.V. positivity and AIDS. To help you understand more easily and to make my point more precisely, I will explain to you certain basic important principles, sometimes referring to the problems of eyesight.

If each of us create our reality, we have to talk, write or describe our experiences with words reflecting that idea.

Often, people accept this idea of creating their own reality but do not really integrate this idea into their way of talking. In fact, they will say :

> -« *He upset me..., She manipulated me..., I had an accident...* »

Now, if they really « owned» the idea that they create their reality, they would say, instead :

> -«*I allowed myself to be upset..., I allowed myself to be manipulated... I created a particular circumstance in my life...*».

In fact, this new way of talking then **REALLY** reflects the idea that they create their reality.

I am very aware that this idea may seem outrageous at first. At least, it was for me when I heard it for the first time. Nevertheless, if you choose to leave your prejudices aside, you will realize that when you describe a symptom[1] with words that reflect the idea that we created it ourselves, that we do are literally doing to the body, what we were figuratively doing in the consciousness. So, in my vision improvement workshops, if a person is myopic, *(seeing better what is close than what is far away)*, I explain *(by describing the symptom with words reflecting the idea that person created it him/herself)* that on one hand he/she « chose » to see what is close and that he/she « chose » to not see what is far away ». This implies a kind of turning in on oneself, as if the person was distancing himself

---

[1] A Symptom can be a pathology, a state of being, or even a circumstance of life. Not seeing clearly is a symptom, seeing clearly is another symptom. Being in good health or not is a symptom, being happy or unhappy, being lucky or unlucky, for me, are also symptoms.

from the outside world, choosing to see what is closest. This is what enables us to say that myopia *(short-sightedness)* is connected with an emotion which can trigger a movement of « contraction » : fear.

When I myself heard that idea for the first time, I realized many things. I realized how, at the time I had to wear glasses, I was living on the one hand the aggressions and humiliation in the boarding school, and on the other hand, I felt bad about my homosexual drives. Because of that, I was turning in on myself, and because of my perception, thinking of the outside world as dangerous, that it was not safe for me to be <u>out there</u> what I knew to be <u>in there.</u> All the symptoms my body was creating were actually attracting my attention and inviting me to change. My body was telling me :

> *-« But after all, Patrice, get out of your bubble, stop seeing your (distant) future blurred, realize that your future is wonderful, stop being afraid of others and the outside word... »*

With this way of looking at physical manifestation, you realize that you can see, for every pathology, a certain « way of being » associated with each symptom.

Therefore, if someone wants to get rid of a pathology, he must first let go of the « way of being » that created that symptom.

He must get rid of the mental attitudes, and beliefs, which attracted toward him, like a magnet with selective polarity, the pathology or the circumstances which became exteriorised physically.

This is why healing **<u>IMPLIES</u>** change.

And as I like to say :

> *-« There are miracles... but there are no miracles... »*

If someone heals, It is because he or she has changed… and not only physically.

As everything is a state of consciousness, he/she has in fact changed in his/her consciousness.

These basics now explained, let us get back to H.I.V. seropositivity and AIDS.

According to the doctors, H.I.V. positivity and AIDS are caused by a retrovirus which, in general, attacks the human defence system, the immune system. The body, progressively less able to fight against the multiple aggressions of the outside world, then falls prey to all sorts of diseases which generally lead to death.

If everything starts in my consciousness, if I create my reality, a pathology that could lead to death has to start in a decision to die.

The study of the human energy system tells of the existence of *Chakras* or energy centres. According to the model studied, there can be 7, 9, 12 or even more.

In the model that I studied, there are 7 *Chakras*. Each one regulates the flow of energy in our energy bodies. While they are not physical, the *Chakras* interact with the physical body through the endocrine glands *(also 7)* and the nervous system *(we have 6 nervous plexus plus one brain, which means, again, 7 nervous « centres »)*.

These *Chakras* represent also « aspects » of our consciousness. It is as if everything that can motivate you or concern you on earth can be divided into 7 categories. I can, for example, be concerned with my security, my sexuality, my power, my freedom, love and so on…Each of these *Chakras* is in charge of one of these « categories ». If, at a given moment, I am concerned with a certain aspect of my life, this tension produced in a particular part of my consciousness, brings about a tension in a particular part of my energy system, that is, in a Chakra which enters in a state of tension.

We can represent the *Chakras* as solid balls of energy interpenetrating the physical body at the level of each nervous plexus. When a *Chakra* is in tension, this tension is perceived by the group of nerves with which it interacts and from there, the tension is then transmitted through the nerves, to the part of the body managed by that group of nerves.

That is why when someone develops a pathology in a particular part of his/her body or in a particular bodily function, if you know the consciousness « map » that the body represents, you can immediately know what type of tension in that person's consciousness created that pathology.

Once that tension is recognized and identified, the healing process then consists in releasing this tension so that balance (health) can manifest again.

So that you can properly understand the process I am describing, here is a more concrete example :

The first *Chakra*, located physically at the level of the perineum, between your legs, is physically associated, in terms of the group of nerves, with the sacral plexus (which controls your sphincters, your legs, and the lower part of your body. This *Chakra* is associated, in terms of the endocrine system, to the adrenal glands. In consciousness, this *Chakra* is concerned with our perceptions of security, trust and survival. When it is in its natural, or optimal. state, you feel confident, safe, solid, stable and present.

> **Important**: According to the « model » with which I work, I think that health is our natural state, having confidence is our natural state, feeling love is a natural state, seeing clearly is a natural state, and so on...

In terms of that first *Chakra*, if confidence is our « natural » state, then lack of trust or fear are, therefore, you will understand, « non-natural » states.

If, for example, you are afraid, that fear « happens » in a part of your consciousness : the first *Chakra*. This centre of energy is then put into tension. This tension is then perceived by the group of nerves with which it interacts (the sacral plexus) and from there, it transmitted to the parts of the body managed by that group of nerves.

So, what happens when you feel a strong fear ? :

Your legs no longer support you, they start to shake... Sometimes, if the fear is really intense, your sphincters could let go *(Ooops...)* and if this fear is really extreme, you could be « paralyzed », your legs refusing to obey. Also, this fear triggers the secretion of adrenalin *(produced by your Adrenal glands, they too being controlled by the first Chakra through the sacral plexus)* which thus gives you the energy to « run for your life » or to face the danger and fight.

I hope that this short concrete example allows you to better understand the interaction between your consciousness and your body. If you really understand that, you will automatically understand the importance of changing your consciousness to bring about the change in your body. I hope so with all my heart.

In the map of consciousness which I studied, the immune system *(which « breaks down » according to the doctors because of H I V,[1])* is directed by the thymus gland, itself associated with the *Chakra* called « the Heart Chakra» because it is located in the centre of the chest.

This Heart *Chakra* directs our perceptions of Love. It is in part our ability to love and feel loved, our ability to be in a relationship with others. It also represents our ability to accept and the whole notion of acceptance.

---

[1] H.I.V. or Human Immune deficiency Virus, considered by many doctors as « responsible » for H.I.V. Seropositivity or AIDS (Acquired Immune Deficiency Syndrome). However, there are other theories held by some eminent doctors, which we will talk about later on.

The blood, in that map of consciousness that I studied, is also directed by the heart *Chakra.*

Interesting ?

This *Chakra* is associated, also, to the thymus gland (which directs the immune system), and to the lungs, the heart, and n fact the whole chest area..

The element associated with the heart Chakra is Air. (Our lungs are located at the level of the heart Chakra.)

I hope you start to understand what I am leading up to..

H.I.V. positivity or AIDS affects the patient's immunity, his blood.

According to the model with which I work, AIDS or H.I.V. seropositivity is a mal-function of the Heart *Chakra* It is about a dis-function of our perception of Love.

H.I.V. positivity or AIDS are therefore not « sexual » diseases, although sexuality can be, according to some doctors, one of the factors of contamination. In fact, neither the sexual organs nor sexual functioning are affected by this disease.

The association with H.I.V. positivity or AIDS is the following :

> *- The person has the <u>perception</u> that his/her « life style » is <u>separating</u> him/her from the people he/she loves. And if there is no love, he/she prefers to die...*

Speaking of which, if we look at the elements associated with the different *Chakras,* we see that the Earth is associated with the first *Chakra,* Water with the second, Fire with the third and Air with the Fourth *Chakra.*

Now, let us think about this a little.:

How long can we live without food ?

(Earth , first Chakra) : ...   Weeks, even Months...

How long can we live without water ? *(Second Chakra)* : ... Only a few days...

How long can we live without air ? *(Fourth Chakra)* : ... Only seconds...

So, Air, symbolically associated to the notion of Love, is indispensable. Love is indispensable. It is the basis of everything.

There is always air around me... There is always Love around me...

The problem is therefore not the absence of Love (because it is always there, present around me) but really the **PERCEPTION** of its apparent absence.

Again, everything is in our perception. It is something I like to say again and again in my workshops.

> -« *What is happening out there has <u>no importance</u>. What matters is my perception, my view, my way of seeing those circumstances!* »

If we look at what is happening with H.I.V. positivity or AIDS, the person has the perception that his lifestyle separates him from people he loves.

He is telling himself :

> -« *Because of my different sexual inclinations, I am not lovable or not loved.* »

Be it because his family or relatives reject him when they learn about his sexual orientation, or because the person himself perceives himself as being « fundamentally un-lovable » or not loved because of his different sexuality.

And if it is not a different sexuality, it can be different practices, for example the use of drugs which are not socially acceptable (It is rarely the use of alcohol, coffee or pharmaceutical drugs, ...) or again a « life style » that the person perceives as « different » which creates the perception there is no love, that one is not loved... And again, the person may be either rejected by his relatives, by his family, by those he « perceives » as « source of love » perceiving himself as « fundamentally un-lovable » because of his different life style

And without love, or should I say, without the « perception » of love being there, what can we do ? We decide to die.

Without Love, life can not be lived. Or to be more exact, it does not « <u>seem</u> » to be worth living.

And why is that? I think, according to what I experienced up to now, that love is the basis of life. Love is the core of life. Love is life itself. It is both cause and effect, it is the force by which the Universe organizes itself according to our desires, out of Love for us.

Now, that H.I.V. positivity or AIDS is understood, what do we do about it ? How can we change and reverse the process ?

Here are some possibilities.

When I heard these ideas for the first time, I found everything very « coherent , logical, rational » but when I received my diagnosis, I had to integrate these «ideas » into the context of what I was living.

I started to thoroughly and honestly question myself.

If nothing happens by chance, I had to ask certain questions. :

> *-« What was happening in my life at the time I became aware of being H.I.V. positive and on the other hand, what was happening in my life at the time I was contaminated ? »*

In fact, according to the doctors, I had been contaminated when I was 18 or 20, even if I didn't know about it « officially » until I was 26.

I had to find the events, the circumstances I had undergone in the different periods of my life, which could have made me want to die, because of my « perception » of not being loved.

The answers came, one after the other, not all at once and certainly not very quickly, but nevertheless, they came and I understood why I had created all this.

When I thought about what was happening at the time I learnt of the symptom, I could only think of the adventure I had had with that boy some weeks earlier, and Myriam's reaction to the situation. But mostly, it was about <u>MY PERCEPTION</u> of this situation.

Ok, I wanted to be with a man... but I felt good about that.

Ok, I told Myriam about it,... but since clarity seemed paramount to me, I felt good about that.

Ok, Myriam had told me : « Patrice, do what you want to do, but if you want to do it again, I'd prefer not to know. »... And there, on the contrary, I did **<u>not feel good at all</u>** about that.

I did not « perceive love » in Myriam's declaration. I had « perceived » I had done something wrong. After all, she had the RIGHT to prefer not to know if it had to happen again, and I had the RIGHT to accept doing it again, hiding it from her or preferring clarity, not accepting hiding it. This erroneous **<u>perception</u>** on my part had a huge effect on our relationship. I no longer perceived myself as loved, nor accepted the way I was, whereas actually, that was the true situation.. Nevertheless, that unfortunate **<u>perception</u>** on my side had been enough to « close » my heart *Chakra*.

I now realized why, after that episode, the relation with Myriam was not the same. My heart *Chakra*, which, when optimal, allows me to feel loved, connected and close to others, had closed.

Before, when I though about Myriam, I thought « us ». She and I formed ONE entity.

After that episode, when I thought of Myriam, it was « her » on one side and « me » on the other. The feeling of « us » had disappeared and at that time, I did not understand why…

On the other hand, I definitely did <u>not</u> remember feeling <u>so unhappy</u> in that experience that I decided to die.

On that point, something did not « fit »…

I had to search more deeply.

The doctors told me I had probably been contaminated 6 or 8 years before. I had to search for something that had happened when I was 18 or 20.

It is clear that at that time, I really did not feel loved.

That was sure.

It is also clear that that was the time where I <u>plainly</u> decided to die. Actually, to be more accurate, because it is important, it is not that I had decided to die. I had decided I did not want to live beyond the age of 28 or 30, if life was to continue as it had been *(or more accurately, the way I **<u>PERCEIVED</u>** it)*, which means **without love**.

But who could have contaminated me at the time, in response to my deep demand ? Especially as in 1980, it was only the « beginning » of AIDS in France and I had barely started my sexual life !

And, obviously, new realisations came to me.

It could not be the cashier of the gay cinema with whom I had had my first sexual experience, because it had been totally « safe », without any risks.

On the other hand, that had not been the case with the charming boss of this establishment whom I met afterwards.

He had invited me to spend the night with him, and I willingly accepted. He was tender, affectionate and kissed divinely. Feeling I could trust him, we did not take precautions. I saw him again some time later and once again, we did not use condoms… At the time, it was 1980, 1981 and all that seemed so far, so impossible…

Nevertheless, when about a year later, I returned to that theatre to see him, when he walked towards me, I did not recognize him at first glance.

He had lost so much weight ! His face seemed sunken, destroyed.

But it was indeed him, still smiling and affectionate. And bingo, I slept with him again that night.

After that, we never met again. My life was to take an other direction.

Nevertheless, as I searched to « understand » how I had been contaminated, everything was becoming clear !

It is true that in 1980, it was only the « beginning » of AIDS in Europe. Nevertheless, he was in charge of a Parisian establishment frequented exclusively by gays. It was therefore right in the middle of the storm. He had at his « disposal » to live his fantasies, quantities of dashing young men and had explained that he was very happy with that….

When I realized that he was the one that had contaminated me, I went through a short period where I was angry at him. Nevertheless, very quickly, I forgave him, realizing that actually, it had all started in ME.

Remember : I was determined to work sincerely with the idea **I MYSELF** created my reality.

In fact, an illness can come either from the outside, as most people believe, or from within. If it comes from the outside, I am therefore a « victim » of the Universe, under the influence of circumstances over which I have no control. On the other hand, if it comes from within, which means my attitudes, my perceptions and reactions, **THEN**, I CAN CHANGE SOMETHING.

I can take back my power and **CHANGE**.

And thus, I am not a victim anymore... I am a **CREATOR**...and I am responsible for my state.

I am therefore both creator of my happiness **AND** my unhappiness....

This does not mean I have to feel guilty for the state or the circumstance I created in my life...I can simply recognize that I am the one who created it ... and **DECIDE** to change it...

If what I created in my life does not suit me, **I CAN CHOOSE** to change it...

For my part, I realized that I had attracted this experience of H.I.V. positivity to me, somehow to « punish » myself for living something which society told me was « bad ».

Not only was society telling me that it was « bad » but, also, I, Patrice, I had not only wished to live this homosexuality, but **ON TOP OF THAT**, I liked it!

I had somehow to punish myself for living something I wanted, while at the same time I felt guilty for wanting it.

I had therefore attracted that person who contaminated me, like a magnet, so that my body could attract my attention, through the disease, to the fact that it was necessary for my **survival** that I change the perception I had of myself and that I finally feel **LOVED**.

I had attracted him to me, at the perfect time when I had taken the decision to die if life was to continue being what it had been. Which means a life of solitude. A life without Love. Or more accurately, a life in which I did not perceive love. A life in with I felt so alone and unloved.

Actually,,, I now believe that one **cannot** develop a symptom unless one has developed first, in one's consciousness, the state of togetherness with this symptom.

As Etienne Daho says so well in his magnificent last album « Corps et Armes » (Body and Weapons (play on words in French with Corps et Ames which means Body and Soul)) :

-« There is no chance,... There are only rendezvous,…No coincidence »

And even if it is in a very different context that this singer pronounces this beautiful sentence in his very first song « Overture » , we know that anyway, what is true, IS TRUE, by its very nature.

Any time, any place, and any context…

He therefore came, perfect, at the perfect time, to make me live this perfect contamination so that at a perfect moment, I could become aware that it was necessary to change.

I actually realized how lucky I was to know about my contamination at that perfect moment.

I had been working with Martin for about 6 months and I had at my disposal wonderful tools which I had <u>already</u> recognized as being very powerful, telling myself, that some day, I would use them to help people who had either H.I.V. positivity or AIDS.

Everything was in fact perfect !

I just had to use these tools on my self!

Obviously, I was upset for a while, but reason allowed me to recover rather easily.

Had I known about my contamination some months earlier, I would not have had the knowledge I had and I would probably have been drawn into the infernal circle of terrible beliefs constantly projected about H.I.V. positivity and AIDS. I would probably have accepted the AZT and probably would have managed to fulfil my « contract » that is, manifesting the decision taken when I was 18. I would probably have managed to « leave » as planned by the age of 28 or 30, exhausted and weakened by all the secondary effects of this drug[1].

I realized the perfection of my meeting with Martin.

Actually, I never did anything to meet this being.

To me, who was living this situation from within, it was a bit as if, with His great blessed Hand, the Great Being had seized me by the collar of my shirt to put me where I was. He had PUT me in Nick's arms, so that he would say some words that were to change my life forever… which was to make me aware of my abilities as a healer…which would make me interested into healing … Which would make me meet Martin, so that what was to happen did happen.

I found Martin's path remarkable. In fact, he went through an experience that could have been terrible. He had a malignant tumour in the spinal cord, and doctors had condemned him to death within two months, having no treatment to offer him. He had thus to find the solution within, not being able to find one outside.

And he healed himself !

Which gave him a perfect credibility as a teacher of healing. Not only did he say that anything could be healed, he **PROVED** it.

I could see my own scenario unfolding, slowly but surely…

---

[1] I quote: « … Remember that AZT is not a new medication to fight AIDS. It was proposed as a cancer chemotherapy more than 20 tears ago, and was rejected by the FDA (Food and Drug Administration) because it was too toxic. As medicine is held in place by practice and not by results, and as AIDS was considered an incurable disease, AZT was accepted as the official treatment (this is called profiting from death). In fact, AZT provokes an immune-depression (that is really the last straw !) with anaemia, lymph problems, toxic hepatitis, etc... Moreover, AZT has been called into question among us and becoming more and more discarded. But, attempts are being made to pass it on to the Third World at Sale prices...» End of quote. Extract from an article published in « Vérités Santé » number 63 Saturday, 29 July 2000 **« AIDS, a Political Scandal»** by Alfredo Embid (editor-in-chief of the Spanish magazine « Medicinas complementarias » which consecrated an issue to a dossier named « South Africa revolts against the AIDS orthodoxy».

Having met Martin and realized the potential of his method, I had told myself I would be specialist on H.I.V. positivity or AIDS, before having my own « entry ticket » in that club !

My path was becoming clear.

Just like Martin, having gone through the process of the disease would give me a much greater credibility when I would have to help people as a result of my own experience.

When, two years later, I started to teach workshops on improving eyesight, I noticed that the fact I had worn glasses myself made me much more credible to these people suspicious about this alternative approach to health.

I had to change and quickly...

To heal from a disease that could lead to death requires adjustments.

First, it can be important to remember you decided to die

For this part, no problem, it was easy. I could not deny the deep decision I took when I was 18.

Then, you have to decide to live.

There, already, there could be a difficulty. Actually, if to decide to live means I will continue to live in the same circumstances as those which made me want to die, I will therefore have no desire to live any longer in these circumstances.

And this is a **PARAMOUNT** point. I would have to be able to consider DIFFERENT CIRCUMSTANCES IN LIFE. Circumstances in wich I would want to live.

And that is the problem for many people : they feel **UNABLE** to consider other circumstances in their lives. They function with **such limiting beliefs** that it seems « inconceivable » there would be a way out of their situation.

And this is where I can really help people. That is what is happening in the workshops I present.

And as I am doing this right now, let me offer you another way to look at the word.

I offer you a new vision that allows you to perceive a word that already exists but that your eyes may not yet have perceived.

A world in which there is always a solution to a problem. A world in which I sincerely believe that if a door closes somewhere, a window is opening at the same time, somewhere else. You just have to search for it and find it…

And as Richard BACH[1] so wonderfully says in his book, « Illusions, The Adventures of a Reluctant Messiah » :

-« There is never a problem that has no gift for you in its hands. You look for problems because you need their gifts. »

I had therefore to consider new circumstances in life. Circumstances in which I would feel recognized and especially **LOVED**.

And I realized I would also have to change the image I had of myself.

And quickly…

At any rate, if I really wanted de heal and Live !

---

[1] Richard Bach is the author of many books, including *« Jonathan Livingstone Seagull »* published by MacMillan (1972). This books tells the story of a seagull who wants to fly always higher, further, faster. *« Illusions, the Adventures of a Reluctant Messiah »* is published both in hard cover (Dell Publiching) and by Mass Market Paperback. All of Richard Bach's books are a wonderful souce of inspiration for someone who wants to change.

CHAPTER 15
En route to Healing...

I decided therefore to do everything that seemed useful to achieve my healing.

It is true that at the time, I easily felt « down» and I often had intestinal problems. Up until then I had not made the connection..

My wide reading had led me to discover a wonderful woman, Louise L. Hay[1]. *(Ahh yes, another « wise » woman who was to put me back on the path...)*

She had produced a beautiful book « You can Heal your Life », published in France under the title, « Transformez votre vie » (Transform Your Life), which is not an exact translation of the English, : « You can HEAL your life » (It is true that France is a rather backward country in this area and very sensitive to the concepts of « healing », or « healers »)

In this book, she explained, amongst other things, how she had healed herself of cancer, using tools of mind control and others she had put together.

I found she had a very interesting approach to health.

She said, for example, that one the reasons why we created « symptoms », was in order to attract something to us, a particular advantage. I could only agree with this idea. In fact, if I am feeling bad, the fact that I complain about it, moaning and groaning, for all to hear, could allow me to attract some of the love I really need !

She also worked a great amount with the notion of forgiveness. It seemed to her necessary to forgive in order to change. According to my own knowledge, I could only agree with her.

---
[1] Louise L. Hay is the author, amongst other books, of « You can Heal your Life » published by Hay House, and « The AIDS book » (Alibris).

In fact, if everything is perfect, how could I harbour resentment towards a person or a situation ?

Another notion that seemed very important to her was that of loving ourselves. She encouraged people wishing to heal to repeat, amongst other things : « *I love myself...* ». There again, I could only agree.

I had bees asking myself questions about what we sometimes call the « power of love ».

In particular, I had decided to question this commonly accepted sentence: « **Love heals** »

In fact, I believe you should <u>never</u> accept something just because someone tells you it is true. We should, on the contrary, doubt it. Doubting is putting the idea to test. And if finally, we cannot prove it false, we have to accept the probability it might be true. At that stage, it is time for you to experience it. I can tell you something is true but before you have lived it <u>yourself</u>, you cannot <u>know</u> whether it is really true.

I remember that at the beginning, I was very resistant to all of these ideas. In fact, I even wanted to prove them wrong. But, finally, not being able to invalidate them, I started to **REALLY** believe in them..

That's why I sometimes say that sceptics make the best believers.

So I was wondering why they say « *Love heals* ». It is true that, after all, this sentence was only a belief ! Why not : « *cabbage heals* » while we're about it ?

Turning this idea round and round, I wondered :

What is the physical process that heals me ? The answer was simple : the body's defence system.

And what controls the body's defence system ?

Again, the answer was simple. It is the thymus gland that controls the immune system.

Now, energetically speaking, with what is the thymus gland associated ?

Answer : The heart *Chakra* !

And to what does the heart *Chakra correspond* ? : to the perceptions of Love ! **BINGO** !

Ok now, it is clear ! I could accept the idea that love **really** healed.

My Love for myself heals me ! The Love I have for someone else heals him/her (provided, of course, that the other accepts or perceives that Love, of course !)

But let us get back to Louise Hay. She proposed to those who REALLY wanted to change that they follow this kind of ritual, a succession of statements you had to repeat like a *Mantra*[1].. A sentence like :

> -« *I am willing to change, I am willing to let go of the need of (here, you can put the situation or the illnesses you want to get rid of), I am willing to forgive, I forgive, I forgive myself, I love myself and.. (here put a sentence describing what you want to live instead.)* »

For me, this sentence became :

> -« *I am willing to change... I am willing to let go of the need for AIDS..., I am willing to forgive..., I forgive..., I forgive myself..., I love myself and my T4 cells are more and more numerous...I am willing to change... I am willing to let go of the need for AIDS..., I am willing to forgive..., I forgive..., I forgive myself..., I love myself and my T4 cells are more and more numerous...I am willing to change... I am willing to let go of the need for*

---

[1] *Mantra* is a Sanskrit word. A *Mantra* is a word, a sentence, or an idea repeated continually. Repetition is a ritual which exists in all religions. In the Catholic religion, reciting with prayer beads, or a rosary, is a form of *Mantra*.

> *AIDS..., I am willing to forgive..., I forgive..., I forgive myself..., I love myself and my T4 cells are more numerous... I am willing to change... I am willing to let go of the need for AIDS..., I am willing to forgive..., I forgive..., I forgive myself..., I love myself and my T4 cells are more numerous...and so on... and so on...*

Like a chant, I repeated it over and over again...over and over. In traffic jams (great, I will have time to think about my healing !), walking in the street (great, another chance to think about my healing !), waiting in a queue (and yippee, there we go again !) and so forth, and so on...

I quickly noticed a definite improvement in my intestinal tract and when I did my test again, my T4 cells had almost doubled !

This obviously encouraged me to continue.

Trusting greatly in Vicky Wall and in her abilities, I decided to go and see her in England and this time to ask her for an Aura reading.

As I explained what was worrying me, she looked at me for a long time, as if I was going through a scanner with her eyes and she said calmly :

> -«*Don't worry. There is indeed a little spot in your aura, but I don't see anything serious for you. On the other hand, I have to tell you one thing :* **Your healing happens through the healing of others.** *It is by healing them that you will heal yourself.* ».

It was only much later that I was to understand what she meant by that.

Amongst the different approaches I used, I would also learn to speak in another way.

I learned to not identify with the symptom. Actually, many people have a tendency to identify with the symptom, to possess it. They will say for example :

-« *MY myopia, MY astigmatism...* »

Using this possessive pronoun, they « possess » the symptom.

It is more appropriate to say :

-« *THE myopia I had, or... THE astigmatism I had...* »

In this way, through the words we use, it is possible to put some symbolic distance between the symptom and us, and then it is more easy to get rid of it. I therefore learned to say :

-« *THE H.I.V. seropositivity that I had manifested or that accompanied me...* ».

In this way, it was more easy to be detached from it, having not identified myself with the symptom.

It is also one of the ideas in I teach in my workshops :

-« *Do not define yourself in the present or future, according to past values. And this especially if you do not wish to keep or develop these characteristics in your present or future !* »

In fact, we have a tendency to define ourselves in the present moment according to past experiences of ourselves.

For example, a person will say :

-« *I am shy.* »

Actually, what she really wants to say is :

-« *I was shy.* » *or to be more precise :*

-« *The experience I have of myself is of having been shy.* »

Nevertheless, talking or speaking that way, what he/she really means, because of the words he/she uses is :

-« *I WAS shy, I am now and I probably will be tomorrow.* ».

This, in an implicit way and also because of the beliefs he/she holds in terms of his/her state.

In terms of myself, it became paramount, **for my own survival**, that I **stopped** seeing myself as having a problem but rather as having had one. If I thought of the symptom, I forced myself to say :

> -« *I had a problem with my immune system, I had few T4 cells, and so on..., but, from now on, everything can be different* ».

And <u>even</u> if I do not know how It can be different, I HAVE nevertheless to believe that, one way or another, it can **really** be different.

However, it is not always easy, especially if you are permanently saturated with limiting beliefs... This is one of the major problems facing a person who has a life-threatening illness: <u>**Fighting against the mass of limiting beliefs which surround us or are imposed upon us every day.**</u>

These beliefs are sometimes presented by our doctors *(we have to forgive them, because it is the result of the pathological[1] model they were taught.)* But sometimes, it is worse : It is people who claim to love us who harass us with thoughts like : « *You don't believe this sort of « bullshit », do you ? »* *(We have to forgive them too, because they are just victims of the limiting beliefs they were taught or they chose. And for them, it is a clumsy expression, it is true, of their Love for us.!)*

These people do not realize that in not morally supporting us, they are pulling us downwards... where, a priori, they would not want us to go.

For my part, I had no choice. Or more accurately, because I **ALWAYS** have a choice, mine was very simple.... If someone

---

[1] For a traditional doctor, it is « inconceivable » that a physical body remain healthy. This is because everything medicine has learned was learned by studying sickness or diseases. The sickness or disease is therefore the « reference model » for medicine.

was unable to support me in my process of healing, being **AT LEAST** neutral towards my alternative approach, that person had NOTHING to do with my life.

That is where I started to realize there are no neutral thoughts.

The person was either **WITH** me or **AGAINST** me.

Jesus said as much to his disciples when they wanted to stop someone « driving out demons » in His name, since that person was not one of His followers :

> -« *Forbid him not: for he that is not against us is for us.* »[1]

Actually, it was as simple as that !

If the person was « with me », I could tell him :

> -« *You are with me. so WELCOME INTO MY LIFE !* »

If not, it was rather :

> -« *You are against me, SORRY, YOU HAVE NOTHING TO DO WITH MY LIFE ! I have already enough fears to deal with, without having to deal with yours as well !*

In fact, if in the first place, I CREATE MY REALITY, in the second place, those around me can participate in the creation of my reality, and this obviously, <u>if, and only if, I am open to their creative energy.</u>.

This is a process that is called co-creation and this is what happens when a « healer » and a « patient » choose to unite in order to create a scenario that is pleasing to them both : To see the disease disappear.

This is why, for many years, I chose not to talk too much about my experiences, preferring to tell them in confidence only to those I knew were positive. Anyway, these experiences were past and I had no desire to re-energize them in the present.

---

[1] Luke 9:50

And this was a wise decision. I remember one day meeting a woman who had been in Martin's classes saying to me in a surprised tone:

> *-« Say, Patrice, you look great!... So-and-so told me you were very very sick ! ».*

With such thoughts, this « So-and-so» was keeping me in the illness !

A true healer has a function, I believe, which is, if not to <u>know</u>, at least to hold in his/her consciousness the fact that the other feels better or is healed !

Well, yes, this « So-and-so » had ATTENDED a workshop. But their attitude revealed that they had understood nothing, nor had they integrated these precious ideas, that was sure.

I think that it is also important to remember that, whatever symptom we have, somebody, somewhere, has already been healed of it. Or at least, somebody did not see the symptoms develop as doctors predicted they would. And this, <u>WHATEVER</u> the symptom !

This is why, as the years passed by, I got my hands on different books telling the story of those who healed from H.I.V. or AIDS, or met people to find out how they did it. Sometimes, I would find inspiration. Two books, that we will talk about later, seemed particularly interesting to me: *« Healthhope Pub House*[1] *»* and *«* Deadly Deception[2]*».*

After all, as I often say, in the long run, it is not really important how you get to healing. The important thing is to get there.

In the same way that we are physical, mental and spiritual beings, we can heal using tools which are physical (traditional

---

[1] « Roger's Recovery from AIDS: How One Man Defeated the Dread Disease... » by Bob Owen, published by Healthhope Pub House.

[2] *«Deadly Deception»* by Doctor Robert Willner published by Peltec Publishing Company.

medicine, homeopathy, surgery, herbal therapy, food hygiene, acupuncture and so on …), mental (relaxation, reprogramming of the mind, and so on…), or spiritual (meditation, prayer, rituals and so on …).

In fact, use EVERYTHING you think can help you, be it physical, mental or spiritual tools and, why not, all three together.

If you think about it for a while, which is the link that unites a therapist to his patient ? (Whatever name you give to the therapist : doctor, Homeopathic doctor, Surgeon, Herbal therapist, Acupuncturist, Magnetiser, Healer or Guru, and so forth …) The link is « BELIEF ».

The therapist BELIEVES, or even better, KNOWS that his « method » can help the patient and the patient himself BELIEVES, or even better, KNOWS that THIS SPECIFIC TECHNIQUE can help him.

Again, beliefs, beliefs, beliefs,….

Wonderful beliefs that can either free us or enslave us.

Remember one thing that appears more and more important to me : The important thing is not the path that leads to somewhere but rather the final destination !

And without knowing it, I was getting closer to my Final Destination !

CHAPTER 16
Accept the unacceptable...

Amongst the different processes I had to go through, one of them appears to me important enough to look at it separately.

In order to understand this mechanism, I have to present certain metaphysical aspects with which I was working.

In the physical world, we are taught that the cause is out there and that the effects are also seen out there. We are taught, for example, that a virus or a germ brings about a disease, that heredity brings about an illness, that an accident brings about a wound and so on...

According to this model, the cause of the problem being out there, the solution of our problems is also therefore to be found out there. We should therefore take these medicines, these substances, this advice out there to change something which is, according to this model, external to us.

Metaphysics, contrary to physics, tells us that EVERYTHING that happens out there is an EFFECT of a cause that is in ourselves...

From this principle we can derive a kind of formula allowing to create something.

This metaphysical law is :

$$\text{Image} + \text{Certainty} = \text{Manifestation}.$$

In order to manifest something, according to this principle, you just have to create a precise picture of what you want and then add certainty, confidence.

The more precise the picture, the greater the certainty, and the faster the manifestation.

This principle is very simple and it is one the basic tools I decided to use for my healing. I knew it worked because I had already used this same principle to create certain things in my life.

Nevertheless, with metaphysics, you have to be very precise and take care.

Why ? Because when a person is confronted with an illness that can generally be considered as serious, that person has a VERY clear picture of what could happen *(the doctors have taken care to inform him/her of what could happen !)* Moreover, he/she is afraid that picture could come about.

Now, fear is a certainty, a belief, a faith in a negative future.

Which means that, metaphysically speaking, we can create <u>just as easily</u> what we want as what we fear !

And this a <u>very important</u> variable, of which we must be very aware !

Here is an example that will illustrate, I hope, the importance of being « aware » at the same time both of the « pictures » we hold in our consciousness and of the « certainty » we hold towards these pictures. Do we have positive or negative certainties ?

We have all lived, I think, a scene like this one : We have been lent a magnificent set of glasses. Everything has gone fine and we are doing the dishes. And just as we are drying these glasses, a thought crosses our mind : *« Oh... I mustn't break one of these glasses... »*, and, at that very moment, the glass breaks in our hands.

Image + Certainty = Manifestation...

You had a picture *(clear, precise...)* you were afraid *(confidence, certainty in a negative future...)* and **BINGO**, you got a manifestation.

For my part, I was determined to heal and therefore, I decided to use these tools consciously. If I wanted to heal, I needed to see myself as being healed and believe it.

The problem was fears. Those fears which, like an emotional glue, were constantly bringing back certain images to my consciousness.

What I am afraid of ?... Of **THAT** ! And I guess you can imagine I had a <u>very clear picture</u> of it. And this very clear picture, added to the fear which is a certainty, could only manifest it.

Therefore, in order to get of out of such a situation, one has to go through a particular process. A process of **ACCEPTANCE**.

I have to accept the <u>probability</u> that, amongst <u>the infinite possible futures that available to me from now on</u>, well, this future I am afraid of <u>might</u> happen ! It does not mean it <u>WILL</u> happen.

In the same way, I would like you could understand, that it is not because someone « predicts » something that that prediction is true. And this is so, whether it be a doctor, an astrologist, a « medium» or even a meteorologist…who is doing the predicting. The only thing that is TRUE, is that he/she said it would happen. That part was really true ! The prediction itself can be erroneous and due to « unconscious projections of our soothsayer ». The prediction is either wrong or right !

Personally, I like to see consciousness as being logical, rational, mechanical, sometimes comparing it with a car with its rules and its functioning mechanism.

Then, if a person chances to predict something for me, I choose to understand something a bit like this :

-« You see, Patrice, I believe your « vehicle » is going...
straight into a tree… (this part is the prediction) therefore, if you continue to do what you have been doing until now, and you let go of the driving wheel and of the pedals… you will land up against that tree… ».

Ok, I do agree, BUT I am in control of my vehicle.

And if I was not in control of my vehicle, having settled comfortably in the passenger seat, which means considering myself a « victim » of the Universe, suffering outer circumstances, I can now <u>choose</u> to take back control of my vehicle. I can CHOOSE to take back control of my life and can AGAIN GET BACK in the driver's seat. And n this position, I can NOW change something *(brake, turn the steering wheel...)* and give my vehicle, and my life, another direction !

You understand now ?

I KNOW anyway that deep inside us, we all know what is right for us and what isn't.

We KNOW all of the decisions we have taken.

We are conscious of all the choices we either made ourselves or let others make for us. In the end, it comes to the same thing, because that too was our choice.

Because of that, if someone predicts something that is true, I know it, I RECOGNIZE it *(I Re-cognize it, I know it again)*, because it is just « confirming » something I already know ! *(And that actually I had already decided !).*

That's why all that remains to do is to change!

And to thank the person or the symptom that allowed me to «remember » that decision I had taken in the past and that I am now bringing into being in the outside world.

Fore-warned is fore-armed.!

I <u>have</u> to do something differently ! That is why I said healing IMPLIED transformation.

A Sufi proverb comes back to me :
« If you keep doing what you have always done, you will keep getting what you have always got ! »

Something to deeply meditate upon...

But let us get back to the metaphysical process of transformation :

$$\text{Image} + \text{Certainty} = \text{Manifestation}.$$

Generally, when you totally accept that that picture you feared could manifest, you go through a period of intense emotional release. Just as if you were living it...

But once you have « **accepted the unacceptable** » you are free !

Once the possible future TOTALLY accepted *(because, anyway, it could happen, couldn't it ?)*, you can then focus fully on the picture you would like to live instead !

Fear having disappeared, it will no longer bring that negative picture back to your consciousness and you will be free of it.

This process can nevertheless take a certain time but, eventually, you will be able to say without any emotional reaction :

-« Yes, it is true... It could have happened to me that ...(here, put what the doctors, or others, predicted, that you do not want to live...) but, for me, actually, it will be like this.... (and here, you put everything you would like to live instead !) »

I hope that the understanding of this principle will help you to change some situations in your life, because, actually, it can be applied to create anything !

And always remember :

« If someone has already done it, someone else can do it...»

It is just about deciding to do it, and may be, it is about learning to do it **BUT MOSTLY, IT IS ABOUT DOING IT !** Because **NOBODY** can do it for you.

No more limits here, except : your own fears or beliefs.

CHAPTER 17
And now, what will I do ?...

What was great for me, in this experience, in spite of everything, was that I had close to me the precious help of Martin and his own experience. Knowing it by heart, having translated it so often during lectures and workshops, I could draw inspiration from it..

After the surgery that was supposed to remove his cancerous tumour, the doctors explained to Martin that the surgery had failed. When he asked what treatment they would prescribe, they explained that there was none. Chemotherapy was not appropriate for a bone-marrow tumour in this area of the neck, radiotherapy could not be used either, and the surgery had failed.

When he then asked who would happen, the doctors told him that the result would be fatal, because of the nature of the tumour and its location. To the question : « *How long?* », they answered that it was a matter of one or two months, unless a sudden sneeze speeded things up...

Charming !

Feeling himself condemned, Martin wondered :

-« *If I have one or two months left to live, how would I like to spend the short time I am allowed ?* »

The answer was simple and easy :

-« *Being happy.* »

I asked myself the same question, even if, *a priori*, I was not facing such a tight « schedule ».

Even so... Who, here on earth, can tell me with certainty when he is going to die...?

Same question..., same answer...

Since for the past two years, I had been training myself in the techniques of healing, I realized more and more that transmitting these ideas filled me with joy.

On the other hand, I had healed my sight thanks to this method and I was starting to think seriously about « one day», starting to teach and transmit myself these ideas of improving eyesight.

The fact of learning I was H.I.V. positive only speeded up my decision.

I told myself :

> -«*If I have « x » months or years to live, I would prefer spending them doing something that really makes me happy.*»

I therefore decided to stop my salaried activity.

But when ?

In order to mark clearly my intention of living doing something else, I asked Martin some months later the authorisation to become an instructor of his Vision Workshop, to which he agreed.

At the time nevertheless, it was only the « beginning » of my opening-up process and I had still strong limiting beliefs about money.

It is the period of my life I explained in Chapter 10.

I had decided to open myself to receiving money for doing what I loved doing and the Universe began to really support me in that decision.

Each month, my income coming from healings or translation became an increasing part of my total income. And I realized that even if this income was less than my salary as Quality-Controller in Catering, it was nevertheless enough to pay basic expenses like rent, telephone, and so on…

It was on Saturday July 7th 1990 that I had « THE VOICE »[1]. This intuition pushed me into finally taking the leap and leaving the workaday world.

I had gone to the wedding of a friend, Françoise, whom I had met some years earlier during the theatre courses. On that day, this voice, which I had already heard in the past, declared to me :

> -« Patrice, you can stop working now. We will see to it you live from now on doing what you love :
> Healing. »

This idea came upon me with such strength and such certainty that **NO DOUBT** could remain.. It was sure. It was going to work, the Universe would make me earn a living from healing.

And I realized I had to hand in my resignation as soon as possible ….

I still had to be patient and wait until the coming Monday.

At my work place, I made an appointment with my supervisor and told him my intention to stop work and to ask at first for a year's « sabbatical ».

It was July 9th 1990.

The system required me to give three months notice.

The date of my « retirement » from the work world was fixed for October 9th 1990.

The day of my 28th birthday !

For more than two years, since I had started Astrology I had been wondering :

> -« But what is going to happen for my famous « Saturn return » when I'm 28 ? »…

---

[1] Astonishing Synchronicity again or coincidence, it is exactly 10 years later, July 7th 2000, that I write those lines !

Well, now I knew !

What a gift ! What a perfect synchronicity !

I realize now how everything was perfect and nevertheless normal. For more than two years I had been unceasingly energizing in my thoughts a strong transformation for my 28 anniversary ! It could only be strong.

This was also the period I started to wonder about the relationship I felt with Jesus when I did laying on of hands :

-« But what is it going to happen when am 33 ? ! ».

And this is how I started to energize this new symbolic date which I hoped would be important.

And over the next 5 following years I had the opportunity to reenergize in several times !

Once I had given notice to my employer, I started to organize my life as a young « retired » person.

I had been contacted by Daniel, who was organizing workshops in Belgium. He knew that I wanted to start teaching and offered to organize a first workshop. A date was fixed : September 29th and 30th 1990.

I found that date « interesting ».

One of those synchronicities which, each time they happened, touched me deeply, revealing to me a little more the perfection of the Universe.

September 29th was Saint Michael's day, an Archangel for whom I had a particular affection. What I had learned, which made him even more appealing to me was that he was the one who « cut » between good and evil, working on the « blue ray », the one of Divine expression.

I felt honoured to be placed under his « protection ».

As the workshop date drew nearer, I began to have doubts:

> *-« What if I forget something important... What if I don't know what to say anymore... ».*

After all, I would have to spend two whole days talking to these people who had legitimate expectations...

Finally, the workshop date arrived and any doubts proved to be totally unjustified because the workshop went by marvellously both for all of the participants and for myself.

D-day, where I was to quit my job, also arrived.

October 8th was to be my last day of work.

My new life as young retired person could start on my 28th birthday.

I had treated myself, as a birthday present, a seat for the show of the « Cirque du Soleil ».

This magnificent show was beautiful and really magical ! I could again perceive therein a synchronicity, a sign that the Universe was encouraging me in my decision.

This wonderfully harmonious show held a message that was clear to me :

> *-« Dream your life and live your dream ! »*

To sum up, for those of you who didn't have the chance to see the show, here is the subject :

A group of « tourists » arrive on stage. They all seem heavy and sad, dressed in their dull raincoats or their faded coloured dresses. Suddenly, as a mist invades the scene, elves with brilliant colours joyously spring from the fog and metamorphose the whole group.

Each of the characters are then transformed. An old crippled man becomes a contortionist... A man becomes a rope walker... A woman becomes a clown... each of them seeming to manifest a potential they had not yet exploited.

And as the show ends in a whirlwind of colour, each character becomes again what he was before. With a little difference though : They can « find again » that magical state they had lived. Simply by a small effort of centering and remembering !

For me, as I was watching this superb highly symbolic show, my eyes filled with tears of emotion, I could see and hear the Universe telling me, as I was starting my new life :

-« Bravo, you made the right choice ! Live your dream and dream your Life, for EVERYTHING is possible, if you believe in it !

I had on top of that the strange impression that ALL THAT existed <u>ONLY</u> for me ! And in a way, it was true.

I was to see this show again 14 times !

It gave my the possibility to push back even further some of my limits.

One of the principles I was working with *(and still do)* is :

-«There is nothing you cannot do, there are only things you have not yet learned how to do ».

And as I was looking at the show, seeing a juggler with his balls and another person riding the unicycle, I heard myself say :

-«This, this it is something that you cannot do. »

And the very moment I thought that, another part of me said :

-« That's wrong. You just have not yet learned how to do it. So, stop complaining, learn and <u>do it</u>. !»

As a sort of challenge, I bought a unicycle and some juggling balls and proved to myself within weeks that this sentence was really true. And those of you who saw me riding on the unicycle on Santa Monica Boulevard at that time could have seen that, as I came there to see Louise Hay, Deepak Chopra or Marianne Williamson when I found about having been H.I.V.

positive and when then I flew to Los Angeles to meet these wonderful people.

« There is nothing you cannot do. There are only things you have not yet learned to do. »

This is a **fundamental** idea in many fields.

In the context of improving eyesight, for example, if someone says : *« I can not see clearly.»*, he defines himself as unable to… and therefore, will have that experience.

Instead, if he says *« I can see clearly, even thought right now, I do not have that experience… »*, this person can then expect to see more clearly, seeing himself now as able to see clearly.

And that is all that's needed.

We need to start to perceive ourselves as capable of much more in order to manifest it.

Once again, it is simple. Not always easy, but it is nevertheless possible.

I thanked Heaven again for the experiences it was giving me.

It was only much later after that I realised one of the other gifts the Universe had given me when I quit my job.

Having taken my leave of the « security » that my work represented OBLIGED me to trust the Universe. I had « no more choice ».

Before, I could always rely on the « security » of the fact that, working or sick, my salary still arrived each month.

But now that I was responsible for myself, I had to trust the Universe.

In fact, the total of my funds was about 2 000 francs (about 300 €), because I had borrowed some money from my employer to buy a car.

I knew that the revenue of the workshops I was to translate between October and December would allow me to last until January but after ... ? What was going to happen ?...

In the States, there is book which made a strong impression on me, although I never read it. For me, the title was enough.

« You can't afford the luxury of a negative thought »[1],

I was feeling in that exact situation. As I said previously, they are no such things as neutral thoughts.

I was either **WITH** me, or **AGAINST** me through my thoughts ! I had therefore to be very aware of them, as I still need to do today.

And with my mania for dissecting everything, as I was analysing this sentence, I said to myself :

-« How come, I cannot? I am free! Free to think what I want to think, free to say what I want to say, and free to do what I want to do ! »

And, obviously I am free to think what I want or to do what I want, including having negative thoughts !... But I must be ready to take the consequences ! It is as simple as that.

A thought brings about an action, an action brings about a reaction. Everything is there.

Do I really want to receive the fruits of my thought, of my word, of my action ?

If yes, no problem, I may continue…

If no, for my own comfort, I had better stop immediately…

This is sometimes surprising in certain people's behaviour.

They expect something different from the Universe, while they keep spreading their fears or their limits, through their thoughts, words and/or actions.

---

[1] This book by John Roger and Peter McWilliams is published by Harper Collins Publisher.

I sometimes like to formulate it this way :

« If you want to harvest wheat, sow wheat ! Some people who are probably crazy or, to be kinder, let us say, asleep or bleary-eyed, continue sowing corn hoping to one day harvest wheat ... It is madness. <u>It cannot work</u>. This is simply automatic. There is no notion of judgment here, please understand. It is purely mechanical. Open your eyes, LOOK and SEE. Wake up ! If you want to harvest wheat, sow wheat. ! »

One of the transformations that was to help me most was to « feel » more and more the presence of this benevolent strength that was always accompanying me and towards which I could always turn in case of problems. *(Years afterwards, I now realize the benefit of turning to it, even when there is no problem !)*

When, in the past, I heard people thank this « God » for what they had, it would make my blood boil.

I said to myself :

-«Stop this bullshit ! If I have money, it is because I get up every morning at 6 o'clock to be on the job at 07.30 !!! »

And as I came from « so far » *(and so, I can assure you, everything is possible !)* I was becoming more and more aware, having surrendered to Providence, that IF I had what I had, it was only BECAUSE that energy, that strength, that GOD I started to perceive some times had **<u>INTERCEDED</u>** for me.

I perceived more and more the marvellous « Perfect Cosmic Orchestration » that the Great Cosmic Conductor was leading every day.

CHAPTER 18
Around the world...

After having presented my first workshop in Belgium, a friend offered to organize another in February.

I was very happy, because I told myself,

-« Well, apparently, you will be able to keep going financially until at least February or March now.

And that's how I lived in the beginning. I <u>always</u> had what I needed but <u>very rarely before</u> I really needed it…

Often, I received what I perceived as being « a miracle » just before I really needed it.

At the beginning, I gave workshops in Lille *(in the north of France)*, Paris, Namur or Brussells *(in Belgium)* and alongside my own workshops, of course, I continued to translate Martin's workshops.

Talking of which, you may remember how I had « decided » to become Martin's sole interpreter (see Chapter 10)

I had a pleasant surprise, barely three months after having taken my « retirement » from the world of work, when I received a phone call from Pierre, who was translating Martin's workshops in Belgium. He told me :

-« Listen Patrice, I'm going to stop translating Martin's workshops as I'm starting to teach my own. Could you take care of translating workshops in Belgium from now on ? »

You bet I could !

I was so happy with the gifts I was receiving from the Universe ! Everything was really working ! I had decided to become the sole translator, and I was going to be !

Actually, I must honestly say that I now thank the Universe for never having given me the job of translating workshops in the south of France, Yves's « territory ».

In fact, if I had had to translate these summer workshops, I could never have gone to teach my own workshops in the far-off countries I was about to discover later.

And on top of the gift that these extra translations meant, the Universe was teaching me a beautiful lesson.

It was teaching me to have SUCH FAITH, that I should act as if I already had what I wanted, even though, physically, it seemed as if I didn't yet have it.

I had left my job without any proof that my future was secure.. Nevertheless, my experience was telling me that I was right to have this sort of « blind » confidence.

In this regard, this saying existed already, about 2000 years ago, from a certain Jesus. (I quote: « *Therefore I say unto you, What things soever ye desire, when ye pray, believe that ye receive them, and ye shall have them.* »[1]).

And if all of that was just bullshit ?

But let us be serious again.

At the time I stopped working, I had no physical security to hold onto ! My total bank balance was only 2 000 francs (about 300 €), I had no savings and my only « sure » income was coming from translations or workshops that went barely till January, which was 4 months away.

On the other hand, I had had « **THE VOICE** ».

This Voice so strong, so sure, so soft, that had told me :

-« You can stop working. We will make you earn your living doing what you love. »

Having trusted that voice, putting my trust in It instead of in external physical appearances, I was demonstrating my faith.

And God, always keeping his promises, was proving it to me, but only after I had taken the first step myself in faith. I heard

---

[1] Mark 11:24

later in India that if we take ONE STEP towards God, he will take 100 towards you. This statement now seems to be absolutely correct because I live it permanently.

And actually, it is true, He will take a hundred towards me, but only <u>after</u> I have taken one. And that one step, I am the only one who can take it.

A bit like Indiana Jones in « The Raiders of The Lost Ark », the hero seeking the « Grail », has to make his own step in faith into the void, to realise after, <u>but only after</u>, that that void was only an illusion.

As I often say in my workshops, the Universe seem to push us to the edge of what seems to be a bottomless precipice, which we later perceive as just a small step, <u>BUT ONLY AFTER</u> we have crossed it.

Before resigning from work, this decision I knew I had to take some day frightened me, what would I live on ?.... and if all this did not work ?...

Nevertheless, once the decision was made, I realized that the precipice into which I had to throw myself was just a simple step to go down *(or may be go up !)*.

Actually, I often wondered afterwards :
-« But why did you not do it earlier… It was so easy after all. »

I now know that I did not do it earlier because the time simply had not come, I just was not ready. I know the Universe functions in an ordered way, with rhythms, seasons, cycles and that everything always happens at the right moment, never before ! So why worry ?

I felt so fortunate to be able to live these experiences that, at the time, I did not dare ask MORE of the Universe.

It is a lesson I learned later.

Daring to ask for more.

And as I reconsider all these experiences before telling them to you, I once more feel filled with gratitude towards the Universe for the « luck » I have.

Nevertheless, I know this « luck » I have did not come « by chance ».

It is just a state of consciousness which flows from a simple decision.

A decision you can take at any time !

A decision that I hope, you will also take !

As my teaching activity started to intensify, I started to think differently about an idea we have already discussed:

I told myself :

-« Since I am free and EVERYTHING is possible, I can either : choose to do something I do not like doing….and let myself be paid for that … or choose to do something I REALLY like doing… and let myself be paid for that. »

For my part, I had made my CHOICE and the Universe had fully satisfied my expectations.

Nevertheless, I wished to push this idea even further … For fun… …To see how far I could go…

I decided therefore, that if I was free, I had the choice to do what I really like in <u>a place I did not really like</u> and let myself be paid for that OR, I had the choice to do what I REALLY liked…, in <u>a place that I REALLY liked</u> and let myself be paid for that.

Again, I made my choice.

It happens that I am a great lover of orchids. Having travelled very little up till then, I DECIDED that it would be nice if I could now give classes in exotic places where orchids grow and there are sunny beaches…

Love is the Key...

Some time later, as I was translating a workshop for Martin in Belgium, a participant approached me during a break :

-« Hello, My name is Philippe. I live in Noumea and I saw you were teaching vision improvement workshops. Would you like me to organize a workshop for you there ? »

At the time he spoke, I must honestly say I did not even know where New Caledonia was ! On the other hand, « Noumea » sounded exotic to my ears and we agreed on a first date.

When, some weeks later, I was making my flight booking, I got quite a shock. The fare was more that 15.000 francs (about 1 500 €) ! It is true that at that time, air fares to these destinations were still prohibitive.

At that moment, I doubted, wondering :

-« Do I really want to go there ? Will I invest such an amount without knowing in advance how many people will be there and whether organization costs will be covered ? »

I decided nevertheless to trust the Universe. Anyway, it was what I had chosen to live and demonstrate !

The Universe was giving me an other chance to test it...

So I paid for the ticket, asking my friends up there :

-« If this workshop brings me **at least** enough to pay for my trip and my expenses there, already that would not be so bad ! »

Not having such an amount available, I bought my plane ticket with my credit card, trusting the Universe that by the final payment date, the money would have been credited to my account...

And, sure enough, I was to come back from my first workshop in New Caledonia having earned 500 francs (about 76 €) after the trip and organization expenses had been paid.

I received **EXACTLY** what I had asked...

I had asked and received. Yes, of course I had received, but <u>in accord</u> with what I believed I would receive !

This realisation is **extremely important**

Yes, I can have EVERYTHING, Yes, I can create anything, Yes, I can obtain everything I want by changing my beliefs.

However, there is a limit. A limit you have to know if you want to go beyond it.

I must ALWAYS allow myself to BELIEVE this new belief is TRUE, that I CAN REALLY get what I ask for and that I DESERVE to receive what I want.

This a variable of **paramount importance** in the mechanism of creating our reality that often poses a problem for many people.

Do you REALLY believe you <u>CAN</u> get what you want ?

Do you REALLY believe that you <u>DESERVE</u> to get what you want ?

If you succeed in managing these variables correctly, I assure you that your transformation will be rapid.

I think that they are rules, laws, simple principles that rule the Universe and when we start to understand them, we can then consciously use them to our advantage.

It is a bit like a precise apparatus where you have to know the user's manual.

Unfortunately, we did not all receive this manual at birth.

Certain people have it automatically, sometimes without even knowing that they have it and therefore seem to succeed at everything they touch.

Others, like me, did not have it. I had to look for… and find this user's manual.

So, for example, in the same way that there are rules to know and obey when you drive a car, so is it for consciousness.

In a car, you know that you CANNOT accelerate and brake at the same time if you want to drive it in the best way.

You could of course tell me you CAN accelerate AND brake at the same time because these are two different pedals and you have two feet.

And of course, you COULD do it.

But, do you CHOOSE to do it ? NO.

So is it with consciousness.

I cannot WANT something and BELIEVE, at the same time, I cannot get it. It is purely mechanical.

Again, you could tell me :

-« Of course I can , since I am free !... »

And, this is sadly what many people do.

And it is true, that obviously I **CAN** do it.

However, do I choose to do it ? **NO.**

Being free does not mean doing anything at all!

It is sometimes sad to see so many people persist in WANTING something while they hold onto the idea that it is either « difficult » or « impossible » to get. *(This word « impossible » should be banished from your vocabulary from now on if you <u>sincerely, deeply</u> want to change something in yourself or in your life.)*

Mechanically, unless these people realize what they are doing, unless they OPEN their eyes to REALLY see, unless they wake up from their stupor, they can not get what they want.

These people should first AUTHORIZE themselves to believe that it is possible for them to get what they want, WHATEVER IT IS.

Having for my part, realized that I had created the experience of Noumea, I decided to make a new decision.

I <u>decided</u> that, <u>even</u> if the expenses could « seem » high, according to my <u>still very limited perception</u>, the Universe would see to it that the income was always more than the expenses, so that it could not only cover the expenses of basic organisation, but there would be <u>more</u> left to pay the expenses I had to face with my new- born training company.

If I were to have more expenses, I decided that it HAD to be because I would have more income.

And that, of course, is what I had to live afterwards.

Clarity is a fundamental value for me, and I had decided, to be « clear » in the organism in which I lived, to respect the « rules » within this organism and to teach within an « organic » structure, within that organism.

If I did not live in an « organic » way within my organism, it would reject me, I was sure of it. This is what happened for many of my « colleagues» who preferred to work « cash in hand».

If I want to be integrated within an organism, either I accept its laws, or I change organisms.

Otherwise, my « non-organic » functioning within this organism will make this whole organism mobilize itself to « destroy » me.

This important realization obliged me, moreover, to revise my « beliefs » about food.

This is what I will tell you about next …

CHAPTER 19
I eat, therefore I am...

Since the beginning of my transformation, I had decided to become vegetarian, my readings having convinced me that it could only be beneficial for me.

In fact, these writings taught me that foods participate in our state of mind, and if we take in different qualities of food, different emotional qualities will then take their place in our consciousness. Body chemistry *(through food)* brings about a certain « chemistry » of thoughts, of consciousness.

So, if you absorb a lot of coffee, a highly exciting substance, you will probably have difficulties falling asleep or having a refreshing sleep or will be easily excited or even irritable.

I had, at the beginning of my own process, felt so bad that I was determined to do anything I could in order to get better.

Anyway, I had NOTHING to lose, on the contrary EVERYTHING to gain.

I wanted to change the chemistry of my thoughts, and therefore, I changed the chemistry of my body, through different food.

Nevertheless, some years later, when I met Martin Brofman, I had to reconsider everything again. In fact, he was teaching, amongst other things, that it is important we never give power to something outside of yourself.

And that idea seems to me very important.

Here is an concrete example in terms of improvement of eyesight.

Some people tell you that you should eat bilberries in order to promote good vision. Even if this is true, on a purely physical level, I think this is limiting.

Let's imagine for example, that the person to whom we tell this wants to heal his/her sight. Unfortunately, that person with limited income cannot afford to buy bilberries because they seem too expensive to him/her. That person could say that he/she <u>cannot</u> heal. And personally, I think this is limiting.

I sincerely believe that if a person wants to heal, he/she can heal, either with physical « tools » *(bilberries or Hatha-Yoga for the eyes)*, or with non-physical tools *(visualization, reprogramming of the mind or even prayer....)*

Remind yourself that in fact :

-« There is nothing I cannot do, there are only things I have not yet learned how to do » and « every belief which limits me can always be replaced by an other belief reflecting more my true unlimited nature. ».

According to Martin, it is not really the substance that I ingest that is important but more my « relationship », my beliefs, towards what I am eating, that will determinate the effects of this substance on my body.

According to this theory, I could therefore ingest any substance without fearing a negative effect, if I had decided it was so.

Personally, I am sure everything here is true with nevertheless one « reservation » : <u>It all depends on my level of consciousness or my beliefs</u>.

I had read a fascinating book : « *Autobiography of a Yogi* »[1] by Paramahansa Yogananda. In this wonderful book, Yogananda explains how a disciple of the Master of his Master « doubted » the « realized » consciousness of his *Guru*[2]. In order to test the state of awareness of his Master, he offered him a glass of quicklime, a particularly toxic substance. The Master took the glass and drank it without any problem, while at the same time,

---

[1] Yogananda is a Indian Master who introduced Kriya-Yoga to the United states. His book, *« Autobiography of a Yogi»*, is published by Mass Marketing Paperbacks, and the Self-Realization Fellowship.

[2] *Guru* is a Sanskrit word meaning « spiritual master ».

his disciple was « burned » from within, as if he had himself swallowed the poison.

I am deeply persuaded that my awareness, my perception of a substance is more important that the substance itself. Nevertheless, it all depends of my level of consciousness.

Here is an example I sometimes use :

Imagine my car is a diesel car. It has certain rules of functioning and I am supposed to « feed » it diesel, if I want it to remain « healthy ». Is that clear ?

Nevertheless, I KNOW that if Jesus was here now, he could drive my vehicle if he put in petrol, water, oil, or even nothing at all. His consciousness allows him to transcend matter, which He recognizes has a divine nature. For Jesus, for whom EVERYTHING is God, whether he « nourishes » my vehicle with God in the form of diesel, or with God in the form of water, or with God in the form of air, in the end, He is always nourishing my vehicle with God. You understand what I mean ?

The day when I have myself realized and totally accepted my TRUE DIVINE nature as well as that of the whole Universe, I could allow myself to function with or without food, as numerous people have done and are still doing on earth.[1]

In the same way, my body function according to certain rules. And while my consciousness is not enough « realized », I have to « obey » these rules, until my consciousness can « transcend » them..

Coming back to the subject of food, we know, for example, that in order to digest in an optimal way and facilitate the job of

---

[1] See for example, among the mystics, the case of Marthe Robin or Therese Neumann. In his *« Autobiography of a Yogi »*, Paramahansa Yogananda cite the case of a woman, Giri Bala, who at the age of 68 had neither drunk nor eaten for 56 years. He says of her : *« She proves that man is spirit in truth and can live from the eternal light of God »*. In a more « earthly» area, Jasmuheen wrote a book an that subject : *« Living on Light»* published by Koha Publishing.

digestion and assimilation, it is best not to mix certain foods together. This discovery is the base of the Shelton[1] method which inspired many people who use the « dissociated » diet.

My body, as an organism, has its own rules on inner functioning.

Obviously, I, Patrice, am not that body, although that body is a part of me. I am first of all the consciousness inhabiting that body.

Unfortunately, I regret to inform you that up to this day, the consciousness that I am has not fully realized and accepted its divine nature and that of the entire Universe. The consciousness that I am can KNOW it intellectually but has not necessarily REALIZED it.

According to the principles we talked about previously, if I want to live in harmony with my body, I MUST respect certain rules of functioning. If I do not respect them, my « non-organic » way of functioning will see to it that my body rejects me…, perhaps with an illness.

I decided therefore, until a new situation developed, to respect the functioning rules of my organism and to facilitate its task, and to become vegetarian again.

This vegetarian diet, along with my new decisions and my changes in consciousness, allowed my body, I am sure, to detoxify and my immune system to function better.

In the book published by Healthhope Pub House, « *Roger's Recovery from AIDS* », the author, Bob Owen, who is a doctor, tells how he decided to help an old friend to be cured of AIDS. The book's approach to HIV-positivity and AIDS is very interesting. The author explains that when he saw his friend come into his office suffering from what was diagnosed as

---

[1] Herbert Shelton was a nutritionist suggesting a particular food hygiene for better health He is the author of several books « *Food Combining made Easy* » and « *The Fast»* (Willow Pub) where he explains how a modified fast can heal many illnesses.

AIDS, with Kaposi Sarcoma, loss of weight, and so on... he was extremely upset. At the time, in 1986, nothing was really known about the disease.

By studying the eating habits and behaviour of his friend, he understood how his immune system was so weakened that his body became prey to all sorts of opportunistic diseases. he understood that coffee and cigarettes, which he used and abused, drugs (both legal and illegal), and stress had ruined his defence immune system. With his friend and patient's agreement, he prescribed a strict diet of fresh fruit juices for several weeks. After a very difficult period of cleansing and detoxifying of the body, which often happens with long fasts, his friend's skin became soft and pink again and all the illnesses finally disappeared.

I found the book interesting in many respects, because, besides the change in diet, a definite change happened in this person's life.

He now felt loved.

His doctor friend had to hire a full-time nurse to take care of his friend, and they fell in love with each other.

This story confirmed what I already knew in term of the importance of feeling loved if you are H.I.V. positive or have AIDS.

Personally, I too had to make sure to feel loved at all times.

In fact, I had decided to die because I was not feeling loved and, as I had decided to live, I had to start envisaging new circumstances of life in which I would feel loved.

Moreover, if I had felt cut off from my « Love sources »[1], I would have to find others.

It was IMPERATIVE that I find others if I REALLY wanted to heal.

---

[1] See Chapter 14

As soon as I perceived Love around me, I used it for MY HEALING.

-« Look, two people kissing in the street or looking at each other tenderly : That's Love, and that Love helps me heal. »

-« Look, somebody smiles at me and gives me a compliment : That's Love, and that Love helps me heal. »

-« Look, somebody makes a reproach or judges me : Thank you, because this too, is Love and that Love helps me heal. »

Please understand : I, Patrice, I **CHOOSE** to see it as an expression of Love. Because it might really be one. Some people have sometimes very « original » ways of expressing their Love ! Finally, you have to understand this it is not really important, as everything is in my perception ! And if I REALLY want to heal, I have to <u>choose to perceive</u> love all around me.

Not only should I see Love all around me, but I had <u>TO LET IT ENTER ME.</u>

That was not the easiest part at that time.

To see Love was relatively easy.

To let it in was more difficult. My self-image was such that I did not feel I deserved it.

One of the effect of H.I.V. positivity was for me to see clearly one of the beliefs that was deeply ingrained in me.

In fact, if a belief brings about an experience, if I live a particular experience, I just have to observe my perception of that experience to uncover the belief that created it.

It is interesting to see how this disease affects different people in different ways.. For example, for some, this disease has not the least effect on their sexuality. For others it does..

This was the case for me. It was actually normal because I did not at that time allow myself to fully live my homosexuality.

On top of that, after the announcement that I was sero-positive, I had been feeling « rotten » on the inside.

I had developed this self-image years earlier because of the humiliations and aggressions at boarding school. I used to say to myself :

-« Patrice, you must be a person who really is, fundamentally bad to attract that to you.».

I had <u>believed</u> that so much in the past that my body was now allowing me *(thank you, my body !)* to manifest it physically.

I had had such a negative image of myself that for a long time, it was <u>impossible</u> to consider being intimate with someone. I thought that I was rotten *(literally rotten, with my body crawling with this virus)* and that my simple presence was enough to « contaminate » them.

However, at that time, beyond my perception of appearances, my body was doing me a GREAT service. It was externalising for me the belief I had within, so that I could SEE it clearly, so that I could realize it was not true, *(because obviously, that belief did not make me happy)* AND FINALLY, so that I could change it.

And I needed a lot of persuasive effort, and repeated affirmations to progressively cause that image to fade away.

However, please be aware... I am not saying here that this thought pattern is the same for EVERY person who has been H.I.V. positive or has had AIDS. But I do think it could be common to many.

In fact, each person that had been concerned with H.I.V. could honestly question himself on how the discovery of his serology affected his life. This would allow him to better understand certain beliefs that generated these experiences, so that he could then put a stop to it.

For my part, I had to accept that Love I perceived around me, accept it, and let it enter inside me to nourish me.

I had to totally change my self-image and perceive myself more and more as a « good » person, who deserved to be loved.

And as I was teaching people to get rid of their glasses and change their view of the world, I understood more and more why Vicky had told me some years earlier that my healing was achieved through the healing of others[1].

As these people, to whom I was able to transmit my knowledge and my beliefs, thanked me for the help I brought them, I had to ACCEPT that, as time passed by, I COULD NOT be as « bad » as all that.

If so many people perceived me as a « good » person, I had to accept that they might be right.

Their perception of me helped me to create a new self-image.

And this is when I can again feel filled with gratitude for the perfection of the Universe.

And as, in my perception, I was there, to help <u>THEM</u>, I now realize that actually they were there to heal <u>ME,</u> reflecting in a tangible way this new image I knew I had to develop for my healing. And I would like to take this opportunity to thank all the people who have been in my workshops for the subtle but nevertheless very important help that they gave me without knowing it.

Each « Thank you », each word of gratitude they gave me was actually an antidote progressively dissolving the terrible poison that could have killed me : **« The perception that I was neither lovable, nor loved... »**.

Of all the books I had read, one in particular attracted my attention.

---

[1] See Chapter 15

It was the book *« Deathly Deception »* by the Doctor Robert E. Willner, Peltec Publishing Company.

In this fascinating book, several eminent doctors explain the lack of foundation of the theory that H.I.V. is responsible for AIDS. In this book, a quotation from T.C. Fry, author of *« : AIDS : The Great Hoax »* is particularly revealing.

-«... The presence of H.I.V. in the frame of this disease (AIDS) is no more a proof than flies in garbage are a proof that flies are the cause of the garbage.».

In that book, I learned that, it is not because we can sometimes detect H.I.V. when people develop one or several pathologies associated with AIDS, that H.I.V. can be held responsible. Many people can develop one or several illnesses associated with AIDS without <u>EVER</u> having been in presence of the so-called « culprit » of which we find no trace in their bodies.

This book explained that H.I.V. could in no way create such illnesses. At worst a sort of little « flu », that heals all by itself in a few days.

When I learned that, I must say I was at the same time astounded and filled with gratitude.

So I had been right when, years earlier, and even before learning from these eminent doctors, I had decided that :

-«H.I.V. positivity or AIDS was actually a quite small unimportant disease, like a sort of flu that comes one day and goes another, as easily as it came. »[1]

This book is really a goldmine of information which should be made known to the public, and I highly recommend it to all of you.

The real problem, according to these doctors, was the weakening of the immune system.

---

[1] See Chapter 14

This weakening can come about very simply. All it needs to trigger it is eating food that is toxic or low in nutrition. Add to that repeated stress, pollution and you are sure to have all of the necessary elements to suppress your immunity.

Personally, I would add this while we are on the subject : Add to this an emotional desert, the difficulty of communicating in industrial society as ours, where everyone lives more and more for themselves, separated from others, a poor self-image, in fact, everything that a society based on fear excels in creating, and you now have the needed elements present.

You have all of ingredients which are certain to weaken, either your thymus gland, or you heart *Chakra*, it amounts to the same thing..

You can be sure, without any doubt, you do not need H.I.V. to destroy your immune system !

During my readings, I found another particularly interesting book, which served only to confirm everything I had already read, although adding an other aspect.

This book « *The cure for H.I.V. / AIDS* » is written by Doctor Hulda, R. Clark[1].

This woman doctor, just like many of her colleagues whose approach threatens the profits of the powerful pharmaceutical laboratories, was obliged leave the United States and to practice in Mexico, which is more tolerant.

Here are some words of her theory :

She explain how modern food, stuffed with various chemicals, little by little destroys our thymus gland and therefore our immune system. She quotes, for example, the traces of Benzene found in numerous dairy products which accumulate in the thymus gland as time passes until it reaches a critical threshold,

---

[1] Doctor Hulda, R. Clark wrote many books « *The Cure for all Diseases* » published by Mass Market Paperback

may be lethal, preventing the thymus gland from functioning normally. *(She explains that benzene and its by-products are part of the powerful solvents used to clean various machines for sterilizing or processing milk.)*

She also cites the devastating effect of heavy metals in the body, particularly the thymus gland. The presence of these heavy metals *(mercury, silver, pewter, copper, zinc)* in many dental amalgams where they are continually ingested by the body in the form of vapours or particles, incite her to encourage everyone, as soon as possible, to remove these small time bombs implanted in our teeth without our knowledge.

The damaging effect of these amalgams have since been confirmed by Dr Murray Vimy, a research scientist at the University of Calgary *(Canada)* and an expert for WHO, as well as by Dr. Dietrich Klinghardt[1].

She also explains that H.I.V. *(we have not mentioned it for a while !)* is often found in a parasite living normally in the intestines. This parasite is theoretically supposed to stay in the intestines. However, if the thymus gland is weakened by toxic chemical substances, drugs, stress, attitudes and so on… *(as we have already discussed)*, this parasite migrates to the thymus gland where its presence is even more disruptive.

She has successfully prescribed extremely simple disinfecting cures, based on cloves, extract of husk of nuts and root of wormwood, which are all three powerful disinfectants.

Recently, a new disinfectant treatment based on Curcuma[2] brings about astonishing results, the patient's viral loading[1] diminishing in only a few weeks.

---

[1] Dr. Dietrich Klinghardt has presented a conference on this subject, which is available on the internet site : http://www.amalgames.com

[2] Curcuma, often called « Indian Saffron » is one of the spices in curry. It is manufactured from the plant rhizome. Curcuma is known for its disinfectant virtues, but it also has other properties.. anti-oxidant (anti-free-radicals...), anti-inflammatory,(Flu, Rhumatism, Arthritis, Diabetes...), anti-viral for all sorts of viruses, (Herpes, Zona, Hepatitis B et C, Colds...). It also has an effect on Cholesterol.

Love is the Key...

It is disappointing that, although all over the world there are many « long time survivors »[2], as well of numerous books recounting their experiences, so little attention is paid to these cases.

It is true that for the pharmaceutical laboratories, which, let us not forget, thrive on diseases, there is such a high commercial stake that these super powers are concerned lest the general public know that these « long term survivors » often succeeded, without any drugs, using either a nutritional, or behavioural approach, or both of them combined.

Moreover, it could be asked whether, in certain quarters, some people would prefer to see « certain sections » of the population, considered « embarrassing » disappear in this horrible way.

It is astonishing to note that, instead of asking the only sensible question in terms of H.I.V. positivity or AIDS, which is « How can we strengthen the patient's immunity ? » many of the researchers insist on the question « How can we destroy H.I.V. ? »

It remind me a story heard in India during one of my later journeys there:

An old woman is bending over, under a street lamp, apparently searching something. A man passing by offers to help.

-« What are you looking for ? Can I help you, Madame ? ».

The woman answers :

-« I am searching for a needle that I've lost. »

Having searched in vain, the man then asks the woman.

---

[1] The viral loading is one of the « markers » which allow doctors to measure the illness's progress. It corresponds to the number of viruses present in the body and is measured by different techniques, after taking a sample of blood or plasma.

[2] « Long-term Survivors » are those who, with or without the help of medical treatment, have survived or continued to live well beyond what standard medicine considers as « normal » for HIV or AIDS..

-« Where did you lose it, this needle ? ».

-« At home, in my house », answers the woman.

-« But why are you searching for it here, under this street lamp ? » says the man.

-« Because, at home, there is no electricity and everything is dark. »

It is not because it is more easy or convenient to look somewhere that I will find the solution there.

I must look for my needle where I lost it.

I have to find my immunity where I lost it.

My goal here is not to argue about the subject but to suggest that sometimes you look « beyond » the information we have been given.

What I can honestly say, on the other hand, is that, all this readings, all these realisations added to my metaphysical awareness <u>REALLY</u> helped me and I <u>KNOW</u> that it is not by chance, 20 years after having been contaminated, that I am, more than ever, still ALIVE.

CHAPTER 20
Travels, Travels...

Years passed by, and I enjoyed playing with the Universe. I was giving it tests, challenges.

Having started to teach in New Caledonia, I set other goals for travelling..

Do not we say « Travel educates Youth... » ?

As far as youth, I do not know... What is sure is that travel « educates » !

I was constantly learning...

Thanks to Philippe who organized my workshops in Noumea, I noticed I was making great progress in my communicating and teaching.

Philippe had had the opportunity of spending time with Jacques Salomé, whom we mentioned previously, and he helped me a lot in being even more precise and to better understand the « protocols» of relationships to be more efficient for the participants.

Anyway, it was certain I enjoyed travelling.

And since everything was possible, I wished to travel elsewhere, to see other things.

I had flown twice to Tahiti, on my way to Noumea and, after a while, I was telling myself, and my friends of « up there »

-« Well guys, it would be nice If I could give workshops in Tahiti ».

After all, it was on my route and I wanted to get to know this island-paradise.

And by « chance», shortly after a person who had done a class in Paris told me :

-« You know, Patrice, I have got family in Tahiti who could organize a workshop for you there. »

I remember saying:

-« Oh yes, I would like that very much ! »,

but without doing anything except taking their contact details.

On my next trip to Noumea, I reflected:

-« You have just been through Tahiti, why not come there and teach ? »

And again, another person suggested to me a short time afterwards :

-« You know, Patrice, I have some family in Tahiti who could probably organize a workshop for you. »

To which I answered again, but without doing anything else :

-« Oh yes, I would like that very much ! ».

And as once again, I flew through Papeete on the way to Noumea, this time, I felt filed with a very strong DETERMINATION.

-« I have had enough of this now ! I **REALLY** would like to teach in Tahiti ».

And, the day after my arrival in Noumea, when I went to the La Tontouta airport to pick up a friend coming from France for a workshop, she said to me, coming out of the plane :

-« Hello Patrice, it's great to see you ! I just stopped over Tahiti where I used to live. I'm going back to live there and I would like to organize a workshop for you there. Would you like that ?...»

Immediately, I answered :

-« YES ! When ? »

And we immediately settled on a first date.

Again, I had just learned a magnificent lesson.

The Universe gives me everything, it is true.

But I mustn't wait, sitting on my backside, for it to give me everything all ready on a plate...

I must listen to the messages and <u>answer</u>, with a concrete action in the physical world, the signs It is sending me.

Even if I have to trust the Universe, which for some could look like passivity, it is not real passivity.

It is actually an ACTIVE passivity the Universe expects from me.

It expects me to listen to its messages, ready to answer, and, **especially** to answer them.

Twice in the past, the Universe had answered my request.

<u>Twice</u> I had been asked to teach in Tahiti, and twice, two DIFFERENT people had offered me an opportunity.

The Universe had answered me through them by offering this opportunity. One which I did not grasp at the time.

I can now understand why.

Very simply because I did not <u>really</u> want to go to Tahiti ! My desire was not INTENSE enough. I was not yet DETERMINED to go to Tahiti. It was just a slight superficial desire.

And it's an aspect on which I really insist in my workshops.

-« Just how much do you really want to see clearly ? ».

Do you « wish » to see clearly or are you « DETERMINED » to see clearly?

Is it a little desire, so-so, « polite » superficial... or is it a deep decision, emanating from the deepest of your being, like a kind of CERTAINTY that **nothing else** but clarity could satisfy you ?

This notion of INTENSITY is paramount. How much do you want what you want ?

It is thanks to Gita MALLAZ that I would really integrate this concept. This woman, whom I did not know personally but through one of her books and a television show, had a very strong impact on my research. She is one of these « Wise-Women » putting me back on my path predicted by my astral chart[1]. She is one of those « meetings » that have made a deep impression on my life.

Gita MALLASZ is one of those who transcribed the wonderful book « TALKING WITH ANGELS »[2].

In an interview that she gave a little time before leaving her body, this charming old lady was questioned by a journalist who asked her :

-«But you say, that every one of us, we have a Guardian Angel. But for « Mister Everyman », who does not have all of your experiences, haw can he contact his Guardian Angel ? ».

And this little tiny woman, apparently so frail in her armchair, leant forward with an impressive strength as she shouted:

-« But because you are THIRSTY... **Because you're THIRSTY...**and here, she paused….« But if you are satisfied with your life... », she said with her charming slavish accent as she stretched out in her wicker chair : (and here she adopts a nonchalant tone)... « Here I am, walking on the Champs Elysées, I have got my car, my wife... ». And again, leaping up with an incredible strength, for such body looking so frail, she said : **« But if you are THIRSTY, then IT comes .»**

And I KNOW she is right !

She was only confirming what I had already experienced.

---

[1] See Chapter 7
[2] *«Talking with Angels»* by Gita Mallasz, Daimon Publishers.

Whatever I want to get, be it a state of health, something physical, a state of consciousness or even God, Who I think is just a state of consciousness, I can get by this THIRST.

And if I think I am not THIRSTY enough for what I want, I CAN make this thirst grow within.

It's a decision.

It's a choice.

Very simply.

For myself, when I was teaching my first workshop in Polynesia, I had « proved » to myself, once again, that I could get anything I wanted.

Afterwards, as the years passed by, I decided to become « specialist » of the DOM-TOM [1] and according to my decision, I was to be invited over to teach, as well as in New Caledonia and Tahiti, in Reunion Island and then Guadeloupe.

Finally, I energized the desire to get to know Australia, Sydney being only two hours flight away from Noumea

After all, when you have flown more than 24 hours to get to the end of the world, why not do two hours more to discover Sydney, the Australians, the Kangaroos and the Koalas ?

And once again, in the weeks following my « firm , deep and confident » decision, the Universe answered my request favourably.

This how I « trained » the « muscles in my head »…

By testing and re-testing the Universe through certain goals I set for it, I developed more and more confidence in myself and my creative abilities.

---

[1] French Overseas Departements and Territories

Moreover, I felt a growing sense of recognition and gratitude towards what I perceived more and more as a benevolent entity that in the end, only wanted to please me and make me happy.

CHAPTER 21
A wonderful gift...

As I write down this book, I realize it is not always easy to respect linear time.

Each chapter allows me to express an idea or experiences that sometimes happened over several years

So we will go back into the past, some months before I learned I was H.I.V. positive.

I had to go to Belgium to translate a lecture given by Martin Brofman.

More than 400 people where expected at that lecture

As I realized it was February 14th 1990, exactly 3 years to the day from my first meeting with Vicky, I was filled with a feeling of joy and gratitude as I realized one of Vicky's « prophesies » was <u>really</u> manifesting at that very moment.

Of course, these people had come to listen to Martin, but at the same time, I could see my own path as a teacher falling into place.

And as I was thinking of Vicky, I could only think of Nick again. « Because » of him, or more accurately « thanks » to him, I had gone to see her three months earlier[1]

Dear Nick who, without knowing it, through a few words, had changed my life for ever.

It is true that a year before, I had tried to contact him when I was in London again. I realized already, in fact, the extent of my metamorphosis, the paramount impact he had had in my life, and I wanted to thank him.

When I rang him, I could hear there was a party going on at his place. He explained that he was not able to see me but we talked for a few minutes and I was able to thank him

---
[1] See Chapter 3

nevertheless for the impact he had unknowingly had on me through his remark about the colour of my aura.

However, after this perception on February 14th 1990, I REALLY wanted to meet him again.

So when I visited London, I went to Chiswick, the suburb where he lived.

I searched in vain for his home, with only vague memories of where he lived, having been there only twice.

I finally found a house that could have been his, but the person there did not know him. Feeling piqued and disappointed I could not see him again, I returned to Paris.

I had not counted on the magic of the Universe.

Months passed by and I was to learn about the H.IV. positivity that accompanied me.

As I explained before, the relationship with Myriam had rapidly deteriorated and finally we both decided to split, though still living together in the same house.

In the following months, I researched different alternative approaches to health and participated one day in a support group for H.I.V. positive people organized by the American Church in Paris.

There I met a charming American guy named Chris, holidaying in Paris. We met several times and he invited me over to his place, in the USA.

Taking advantage of my end-of-year vacation, I went to meet him in Seattle, where he lived.

I knew that Nick came from Seattle, so, as soon as I arrived at Chris's place, I grabbed a telephone book to look for Nick's family.

Finding a name like his, I rang several times, in vain.

Love is the Key...

Finally, I was to talk to a woman whom I discovered later was his mother.

I explained to her I was looking for this Nick, a fashion photographer living in London and born in Seattle. Did she know him ? Was he from her family ?

After a silence that seemed quite long, she then said « No » and hung up without further explanation.

I do not know why, but the strangeness of this telephone call left me somewhat troubled.

Nevertheless I quickly forgot this incident, making the most of the good time spent with Chris.

We decided then to spent a few days in Los Angeles. Chris had some friends living in West Hollywood, the gay quarter of this huge city, who could play host to us.

I had at the time read Louise Hay's books, of whom we have already spoken[1], and I knew that she was enormously committed to helping H.I.V. positive people.

She had in fact created the « Hay Rides » weekly evenings to support H.I.V. positive people, people suffering from AIDS or their relatives. It is true at that time, in the USA, nothing was done for the sick and initiatives like this one of Louise were very precious.

I decided to go there to meet this exceptional woman.

During these evenings, I met another charming lady, with amazing charisma and generosity, Nadia Sutton[2]. Having made

---
[1] See Chapter 15
[2] Nadia SUTTON is a woman accomplishing remarkable work. She is the founder of the association *PAWS L.A.* which started in 1989. (PAWS, stands for : **P**ets **A**re **W**onderful **S**upport. This association cares for pets of people with serious diseases (AIDS, Cancer...). *Paws L.A.* (L.A. means Los Angeles) helps them by providing food or volunteers to take care of the animals, or free veterinary care for these patients' animals. In fact, Nadia noticed that some of her sick friends, because of the lack of help they received from state, had to go without their medication which they could not buy, so they could feed their pets. At the current time, *PAWS L.A.* cares everyday for 2500 pets belonging to 1300 patients...

the connection, this lady of French background explained that a workshop called « AIDS Mastery » would take place soon. Knowing my own alternative interests, she asked me If I would like to follow this course.

Of course I would ! Nevertheless, its price, although reasonable, was out of my reach, considering my budget for the trip.

As I explained to her my money « problem », she said simply :
-« Would you like to do it or not ? Money is not a problem…».

I accepted her offer, proposing to pay the price once I was back in France.

During the first evening of this course, during the meal, I started to talk to my neighbour :
-« Hello, what is your name ? ».
-« Greg ».
-« Pleased to meet you. I'm Patrice. Do you know Europe ?».
-« Yes », he said, « I used to work in London ».

I explained that I knew London very well, and had often been for my colour therapy training.
-« And where did you live in London ? »
-« In the suburbs… » he said, « in Chiswick. »

Surprised, I exclaimed
-« Chiswick, that's funny, I know it very well. I have a friend, who of course you wouldn't know, who lives in Chiswick. His name is Nick D… »

Greg looked surprised and said :
-« But I know him ! He was my roommate when I lived in London. »

And I was flabbergasted…

I remembered, in fact, that when we first met, Nick had told me we should not make too much noise, because his roommate did not much appreciate it when he brought somebody home.

I could not believe it !

I was in West-Hollywood, in the centre of Los Angeles, in the United States, and here I am sitting next to the room mate of Nick whom I had been desperately searching for year. I had finally found a trace of him !

Thank you, Thank you, Thank you « up there » !

I then told Greg my about my « magical » meeting with Nick, what he had told me, how it had changed my life, my attempts to search for him in London and in Seattle… to end by asking him where I could contact him.

Looking very upset, Greg then told me that Nick had died from AIDS some months earlier.

The shock was terrible.

I burst into tears, shaken by waves that seem to never want to end. One wave would stop for another to start.

After a long while, I managed to calm down and Greg, also distressed, said that in fact, Nick had told him about me.

And, pulling off one of the rings he was wearing, he gave it to me saying :

-« When Nick left, he gave me two rings. I think this one is for you. »

I still wear this ring today and I have hardly ever taken it off, except for repairing or cleaning. It has a highly symbolic value. It reminds me of Nick, and of our meeting but mostly of this wonderful transformation he initiated without knowing it.

As I asked Greg to tell me more of Nick and the circumstances of his departure, he told me of some awful things. He explained how he had been rejected by his family, his mother telling him he was « an abomination ».

I was distraught to hear that and made myself the promise that one day the whole world would know such a being as Nick had lived on earth, and not in vain.

And that the « simple » fact that I had known him for a while had radically changed my life…

I hope my testimony will prevent others from such suffering.

May people understand that, even if their child has different attitudes, he or she is nevertheless a human being and is important as such.

And that, above all, this being deserves and needs to be understood and loved.

In the days that followed, I was in a hyper-sensitive state and as if to get close to Nick, I often touched the stone of the ring that I wore on my right ring finger.

Two days after Greg told me the terrible news, I found myself in the car with Chris, stuck in the traffic of this sprawling city.

I was touching the ring with my thumb, and mentally, I was seeing myself with Nick, him on the sofa, me lying next to him, my head on his stomach, watching TV, as he gently caressed my hair. It seemed I had never felt so good, surrendered and trusting in a man's arms.

And as this sweet memory filled me, on an impulse, I started the car radio.

You can imagine my surprise when I heard, at that very moment, the song it was broadcasting:

« Think of the good time we had together… »

Overwhelmed by this synchronicity, I burst into tears, to the surprise of Chris, who of course did not know what was happening inside me.

And as if I needed other « proofs », the next day, we were stuck again, somewhere in the gigantic highways of Los Angeles, I was to live another unbelievable moment *(unless you lived it, of course !)*

Again, I was touching Nick's ring while looking at it intensely. I thought of him now on the other side. And it was as if I was talking to him. I was telling him :

-« Of course, you are dead, but I KNOW, that despite that, you are here, somewhere observing me…»

And again, moved by an impulse that I « analysed » only afterwards, I turned the radio on again.

And at that very instant, the interior of the car was filed with the wonderful song of Bette Middler[1], whom I did not know at the time :

-« God is watching us…, from a distance… »

Again, struck by the power of this synchronicity, I broke into tears.

The events I was living were moving me deeply..

OK, I knew that there was a life beyond death, but I had never experienced in such a way !

An intellectual knowledge is **NOT** a direct experience.

I had had a deep desire to find Nick again and beyond death, I found him again and he gave me this wonderful gift which I now always wear.

As I thought back on all the events and synchronicities leading me to meet Greg, it was deeply moving.

I had to, being diagnosed H.I.V. positive, go to the American Church to get the information, in fact, to meet Chris there, who came from Seattle and would invite me to his place, then to Los

---

[1] Marvellous for ME, of course, in the light of my experience… Clearly, this song reminds me each time of my time with Nick and what it triggered off…

Angeles. Chris, knowing Louise Hay, had to present me to her so that I could meet Nadia, who was to invite me to the workshop where I was to meet Greg and talk to him during dinner so that he could give me this ring on behalf of Nick, so that way I knew that Nick knew... and had indeed received my message...

When one thinks of the succession of events necessary so that, finally, <u>beyond death</u>, I connect again to Nick, it is mind blowing.

You can understand why, I can only be in total agreement with Etienne Daho on the fact that there is NO chance, NO coincidence but rather wonderful Rendez-vous, as he says so well.

If I needed proofs, I was well provided with them !

But it was not finished yet. Nick had other surprises in store.

When I went to see Nadia a few days later to thank her for inviting me to the workshop and to tell her about my experiences, I found on her desk a book presenting the *«Patchwork for Names Project »*[1].

As I opened it mechanically and by « chance » *(another one !)*, I fell on a page with a picture photo of a patchwork in the name of Nick.

Again, I started to cry like a small child, overwhelmed with emotion.

For many years, I was totally unable to tell this story without bursting into tears, caught up in the emotion of memories.

Nevertheless, I was to be freed finally.

As I was telling someone who had asked the story of my luck ring, I started to feel the emotions overwhelm me.

---

[1] The *« Patchwork for Names Project »* regroups the patchworks created by the friends or relatives in memory of someone who has died from AIDS. This patchwork is also called *« The AIDS Memorial Quilt »* and is now gigantic.

I explained to him that I was going to take a moment aside to relieve myself of the weight of my emotions and that he should not worry about me.

I know that, in fact, if I let myself let go of suppressed emotions, after a while, even if the process takes years, the « bag » holding them will finally be emptied.

During my workshops, I explain to the participants that it is important not to hold back emotions, if ever they surface.

Actually, some people believe they have so much emotion suppressed within them, that if they let them come up, it will never stop.

I explain to them in a rather « light » way with imagery:

-« Even if it were true you had three tons of « shit » or problems inside, each tea spoon you let out is a teaspoon less to take out ! »

And I should know!

I went off alone to a corner to free the emotions that welled up from inside as I though of Nick again.

And suddenly, I was propelled into an astonishing experience.

A being, or rather a shape of light that I knew to be Nick, appeared to me. That light was not a human body but more a kind of living consciousness... And while I was shaken with tears, inside I heard Nick « tell » me, although this happened without words because it was more like ideas, or images which came to me :

-« Patrice, listen... you have to let me go now... I have to go further and the fact you always think of me holds back me here...»

It is true at that time, I found myself very often touching the ring with my thumb, as if to reassure me.

I knew, intellectually speaking, that after a death, the person « leaving » can be held back on the terrestrial plan by thoughts of loved ones , **but this**, this was different, I was living it from **the inside**...

Again, knowledge is not experience.

Somewhere, I knew Nick was right.

In the same way my mother had been attached to me, I had attached myself to Nick and I knew that now I had to « give him back » his freedom.

I imagined taking a pair of golden scissors and after a short « prayer of thanks », I cut the link connecting me to Nick, sending him with much Love to his new destination.

At the moment I cut the « link », the light that was Nick, started to move away.

Seeing him leave and feeling suddenly abandoned, I was again shaken by emotions and tears.

An astonishing thing happened then.

The light that was Nick came back to me and it was as if a kind of « negotiation » started. I already knew, of course, the outcome, but Nick, full of love, did not want to leave me in that state.

Finally, once I had calmed down again and <u>KNOWING</u> intimately that I <u>HAD</u> to let him go, I wished him a good trip saying :

-« Go now where you want to go, and THANK YOU again... »

This time, he left for good and I felt finally at peace, serene and fulfilled from this last meeting with him.

I was extremely surprised to discover the next morning that the stone in shape of a hood covering my ring had broken, even though I had never taken it off..

Engraved in this ring, there was an eagle perceptible under the green translucent stone.

And as I looked, astonished by this new synchronicity, I knew that this eagle was free now, without the stone holding him prisoner, to fly, further, higher…

It was only three years later that I finally found in the USA a jeweler capable of mending it.

I think that it is not necessary to say more here, except :

From the bottom of my heart :

-« Thank you,... Thank you,... Thank you, Nick... Thank you for loving me and THANK YOU for putting me on the path...»

CHAPTER 22
Hervé...

As I was travelling more and more to the French colonies to teach workshops there, continuing at the same time to give the same workshops in France, I was to encounter a wonderful being who was to share my life for almost 5 years.

He came to participate in a Vision Workshop and I found him very attractive.

In order to be better as a teacher, I had to put aside all personal preoccupations for the duration of the workshop.

I had noticed that he had feelings for me, but I tried, for the good of all the participants, to put that aside.

Once the workshop was over, I could allow myself to take off my « Patrice the Teacher » hat, to be just « Patrice »

We were going to go and have a drink after the class with a group of participants and as Hervé was in the room, apparently waiting to see what was going to happen, I invited him to join us in the most « neutral» voice possible.

I was to see him again in the following weeks either to go to the pictures, or to a restaurant.

Little by little, we were getting closer one to another.

I wrote to him from time to time when I was in the islands, but « nothing » physical between us had yet happened.

We were supposed to go and see a movie one evening, but eventually we talked for so long that we had to change our plans for the evening..

I had at home a wonderful video, *« Field of Dreams »* [1] with Kevin Costner, and, having talked about it to Hervé, I suggested he come and see it at my place.

At the time, I lived in a small bungalow that Myriam and I had built in our garden, when we lived together. At the time of our separation, we had agreed to live, Myriam in the house and me in bungalow when I returned to Paris between my numerous flights to the islands.

In the restricted space where I lived, Hervé and I, were lying on the bed, watching this movie.

Although very attracted to Hervé, I felt in a state of « panic » now we were so close to each other for the first time. I remember sitting on the bed, glued against the wall, as if I wanted to be as far as possible from him, now he was so close to me.

Hervé was aware that I had been H.I.V. positive and, although I could not be 100 % sure, he seemed to be open enough not to be afraid of it.

Nevertheless, I was afraid ! A kind of panic..

He was the first TRUE relationship I allowed myself since Myriam.

As I have explained, one of effects of the announcement of H.I.V. positivity had been a brutal and total stop of all sexuality.

Some months later, I met Chris with whom I went to the U.S.A. but he was also HIV positive, which, I thought at the time, made things a bit easier. Nevertheless, my relation with Chris was to be more of an adventure than a real story, although I

---

[1] *« Field of Dreams »* is a 1989 film directed by Phil Alden Robinson. In this beautiful movie, the hero, played by Kevin Costner « blindly » follows a little voice that « talks » to him in his inner consciousness. He surrenders to this voice that makes him take what seem to be enormous risks to finally come through magnificently transformed.

must recognize that, without him, I never would have reconnected with Nick.

It had been more than a year and a half since Myriam and I had separated and I not yet opened myself to a true relation.

I had of course had some sexual relations, but always making sure not to get involved and <u>especially not to spend the night</u> with these lovers.

I was somehow terrified to start one with Hervé whom I found so attractive.

Not being able to count on me to take the first step (in fact perhaps I was afraid of being rejected, even politely, or perhaps also I wanted to be sure he <u>really</u> liked me), Hervé took his courage in both hands to take mine.

I was shivering with fear when some seconds later, he moved very close to me.

But, finally, I was calmed by his touch and, reassured that he really wanted to be close to me, I kissed him tenderly.

My relationship with Hervé remains for me to this day, a unforgettable memory, although he was to leave me about 5 years later.

In fact, and this was a first for me, we had courted for some months, seeing each other from time to time, going to the pictures or to the restaurant before finally finding ourselves in the same bed.

And I found that so romantic… beyond the fact that Hervé was so perfectly attractive.

It is true that with the boys I had known up until then, including Nick who still remains one of the most significant relationships that I have ever had, I was more used to encounters which, very quickly, ended up in a bed or elsewhere, without any further formalities.

I am not saying that formalities are absolutely necessary but they sometimes seem important.

Nevertheless, Hervé and I were to spend more and more time together.

Sometimes, he would come to my place, other times, I would go to his.

As his home was also rather small, we very quickly decided to move in together.

We just had to find a little love nest.

For several weeks, we searched in vain for a place that was suitable for us.

And although we both wanted to live together, there was no way we could find a place…

I started to wonder.

How is it we could not find a place, when I KNOW perfectly that I can get <u>anything</u> ?

After all, I taught these principles and I had applied them and put them in motion in the framework of my classes, of my trips, of my health, my relation with money, and so on…

And as I searched, searched, searched, finally, I was to find the solution. I think that the understanding of this principle could help you too.

When in the past, I had decided on a situation that I asked the Universe to manifest for me, I had functioned with the principle of « simple » creation. That is, a creation asked by <u>myself</u> for <u>myself alone</u>. I was most of the time the only one to be « affected » by it, and that for my own happiness.

But now that I was with Hervé, the process to get what we wanted was not a « simple » process of creation but « co-creation ». We were **two** people wishing for **one** lodging and we were both **<u>directly concerned</u>** by this creation.

If I want to create something for myself, it is easy, as the only consciousness I have to watch is mine. I just have to make sure that the picture of my desire is clear and precise and that my beliefs about it are in accord with that desire.

If I want to create something **WITH** someone, this is very different because here, there are <u>two consciousnesses</u> I have to watch over.

I seriously started my introspection.

I asked myself : « Patrice, what kind of home do you want ? »

And, if I was to answer honestly, I had to admit that I would have liked a little house in the suburbs with a garden where I could put my beehives and my orchids.

I then asked Hervé :

-« Tell me Hervé, honestly, in which kind of home would you like us to live ? »

And he answered :

-« I would like to live in an apartment in Paris, close to a tube station, so I can get to work easily.»

Bingo !

I instantly understood why it was so difficult for us to find. Each of us was secretly energizing a different picture and the Universe could not satisfy us both.

We were putting « it », with our contradictory wishes, in a position of pulling in opposite directions.

I therefore decided to align myself to Hervé's desire and I told myself :

-« OK, no problems, I do agree to living together in an apartment in Paris. »

And obviously, very quickly, having « aligned » ourselves with a common desire, the Universe had to fulfil us.

Whereas before, each time we went to visit an apartment, there were at least 20 people wishing to rent it, we were to find this apartment which, when we got there, had only 4 people, including Hervé and myself..

And while we were all visiting it together, one of the others found it « happened » to be too big, and the other, too small, whereas it was just perfect for us.

I was to spend some wonderful times there with Hervé.

Following this, I presented Hervé to my parents, who both accepted him completely. They of course both knew from the start that I was homosexual and moreover had known Alain when we were together. I am lucky to have parents that had both been to Martin's workshops, may be at first to check out the quality of the method I was going to teach, then eventually to use it themselves.

It was while my mother was in a workshop with my brother that I told them both I had been HIV positive. I think that, thanks to these classes, Mum had understood the vital importance of feeling loved and seeing that Hervé was making me fully happy, she accepted him immediately.

He was totally integrated into my family. He had his present for his birthday, his saint's day, Christmas, and so on…

For my part, time was passing on and I continued to teach my workshops in France and countries overseas.

Sometimes, Hervé would accompany me for his own pleasure… and mine of course…

When I went alone, I was always very happy to reunite with him on my return.

As time passed, Hervé gained more and more confidence in himself as he was working on his consciousness, and, as I had done some years earlier, he too resigned from the National Education to make his own living.

First he helped me in the organisation of my workshops and afterwards, devoted himself more to acting, and then to singing.

But without my noticing, my numerous trips, my selfish attitude not leaving him enough space was to make our relationship difficult for Hervé.

One day, after almost 5 years of communal life, when I returned from a trip to the Islands where I had given some workshops, he announced that he wanted to put an end to our relationship.

As he was talking, I had the impression I was falling down an endless abyss.

I did not understand why he wanted to leave me. Everything seem to be going so well between us !

True, I had had some purely sexual experiences with others and, wanting to be open, I had always told Hervé.

I realize today that even if, intellectually speaking, he could « understand » my actions, at a deep level, he felt hurt.

Although he felt hurt, and somewhere, I still regret to this day that I made him suffer *(indeed!*[1]*)*, this was probably not the main reason for his decision to leave me.

It seems that my « Tiger » temperament *(it is my Chinese astrological sign)*, was difficult for him to live for him who was « Goat ». The image may seem simplistic, but imagine the relationship between a Tiger and a Goat…

I literally « swallowed » or suffocated him, and it was difficult for him to find his place and space in our relationship. And I was at the time too blind to notice.

---

[1] In fact, even though I know that everything that happens is perfect, this does not mean that I can just go on doing what would be « perfect » for me if I then become aware that this « perfect » action would make someone suffer in a way I would not like to suffer myself.

For my part, I had the impression everything was going fine. I felt very happy being with him and I had the impression he was with me.

What was always a pleasant surprise for me and which I had <u>never</u> experienced before was that, even after several years, as I would wake up next to him, feeling filled with gratitude for my good luck that he had chosen, one more night, to be with me.

I had once heard Martin tell me that he had given his daughter a sensible advice when she was 17 :

-« Do not go to bed with a boy you would not want to wake up with. »

And I think I would have liked to go on waking up next to him for many years to come…

Nevertheless, the Universe was to decide otherwise…

Since apparently, Hervé's path was going in an other direction, it meant that mine, too, was going in an other direction.

But where ?

CHAPTER 23
A new consciousness...

Although Hervé had ended our relationship, he continued to stay « at home » for a while.

I threw myself into « work » and the workshops to mask my suffering, arranging to be away from home as long as possible, finding it difficult to bear his presence without being able to touch the one I loved.

Thanks to my previous transformation, Hervé's departure went relatively well, even though his departure caused me suffering for many years afterwards.

Nevertheless, this experience allowed me to realize that though many principles of change were « simple », they were not necessarily « easy » to put into practice. ...

Having lost the incredible source of Love he represented for me, little by little, without really noticing it, I had to reorient myself towards another unending source of Love.

A new inner change was gradually happening to me, thanks to Hervé.

And I must here acknowledge that if he had not left me, I would not have started this wonderful metamorphosis that was progressively falling into place.

I was starting to live more and more often experiences I could only call extraordinary as they happened to me.

May be was it because my sexual energy was reoriented ? I do not really know. But the fact is that I was very happy with this new discovery.

More and more, as I was giving my classes, a « force » of astonishing love filled me as I would come to the part of the class where I explained to the participants how we evolved in our consciousness, as we are on the realisation of our Divine and unlimited nature.

Often, at the beginning, on Sunday morning, as I would get to the explanations of the heart *Chakra*, this « Consciousness of Love » would invade me and I felt transported for a brief moment, during which I saw and felt this Love flowing from me, like a peaceful balm for the students.

Sometimes, somebody would ask me a question and I heard myself answering something that I had never learned.

It was as if, suddenly, I KNEW.

A kind of understanding, or knowledge came upon me and I often found myself moved by what I heard myself say as I would realise its depth, its power and its simplicity.

The first time it happened, I was totally overcome.

Nevertheless, the quality of experience I had lived, even if it had been brief, seemed so beautiful, so intense, so pure, so real that I could not deny it.

This is how, a little at a time, I started to reconsider all of my beliefs.

Actually, when it happened, I had the impression of being inhabited by « another consciousness ». A consciousness I perceived as « Divine » or « Angelic ». In these moments, which I felt were deeply blessed, a patience, an understanding, a peace, a Love of an incredible strength were filling me.

Each time it happened, I would be filled with gratitude.

However, I realize that my gratitude was going to God now, and not to the Universe, as it was in the past.

In my experience, it was the only word that came to mind and that I could associate with this state. I could more and more taste His Divine presence.

I remember that at this time, when I was giving many workshops, I was always waiting for these sacred moments. I used to wonder, when is « it » going to come this time ?

On the other hand, beyond the transformation that was happening in my consciousness, a transformation was taking place in my body.

Hervé's departure had so affected me that I had put on a lot of weight. One day, as if I was awakening from a stupor, I DECIDED to let go of these excess kilos. I had reached the limit of what I could bear.

I had reached what I describe in my workshops in a light-hearted image as « the bottom of my pool of shit » and I could not bear it anymore.

As I often explain, when one has reached the bottom of his pool, what ever its depth, we just need a little push on our heels to have us surface again !

The question one have then to ask, once we have understood and <u>integrated</u>[1] that we can change everything, is :
-« What depth will we tolerate ? »... «When will we decide it is **enough** ?... When will we decide we can not stand it anymore ?... And when will we decide we are READY to do EVERYTHING that is necessary to get better ?...And obviously, when are we going to start doing it.... ? »

Once you have realized that as a human being, you can not tolerate disharmony for too long, *(since we all, I believe, come from a world of harmony)*, when will you choose and decide to restore this harmony ?

For my part, I had decided to get rid[2] of the excess kilos and I was doing everything I believed I should in order to succeed.

I was determined to do it.

---

[1] « Integrate » means for me an idea or a concept is not « intellectual » anymore but « experiential ». It is not my head that knows. It is my body, my guts that <u>know</u> that this « knowledge » is lived, known and experienced from within.

[2] It is important, when you wamt to reduce your weight to say « I want to get rid of the kilos » rather than « I want to lose the kilos ». In facts, words being creative, if I say « lose », it implies I will find it again, because, as a youngster, I have been « programmed » to find again what I had lost.

I started to really watch my diet, eating everything I wanted without restrictions of quantity, applying Shelton's principles[1], already mentioned, that is without doing « forbidden » combinations.

To help me out, I practiced tools for reprogramming the mind, deciding that the food I was taking in was making me slimmer, and that all of the food coming out of me when I went to the toilets were kilos leaving me. Each time I would flush, I could tell them : *« Bye, bye kilos... »*. I worked on several levels simultaneously.

Nevertheless, although I was getting some results, I found this was not going fast enough.

One night, going to the toilets, I was to take a firm, strong and deep decision.

I decided I wanted to recover the weight that I had when I was 20 for my 33 birthday.

And it was only some months away…

As my birthday was approaching, I decided to treat myself to a very special gift.

I decided to offer myself a trip to Israel, in the footsteps of Jesus.

Being aware that the soil of Israel was charged with energy, I decided to prepare myself, physically and spiritually, for this experience I hoped would be important.

Actually, since the age of 28, I regularly wondered as I would see my life constantly improve :

-« But what will the Universe offer to me for this symbolic date of 33 years old ? »

---

[1] See Chapter 19

Knowing the benefits of fasting and having practiced it several time, I prepared myself for this trip with a big long purifying fast.

I started by eating, for one week, only fresh grapes. For the next four days, only fresh grape juice. And for the next seven days, I decided to fast totally and to drink only pure water.

I had organized my fast so that I could very gradually start to eat again the morning following my arrival in Israel, with fruit juices, grown in the Holy Land.

I must say that this fast allowed me to reach my objective by the planned date. I had finally gotten rid of 25 kilos !

Warning : In order to clarify for those who may think that such a fast makes so much weight disappear, this was not the case for me. I had already gotten rid of 18 kilos through my change in diet and the mind programming. This fast helped me to return the 6 or 7 kilos I still had to return to the Universe.

Anyway, I once again had received the manifestation I had asked.

For those of you who would like to start such a fast, I have to warn you. Such intense fasting should not be undertaken in a haphazard manner. If you are interested, I advise you to read Shelton's [1] book, or seek medical advice.

Arriving in Israel, I was to spend my first night in Tel Aviv before driving next day to Nazareth.

My first « meal » of fruit juices seemed succulent to me.

Perhaps, it is by « lacking » or by « suffering from the lack » of something we REALLY appreciate it.

Could it be why we sometimes choose to suffer before being happy ?

---

[1] « *Fasting for Renewal of Life* » by Herbert M. Shelton, published by the American Natural Hygiene Society.

Why are not we able to simply be happy ?

Something to meditate upon !

After Nazareth, I was to go to Mont Tabor then to Tiberiade where I found a small hotel.

The next morning, as I was driving down to the lake, I decided to stop to meditate for a while.

Honestly, I can now say that my original motivation for stopping there was rather twisted. In fact, I stopped with the idea of being able to say to my friends, once returned to France, that « I had meditated by the lake of Tiberiade ! ». Pretty poor motivation I admit…

However, do not we say God moves in mysterious ways?

For this is the way He had chosen to, somehow, make certain I would stop at that very place, at that very moment, so that I could live a transcendental experience.

I parked my car next to what seemed to be a boatyard and went to the shore of the lake, seeing some stones that seemed to be waiting for me.

I sat there and contemplated the opposite shore of the lake.

And, before I could do anything, without understanding what was happening to me, I burst into tears.

And as I was watching this beautiful landscape before me, I cried and cried and cried.

But these were not tears of sadness.

Within, it was as if I had the impression of « reconnecting » to this landscape… with… something… Something I had known a long time ago,… a long time… so long ago… and that was doing me such good …

And very quickly, I was to feel an incredible peace fill my heart and emanate from it. And the more I opened up, the more I felt this peaceful energy grow within me. I had the impression of being in touch with everything around me, even with the hills I saw on the horizon

I felt in me a tangible Love, strong, soft, concrete and real, for everything I contemplated.

Because during this sacred instant, I was not « looking » anymore. I was « beholding ». I had the experience of beholding, of realizing,… of experiencing absolute perfection in everything my eyes fell upon. And I felt blessed, really blessed, myself and everything I perceived around me.

I was to stay in that place a long time, filled with this palpable peace, immersed in that peace.

When, after a long time, I felt myself little by little « come down» from this transcendental state, I felt distinctly different.

Thinking about it afterwards, I understood certain things, especially that my return to the Holy Land was necessary to open up certain energy channels that had been closed.

And if before, I had intuitively felt I had lived in that country in previous incarnations, I had now what seemed to me an undeniable proof.

I had lived this astonishing experience at a time I was not at all expecting it. Not only did I not expect it but on top of that, I could not even imagine such a state was possible, in any case, not with such an intensity.

And I now had the impression that it was THE reason for my trip to Galilee.

It is true that I was to spend some wonderful moments at the different sacred places I visited in Holy Land but none equalled the one lived in that place that was not at all like a holy place, being a few feet away from a repair shop with boat hulls all around.

I had planned to find myself in Jerusalem for the date of my birthday, but when I got there, I found the energy of the holy city quite harsh and, on the morning of October 9th, after a quick walk in the old city, I decided to spend my birthday on the Mount of the Beatitudes and by the Tiberiade lake.

Actually, I had found the energy of he Galilee region much more pleasant than that of Jerusalem. For me, Jesus' presence seemed much more palpable in that region where He spend such a long time and where He wrought numerous miracles.

I now know that, after this transcendental experience lived by the lake of Tiberiade, I was to never be the same again.

As I conducted workshops afterwards, I could feel the new energy channels that had been opened in me and that were allowing me to channel a much more beautiful, much more pure energy, which made me feel wonderfully well and whose appeasing and transforming effects I could see on the participants.

I really felt that now, I had to go « further », but where ?

I realized clearly that I was lacking « something », but what ?

As time went by, I realized that what was lacking me, was the « experience » of what I was teaching.

I realized little by little that, throughout the years, I had taught beliefs that I « knew » to be true but of which I lacked the experience.

I realized I was able to talk for hours of the *Chakras,* of consciousness, of the levels of consciousness, but I lacked the « experience » of what I was talking about…

I understood why, several years before, I had felt that I would have, someday, to go « beyond » Martin Brofman and teach in « another » way, without knowing at the time what it really meant… At the time, it was just a kind of certainty that settled in me.

On the other hand, I felt more and more uncomfortable continuing to teach certain concepts in the same way.

For example, one of the basic idea of the method Martin put together is :

« We each create our own reality. »

And honestly, I found it more and more difficult to say and teach my students : *« I create my reality »* whereas, more and more, I felt that « energy » that I personally felt to be God, who, « had created my reality for me».

Why ?

Because, at times, I lived experiences that personally, I would never have dared ask for ! *(And yet, I was living them to my great delight !)*

And at other times, I would spontaneously experiencing something, again to my great delight, ALTHOUGH I did not even <u>believe</u> in it in the past. And that was going against <u>everything</u> that I had taught. And this was disturbing me to a great degree. I had to understand...

For example, it seemed <u>obvious</u> for many things in my life, that it was <u>me</u> that had created it. But for others, I knew that there was <u>something</u> else that had created it for me. And I can say that, because, at the very moment I was living these experiences, another part of me was instantaneously filled with gratitude towards God Whom I knew was the « cause » of the « Miracle » I was experiencing.

The experience <u>itself</u> was showing me that **at the same time**..

The experience itself was making me REALIZE « The One » that was the cause.

On the other hand, I had taught in the past : *«My beliefs determine my experience. »*. And now, something « was not right » in my own experience.

I would say to my students back then that : « I cannot live an experience unless I have already developed the state of consciousness or the belief. », because I taught that «Everything starts in <u>my</u> consciousness. » Yet, for some time now, I was starting to EXPERIENCE something else !

Suddenly, I started to « live » things I had NEVER believed in.

And I felt uneasy saying one thing to my students while I was experiencing another.

It was as if I had the impression of lying to them… And that was <u>intolerable</u>.

I had to look at everything in me again because something « did not ring true» in the model I had transmitted.

After having thought, reflected and re-worked these ideas, I realized a wonderful thing.

« Every thing that I had taught in the past was true.

is true and will be true for ever. »

I realized that everything that Martin had transmitted to me <u>IS TRUE</u>.

Nevertheless, I lacked a small understanding that I had not yet integrated and that I will present to you here.

It is that « variable » which, <u>according to your the level of consciousness</u>, makes an <u>identical</u> external event seem to have a totally different cause or origin.

I understood that it all depended on what is sometimes called « The levels of Consciousness ».

It all depended on « my level of consciousness ».

And in order that you may understand this, I will now explain to you in more detail what I « perceived » to be these « levels of consciousness ».

CHAPTER 24
The Levels of Consciousness...

Before I can explain to you what I perceive to be the levels of consciousness, let me talk to you again of the *Chakras*.

We have already touched upon them in Chapter 14, yet, I will now go a little bit further, based on what I have already explained.

As we have seen briefly, the *Chakras* have an interactive relationship with the physical body through the groups of nerves and the endocrine glands. They also represent, and I should say so **FIRST**, aspects of our consciousness.

And as we evolve, as we often say « in our consciousness », we could say we evolve « in our *Chakras* ».

We can say that each of us has a « Home *Chakra* » during a particular part of our life, according to what is motivating us in that part of our life.

This « Home *Chakra* » is the one in which we spend more time and the one to which we tend to « return » after having «visited» other *Chakras*, after having spent some time in other levels of consciousness, in other « *Chakras* »...

Actually, really, we are constantly passing from one Chakra to another, according to what motivates us at any given moment. Nevertheless, to help you understand it more easily, I will greatly simplify, structure and schematize a process that is, actually, much more complex.

And again, although this book in not intended to be a workshop or a technical book, I propose to explore with you the evolution of consciousness in the *Chakras*.

But, please understand, this is not to put more « intellectual knowledge » into you, which, in itself has absolutely no value.

On the contrary, I am doing this so that you can make your own parallels to your own experience, to better understand YOUR

OWN path and YOUR different levels of perception so that, understanding it, you can take other consciously aware decisions in order to change your experiences.

So we will now explore the evolution of consciousness, in the *Chakras*, for a baby being born on Earth and growing into adulthood. We could just as well be exploring the evolution of a Spirit incarnating on Earth as he moves towards the realization of his Divine nature.

<u>First point to clarify</u> : I deeply believe, and not only because it has been said throughout time by wise men and saints, *(and not only in the Catholic religion by the way)*, that the <u>main</u> reason of our incarnation on Earth is the realization of our Divine nature. It is, I believe, the reason why we are on Earth. We are here on one hand, to <u>realize</u> our Divine nature and on the other, to <u>manifest</u> it.

And before we realize our Divine nature, there is a path, with steps to go through exactly as a rose bud MUST go through certain phases BEFORE unfolding in the sunlight.

This path is somehow symbolized by the *Chakras*.

Let us start now our «journey » if you are willing.

When we are born on Earth, we are at first preoccupied by our survival. It is the first *Chakra* that deals in our consciousness with the aspects of security, survival, trust.

We can therefore say we « live » in our first *Chakra* for, let us hope, only the beginning of our life ! We have to survive and that is the only thing that motivates us.

The baby will then, in its relationship with its mother, who is supposed to furnish him with a protective and safe environment, determine his belief system about security. He will do this according to the « perceptions » he has had of his mother.

For example, let us imagine a baby being hungry. Nothing more normal. It is vital to eat. Nevertheless, let us imagine that this mother is feeding it and that, for one reason or another, there is not enough in the bottle. Either because it is the war, or because there is a lack, or because the mother simply does not realize her baby is so hungry... From the baby's point of view, outer circumstances do not matter. In **it's** point of view, it will go through the following experience : « There is not enough for me »

And, at that stage, it is just an experience. An experience among all of the others it lives each day.

But if, on the other hand, this experience happens again several times, this baby will probably come up with a belief. A belief which is likely to be : « There is <u>never</u> enough for **Me** on Earth. **My** survival is threatened on Earth. »

Nevertheless, once the baby has « decided » that it is « <u>like that</u> » on Earth, it will validate its <u>belief</u> by attracting, like a magnet, circumstances which will allow it to validate it.

<u>Its belief will now create its future experience</u>. And its « model » of relationship with its mother will become a sort of model of relationship for everything that is reassuring for it on Earth.

And afterwards, the baby becoming a man or a woman will experience lacks concerning what is supposed to sustain its survival.

Which means probably with money, work (which is assuring its security), with its home (which is the safe place).

All of that, because of a « perception », of a lack it lived, true, but that it mostly maintained in its mind.

Of course, he will live that, until he makes an other decision which is more correct.

This is a **very important** dimension.

<u>We can, and this **at any given time**, change our beliefs, to change our experiences.</u> And this, even if we do not have any experience yet of what we want to live instead.

This is a purely mechanical thing.

We must believe for example it is easy to survive on Earth *(obviously, if this is an experience which we desire to live !)* <u>while at the same time our experience</u> shows us that this is untrue !

And why does our experience show us that they is not true ?

Well simply <u>because we decided</u>, initially, and very often in the very beginning of our life, that for us, it was difficult to survive on Earth, obviously according to <u>our own experience</u>.

Sometimes, the mechanism is different.

Sometimes, we <u>have decided</u> that it was difficult to survive on Earth by accepting beliefs which were proposed to us by our surroundings or the society in which we live.

You understand now why I tell you that you must take « this step of faith » It is now obvious ! We must « believe » before « seeing».

And this is often a difficult point to integrate for many people.

They say :
-« If I see it, I will believe it. »

But this **<u>IS ABSOLUTELY NOT</u>** how it works !

To date, even very serious physicists are starting to believe it ! (Indeed, certain experiments on micro particles showed that the attitude of the researcher had an influence on the behaviour of these particles, which behaved as the researcher expected.).

These people should say instead :
-«If I believe it, I will see it ! »

We come back, as you see, to the basic principles of metaphysics, which are : Image + Certainty = Manifestation.

This point now being made clear, let us come back to the evolution in the *Chakras*.

Once this « baby in consciousness » has spent « some time » in his first *Chakra*, he will search for something better. He will « grow ». He will « evolve ».

After some time, he will wonder :

-« But after all, is not there « something else » on Earth that living to survive ? Something that will give me more PLEASURE ? Something more enjoyable ?»

Why ? Because I believe that as spiritual beings, we ALL come from a space of harmony, beauty, of Love.

And, because of that, sooner or later, thanks to this residual memory buried in us, we ALL search for something more enjoyable, more harmonious, more beautiful.

And as this « baby » searches for something better, he will obviously FIND something better.

Did not Jesus tell us :

-« Seek and ye shall find »[1] ?

And what will this baby discover ? He will discover that the pleasure that he can have through food or sex is more interesting that the one he had in just « surviving ».

He then will « move » into its second *Chakra*. Indeed, the second *Chakra* represents, amongst other things, the relation which we have with our body and the sensations or the pleasure that it can give us. On the level of this *Chakra*, it is obvious that this is only a physical, chemical and/or sensory pleasure.

Eventually, it is more pleasant to search for and to get more pleasure through my body than « simply » to survive.

---

[1] Matthew 7:7-8

So, the baby, that once swallowed everything it was given, will now makes its mother understand that, for example, banana tastes better than apple. He will start to touch his body and will discover it can give him pleasure ! And that is more enjoyable than surviving !

After having spent a certain time in its second *Chakra*, motivated by the search of pleasure through food or sex, he will again start to wonder :

-« But, isn't there something that is BETTER than this ?».

And of course, he will find it. He will then move into his third *Chakra (the one of the Solar Plexus)* and realize he has power. The 3rd *Chakra* deals in our consciousness with the aspects of freedom, control, power. It also represent the intellect, the Mental, and what we sometime consider the power of the Mind

This « spiritual baby » will realize he can say « no » for example. And that the simple fact of saying « no » will increase his pleasure.

He says to himself then :

-« Now, I am not controlled anymore by my body which was pushing me to eat, to smoke, or to search sexual pleasure. I am free. If I control myself, if I control the other, if I control my body, my « pleasure » is more intense, my pleasure lasts longer… »

And this « spiritual baby » which now becomes a « spiritual child » becomes for the <u>first</u> time aware of his creative power !

Before this, it « seemed » to him that he submitted to the outer world. From that moment on, he is aware he is participating in it, that he is a creator, that he has power !

He then realises :

-«If I say « no », my mother does not do what she was about to do… I am free,… I can control her… If I say « Thank you », she gives me more… If I cry, she comes faster… I can control my thoughts and thus obtain what I want,...I can visualize...affirm... decree... and obtain what I want »

What I am describing here is actually the base of all techniques called « mind control », I can tell you !

The baby also understands he can control his muscles and his body *(the muscles are associated to the third Chakra)* and, thanks to that, he can walk ! And the fact of walking allows him to discover a brand new universe.

And that is much more enjoyable than living in the second *Chakra*, where my body and my sensations control me !

This level of consciousness of the 3rd *Chakra* is the one that most humans on Earth live now.

It is from this point of view, this *Chakra*, this level of consciousness that arise all the techniques which are called « Mind Control » or which use the mind as a tool to change situations.

From here, too, arises the generally accepted belief:
-« You will earn your bread by the sweat of your brow».

This is what make many people believe they must « do » to get. Whereas they are many other ways... Other paths we will soon explore....

In our society, it is considered « normal » to be motivated by 3 principal things: survival (1st *Chakra*), sensory pleasure and sex (2nd *Chakra*) and power, control or possibly freedom (3rd *Chakra*).

All the state of consciousnesses beyond the 3rd Chakra, in our society, are considered either as extra-ordinary, or even pathological, which is very sad.

Why ?

Because in our Western society, **consciousness has never really been studied** ! We must turn to the East to find the answers there.

But let us return to our « spiritual child » and to his growth…

As much as he feels intense pleasure by controlling himself or others, partly thanks to all that it will create for him, so, after a certain time, it will seem to him that there must be « something else » than just this !

And even if this being radically changes his life by learning to manage the abilities of his mind, after a while, he will miss « something ».

He will finally realize that it is true that he can have EVERYTHING, thanks to his mind, but in the long run, he is alone. Very alone.

In fact, in the first 3 *Chakras*, we are alone.

It is ME and my survival.

It is ME and the pleasure MY body gives me (it is of course not a question of the pleasure my body can procure for someone else, because that is already about a RELATIONSHIP to another, it is the 4th *Chakra* !).

It is ME and my power or my freedom.

These are relatively « primary » states of consciousnesses in which we are not yet aware of the other. On these levels of conscience, the other exists a little bit as an object, without being really recognized as a consciousness with whom I relate.

And this « spiritual child » will then seek the « relationship » with the other.

He will then realize that, TO LOVE or TO BE LOVED, is more pleasurable than what he can obtain or feel thanks to his 3rd *Chakra*.

And he will realize that, whatever the pleasure that control can bring him, even controlling a multinational business, to Love or to be Loved by <u>ONE</u> person only is much more pleasurable…

We are still talking obviously about what one feels, of an interior state of consciousness !

A feeling of pleasure, of satisfaction which fills us from within.

And he « will move » then into his 4th *Chakra (the one of the Heart)*. The one that deals with our perceptions of Love and acceptance.

And during this part of his life, he will be motivated by the search for Love and Relationships.

He will also learn how to accept.

To accept himself, as he is. To accept the other, as he is *(even if he can choose not to want to be with that other!)*.

He will also realize that Love is not an emotion because it does not depend on the outside. He will realize that this Love is a state of being and that it depends simply on the choice he makes to open to it and to feel it.

He will realize that what he perceived « before » as Love was not Love but that it was only an emotion which he felt as a result of something happening on the outside. *(«Wait, someone does that to me, **therefore** I am Loved". "Wait, someone says that to me, **therefore** I am not loved… »)*.

He will realize that the relationship with the other can be expressed with or without sex.

He will realize that Love is in fact a **state of being, of consciousness** which he can choose to experience at any given moment.

And that to experience this Love, it is enough for him to choose to stop judging and to stop projecting his expectancies onto any one or any thing..

He will realize that it is only a question of choice to make and to maintain.

He will then feel what many people call « Unconditional Love »

And the pleasure that he feels will be enough for him!

Yes, it will be enough!

But only for a while.

Why? Because, as complete and as fulfilling as this experience might be or seem to him, he will grow accustomed to his new state and will seek more, always more! Because there is more to feel or experience!

Many people think that this Unconditional Love is the « ultimate goal ». That it is the end of the road.

But this is not the case, far from it, we are still only half way there… There are in fact 7 *Chakras* and we are only at the 4th!

And what could delight him even more than the Love than he feels?

Well, to express it! To let it pour out of him!

Because very soon, he will realize that this Love that he feels is so beautiful, so large, so big, that it cannot be contained..

And he will realize that in expressing it, in « bringing it out » he creates space for even more Love to come in and fill him!

He will realize that to express this love, to make it come out of him by an expression, a word or a gesture, makes him even happier.

And beyond expressing love, he will realize that expressing himself, making something « come out » of him which he has « in him » transcends him.

He will thus move into his 5th *Chakra*, the one of the throat.

The expression of his being will become his motivation.

And, like a singer who sings for the sheer pleasure of singing, the painter who paints for the sheer pleasure of painting, the cook who cooks for the sheer pleasure of cooking, the mason who builds for the sheer pleasure of building, the dancer who dances for the sheer pleasure of dancing, he will understand that to allow something to come out of him make him even « higher » and transcends him.

And as he « lives » more and more his throat *Chakra*, something « magic » will happen.

He will then realize that he is never alone ! Even when he is alone…

He will realize that he is now connected to a « force », a « benevolent being » which gives him everything he wants without any effort on his part.

Previously, in the first three *Chakras*, he was alone, with sometimes superficial relationships with the others.

On the level of the Heart *Chakra*, he felt in deep connection with the other, in his presence. He was no longer alone « horizontally».

On the level of Throat *Chakra*, he is no longer alone, but this time « vertically »..

For the first time, he has « direct » experience of the interaction with the world called « spiritual ».

We are indeed in 5th *Chakra* at the « border » between the physical world, symbolized by the first 5 physical *Chakras* and the 5 elements *(Earth, Water, Fire, Air and Ether[1])* and the spiritual world, symbolized by the 2 last *Chakras*.

When one is in one's 3rd *Chakra* associated with the mental plane and intellect, it is <u>impossible</u> to have a direct experience of the spiritual world.

---

[1] The Ether is the fifth physical element. It is the most subtle. It corresponds to the space between the atomic particles or to the emptiness of outer space.

One can, on the other hand, understand that it is « possible » that God exists, or Guardian angels, or spiritual Guides etc…, **BUT it is not a <u>DIRECT EXPERIENCE</u>.**

It is a process of intellectual understanding.

On the other hand, when one is on the level of his 5th Chakra, the reality of the world known as « spiritual » is COMPELLING, not in the form of a intellectual understanding, but in the form of a REALIZATION.

You have all, I am sure, already lived an experience in your life where your situation seemed to you hopeless..

And yet, when it seemed that nothing more could possibly be done, your problematic situation was solved all by itself, « something » happened.

And then, spontaneously, <u>AT THAT VERY MOMENT</u>, a part of you exclaimed or thought instantaneously « **My God, THANK YOU** » (or something which, for you, according to your beliefs, or your religion, reflects the idea that «<u> something</u> » solved this situation for you.)

Well, <u>at that moment</u>, you were in the throat *Chakra* !

Your direct experiment <u>showed</u> you, <u>revealed</u> to you, <u>taught</u> you, that you lived what you lived <u>THANKS</u> to this benevolent force that you can choose to name in different ways.

For me, the name you give to that being, to that energy has no importance.

Some people, like myself, call it God. Jesus called it the Father. Others name it the Universe, the Force, or what ever …

The important thing is not the name you give it but more <u>to recognize the interaction</u> with that energy, because, beyond your perception, it exists…

Another marvellous thing which also happens when someone « enters » into his 5th *Chakra* is that, at the same moment one has the realization of the interaction with this « energy », one has an <u>immense feeling of gratitude</u> towards this energy.

You « spontaneously » thank it for the grace it bestows on you.

In the catholic religion, this state of consciousness that I am now describing is known as a « State of Grace. ». Someone who experiences it has the experience that, whatever he wants for himself, God wants it for him. It seems to him that he is **always** at the right time, at the right place, for the things to happen in the best possible way.

And then you are never alone anymore, even when you are alone.

This state of consciousness, was wonderfully described by Jesus when he said:

-« My doctrine is not mine, but his that sent me. »[1] or

-« Ask, and it shall be given you; seek, and ye shall find; knock, and it shall be opened unto you : for every one that asketh receiveth; and he that seeketh findeth; and to him that knocketh it shall be opened. »[2] or

-« "Behold the fowls of the air: for they sow not, neither do they reap, nor gather into barns; yet your heavenly Father feedeth them.../... Consider the lilies of the field .../...

Take therefore no thought for the morrow... »[3] or,

-« Therefore I say unto you, What things soever ye desire, when ye pray, believe that ye receive them, and ye shall have them.. »[4].

Another extremely interesting state of the throat *Chakra* is the « perception of the absence of lack », the perception of abundance…

---

[1] John 7:16
[2] Matthew 7:7-8
[3] Matthew 6:26-34 ; Luke 12:22-31
[4] Mark 11:24

Lack is a perception which « exists » in the 3rd *Chakra*. And once you have perceived your lack *(of clarity, health, money, and so on...)* you have the PERCEPTION that you have to DO to have.

In the throat *Chakra*, you do not have any perception of lack... Somehow, you feel complete, as you are, where you are, here and now.

You can <u>of course</u> have desires, but with a great difference : you DO NOT SUFFER from the fact that this desire is not manifest. It is only a desire.

And the PERCEPTION that you have then is that you only have TO BE to have.

And that is a **big** difference!

Before, I had to <u>do to get</u>, now, I <u>just have to be who I am in order to have</u> ! It is enough for me to be simply be, confident and trustful in each moment that I am led by « God », because my experience shows it to me directly.

It is what each one of us feels when we let ourselves be guided by the Universe and perceive and accept the gifts it gives us.

We feel ourselves then in abundance, having always the perception that we have what we need or what we wish, AT THE TIME we need it.

And again, as with all the rest, abundance is only a state of consciousness...

In my personal evolution, whereas at the beginning, I was mainly in my 3rd *Chakra*, when I heard people « give thanks » for the benefits that God granted them, I obviously could not understand[1].

Of course, since my experience « proved » to me that « I earned my bread by the sweat of my brow».

---

[1] See Chapter 17

My experience at the time was just a reflection of my belief...

And years afterwards, when I started to live in my throat *Chakra*, I could then start to really feel filled with gratitude towards this energy I called God, whom I now saw being clearly the cause of what I was living.

I was perceiving the Cosmic Orchestration...

But let us return to our « spiritual adolescent », about to become an « adult ».

And as he spends a « certain time » in his 5th *Chakra*, asking and receiving from this very powerful source, trustful that no matter what he wishes, he will receive it, our « teenager » will gradually create a friendship with his « benevolent source » that he now clearly perceives.

He will test it and re-test it, over and over, always asking for more...

And thanks to this interaction, he will discover a more effective « communication protocol »

Gradually, he will realize that this « benevolent energy » is in fact himself.

He will realize that this « energy » that he PERCEIVED at first as external IS IN FACT, himself.

This knowledge, this realization will make him ADULT and AWAKENED.

He will have REALIZED his own nature and will then have moved into his 6th *Chakra*.

He will then see CLEARLY, how, through his fears, his desires and his beliefs, he created what he lived in his life.

He will then perceive its PERFECTION.

Sometimes, he will see perfection appearing in a harmonious way.

Sometimes, however, he will see perfection appearing in a non-harmonious way.

But it will be nevertheless perfect.

He will see himself as a creator of his own Universe and will also see each person around him as creator of his own Universe.

It is what allowed Jesus to say :

-«I and my Father are one »[1] or

-« Verily, verily, I say unto you, He that believeth on me, the works that I do shall he do also; and greater works than these shall he do; because I go unto my Father.. »[2] or again :

-«Father, forgive them : for they know not what they do... »[3]

The 6th *Chakra*, also called the 3rd eye, for me reflects **TRUE** clarity.

This is the clarity I would like to reveal to you and share with you in this book and in my courses. **The only** clarity that, it seems to me, is really important to develop. Moreover, I believe that it is from this clarity that physical health and clarity devolve…

This particular point of view, is beautifully described by Jesus with the metaphor of a lamp:

-« No man, when he hath lighted a candle, putteth it in a secret place, neither under a bushel, but on a candlestick, that they which come in may see the light. The light of the body is the eye: therefore when thine eye is single, thy whole body also is full of light; but when thine eye is evil, thy body also is full of darkness.

Take heed therefore that the light which is in thee be not darkness. If thy whole body therefore be full of light, having

---

[1] John 10:30
[2] John 14:12
[3] Luke 23:34

no part dark, the whole shall be full of light, as when the bright shining of a candle doth give thee light. »[1]

For it is true that perceived from the 6th *Chakra*, Life is really perfect.

And remember that it is only a state of consciousness!

A state of consciousness that we all can develop at any time! It is again only a choice to make and <u>to maintain</u>…

But let us return to the path of our « spiritual adult ».

He will be in a state of wonder, both at his own nature, and that of each being he meets.

He will then see clearly how, all the beings around of him create their own perfect Universe. He will see how they create their perfect experiences while holding consciously, meticulously, their fears, desires and beliefs.

And, seeing some suffering, he will probably want to awaken them from their stupor to announce his marvellous news.

Some will listen, others will not.

But it will not be important for it will be, in any case, perfect.

And as he « grows » more and more, he will closer and closer to the « other » until this concept of « the other » finally also disappears.

He will then move to his 7th *Chakra* and will then experience total Unity, absolute Empathy, Omniscience and Omnipresence.

And, just as Jesus was a marvellous demonstration, he will cease to identify with his body, his personality and even with his spirit to assimilate, to integrate, and to become again what he really is.

---

[1] Luke 11:33-36

He will then become <u>the only consciousness that really exists</u>, the only absolute and timeless reality…

That which some call « GOD ».

It is what happened, I think, when Jesus, after his resurrection, says to us :

-« And lo, I am with you always, even unto the end of the world. »[1]

And forty days later, during His Ascension, he returned to the Father, while His physical form disappeared in « a cloud»[2].

And obviously, to those who were looking at Him, to those who were attached to the physical world, it seemed that He disappeared.

However, He was not disappearing… On the contrary…

He was becoming again what He had always been, having simply released any sense of identification with His body, His personality and even His spirit.

And He left us, thanks to his experience, a marvellous message of hope, as well as a marvellous map of consciousness WITH his instructions.

Did we really understand it ? I am not sure !

But do we <u>really</u> want to understand ?

Do we <u>really</u> want to change ?

Do we <u>really</u> want to become the most beautiful expression of what we can be?

Some will say YES, I WANT IT !

But how much ?

With what INTENSITY ?

---

[1] Matthew 28:20
[2] Acts of the Apostles 1:9

With what CERTAINTY that they can do it ?

With what CERTAINTY that, if they cannot do it alone, that they can still do it with God's GRACE[1] ! ?

This notion of the « Grace of God » was completely impossible for me to conceive of at first.

-« If I CREATE my reality, GOD has NOTHING to do with it ! », I thought.

But now, since I met Him, everything is different.

Now, I understand how GOD, who, finally, is myself whom I do not yet know, can observe me, and patiently watch me going through my experience.

And if I have a **SINCERE AND DEEP** desire to change, (even if at the same time, I clumsily go on maintaining a whole series of limiting beliefs in terms of my ability to change, believing that I really don't deserve it, that it is too good to be true…), I can see Him giving me the Grace to experience something which I want deeply, simply so that I can have « the experience of it ».

Because He loves me…

Of course, this experience will then seem to me so EXTRA ORDINARY that I will probably refuse it *(having described it myself as non-ordinary at the moment I was living it !).*

But it will have been so beautiful, so fulfilling, so pure, that I will **never** forget it !

And I will then start to seek it again, now, in one hour, in two hours, this evening, tomorrow, the day after tomorrow, again and again, harassing my beloved Father until He gives me again this gift that I know now that I can live, since I lived it, by his GRACE !

---

[1] Luke 18:27 « The things which are impossible with men are possible with God. » ; Mathieu 19:26 ; Marc 10:27

For my part, I can understand why, at a given time, I was no longer at ease saying that I created my reality whereas my experience proved the opposite.

I had moved from my 3rd Chakra to my 5th *Chakra*.

In the past I had taught a technology of consciousness.

A « mental » tool of transformation. A mental comprehension of consciousness, even if it is true that it included « ideas », concepts known as « spiritual ».

But an idea is <u>not</u> an experience. .

An idea is only an idea… And it cannot be transmitted simply by words… It must be transmitted by experience …

However, the mental comprehension had enabled me to create a bridge between the physical world *(and its multiple apparent causalities)* and the spiritual world *(and its single and absolute causality)*.

This mental bridge had given me access to my 5th *Chakra*, from where I then had a direct experience of God <u>being outside of me</u>.

It had enabled me to pass from my 3rd *Chakra* from where I had a <u>intellectual comprehension</u> of the state of consciousness of the 5th *Chakra* to the <u>DIRECT experience</u> of the state of consciousness of 5th *Chakra* ! .

And I can tell you this is VERY different !

So I could no longer say « *I create my reality* » without feeling I was lying.

I had to « render to Caesar the things that are Caesar's and to God the things that are God's »[1].

---

[1] Mark 12:17

I had to accept that, FOR THE MOMENT, and only for the moment, this force, this creative power, this Love, this God, appeared external to me.

I know that one day, I will accept and realize what He really is.

One day, I KNOW that I will realize that « HE IS ME » and that « I AM HIM ».

The day I have released all fears.

The day I have accepted everything, integrated everything.

The day when I stop creating, with my thoughts, my words, my actions, conflict, duality and separation....

I know that at that time, I will realize that He is myself, even if it is takes some time to accept it.

And I know that just as He has created in « His» own image, I must now rebuild myself according to His image, having for so long constructed an image of myself so different from the one that He is and of what I am also, in the deepest part of me...

And I must give myself permission to be, as Neal Donald Walsch[1] expresses so well in his « Conversations with God », **« the most beautiful expression of what I can be... ».**

On this subject, a short story comes back to me :

> - A sculptor is exhibiting his work. he has sculpted a perfect elephant, of such presence and perfection that everyone believed that it was real. Never in the past had such a success been seen. And everyone asked him:

-« But how, how, did you make such a perfect elephant of a rough block of stone ? »

And the artist answered :

-« I simply hewed away from the rough stone EVERYTHING that did not resemble an elephant. »

---

[1] Neal Donald Walsch is the author of the series of 3 books, *« Conversations with God »*, published by Putnam Adult (hard cover), Hodder Mobius (paperback).

And for myself, I know that to this day, I have not yet reached the permanent perception of my perfection and of my Divine nature, although it has been granted that I experience it briefly in certain blessed moments.

However, I must accept my perception for the time being knowing that it will be different,… some day…one day…

To claim now that « <u>I create my reality</u> », when my perception and my experience show me the opposite, would be **arrogance** on my part.

The only thing that remains for me to do is to be **honest** with myself and my perceptions and to seek always to be closer to Him whom I know to be the cause and the solution of everything.

God, my father and my mother, my beginning and my end, my alpha and my omega, my origin and my destiny…

Today obviously, I am well aware that I still have a <u>long</u> way to go !

And yet, remembering where I have come from, remembering how I was years ago, when I was 24 years old, when I began my search, I KNOW that I have already come <u>a long way</u>.

Moreover, I <u>know</u> now that, beyond my perception, I did not follow this path alone.

And so, I also know that I will not continue my road alone… So, why worry ?

All is well…

All is well…

All is well…

All is REALLY well !

So …

Love is the Key...

Thank you !
Thank you !
Thank you !

CHAPTER 25
Amma...

As I continued my introspection to understand myself more fully, I became aware that I had a lack to fill.

As I said a little earlier, I realized gradually that I had acquired a great quantity of intellectual knowledge about consciousness but I had missed some fundamental data: **The experience** of what I was talking about.

Little by little, I felt that I was reaching « the end » of the method which had been developed by Martin Brofman.

As much this method had enabled me greatly to advance, it seemed to me that I had reached a « dead end ». It had to move to the next stage.

This method had been very useful for me to « understand » very complex spiritual principles but it had not allowed me to experience them.

I realized that a « master » can only make you evolve to the point he has reached himself.

And as much Martin had helped me, and I can honestly say that without him, I would probably not be around anymore, now I had to go « further ».

I had to meet someone who was not only « talking » about consciousness.

I was <u>determined</u> to meet someone who <u>lived it</u>. Someone who was the undeniable living demonstration.

I had, of course, heard about of certain Masters, of certain Beings of whom it was said that they were either Sages, or regarded as Saints or Holy Ones, but they all seemed to be so remote and so inaccessible.

It was said that one had to go to India to be able to meet such Beings. A country toward which I had at the time enormous resistances. *(It is true that I was subjected to the mass of beliefs and prejudices that my education had presented to me,... and that I had « unfortunately » accepted at the time.)*

I think that you have already heard that :

-« When the disciple is ready, the Master appears ».

I know now that my intense desire to really experience these transcendental states of consciousnesses I have spoken of was the catalyst of my meeting with the one who was to be my first « True » Spiritual Master.

Not that I am saying that Martin was not one. He is one.

A remarkable Master who teaches us and prepares us magnificently to be able to continue the path peacefully, with other Masters continuing afterwards.

I realize that, as happens in the education of children, there are various types of teachers.

There are professors of schools whose speciality is to teach in nursery school. There are professors of the schools which teach children in primary education. There are then other professors more specialized still for high-school students. Then others for Universities. And still of others for those preparing for Diplomas, Masters' or even Doctorates... There are even teaching professors for future professors, at every level....

And in the same way that we have 7 *Chakras*, we need various types of « Masters » who can teach us, at our own level, with the language customary for this level, to prepare us for the following level...

And all these professors, all these « Masters » know very well that they have to adapt their language to the public they are addressing. One cannot speak to a child about 7 or 8 years old as one speaks with a future professor, as you know..

And at the same time, <u>NONE</u> of these Masters is **more** important than another. Each one is signed up perfectly at a given time, with a given language, with a given pedagogy, adapted to the pupils to whom they transmit their knowledge, sometimes in very different ways.

What was happening to me, was that I was ready to change class, I was ready to move to a higher level and I thus needed a new « professor », a new « Master » who could, based on the acquisitions thanks to my preceding « Masters », take me still further ahead.

This is how I realized, for example, that the Silva Method[1] of which we spoke earlier was a splendid tool allowing in a simple, concrete and reassuring way people « starting » on this path to understand and easily acquire a certain control of their minds.

Once these people have integrated the power of their Minds by the Silva Method or another similar method, thanks to somebody like Martin Brofman for example, they will then start to familiarize themselves with more complex spiritual concepts and to understand their practical, concrete applications to continue their progress on the path.

Once this stage reached, they then have to find other Masters, may be like those I met, may be another type, in order to see and to feel, in the presence of the Master, what an awaken Being really is…

It is all very well to have « learnt» the techniques of parachute jumping on the school benches, one day, I will have to have the experience, by taking a plane and jumping into the void…

Therefore I realize now that, even if I know that there are other paths than the one I followed, and other paths which are probably much faster, without my parents, my tormenters in boarding school, Jean-Marc, Nick, Vicky Wall, Louise Hay, Hervé, Martin Brofman, Lee Pascoe and Michael Dodson of the SILVA Method, without all the people whom I cannot list

---

[1] See Chapter 11

here and who marked my life and taught me, I would probably never have arrived where I am now.

I had thus decided that I needed another professor, another « Master » to go further and it was not long before he arrived.

We have a saying in France saying :

-« If you do not go to Lagardere (the name of a person), Lagardere will come to you »

I can tell you that it is true.

You really do not have to worry.

When the disciple is ready, the Master appears, it is sure !

And no need for you to go and seek him, He will come to you !

I was one day on a plane (which was not very unusual for me at the time since, about every two months, I was in an island under the sun), conversing with my neighbours, a charming German couple who were retired..

I was on the way for the umpteenths time to Reunion island, a splendid island, where I flew regularly.

I asked them the reason for their trip and they explained that they came especially from Germany to visit their Indian Master, a woman named « Amma », who was flying into Reunion Island.

I had already vaguely heard about her, but I asked them for more details, because according to them, she was really exceptional enough to merit a special trip of more than 15 hours in the plane !

They explained me that this woman of about forty had been since the age of 16 in a permanent state of transcendental consciousness and that she spent her life blessing people, comforting them, performing many miracles.

Love is the Key...

I was very interested by what they said and asked them the details of where it would be possible to meet this apparently « extra-ordinary » woman.

Once arrived in St Denis, I was to meet the friends who organized my workshops and, quite honestly, I forgot about Amma.

I had as usual of a few days of « acclimatization » before giving the presentation conferences of the workshops and so was making the most of the Reunion Island beaches.

One morning, on the beach under a blazing sun, I started to get bored when, all of a sudden, I thought about Amma again.

I did not know it yet, but in fact, she was calling me, giving me a first « phone call » !

I was close to St Gilles and the people I met on the plane had told me that Amma would be near St Louis, in the south of the island.

I was only about 20 miles away and started to search for « The House of India », where Amma was supposed to be. After some time, I found this small house and parked in the car park.

Stepping out of the car, I was bathed in Indian music that was coming from the house.

Today, having sufficiently bathed in this music and having understood its importance, I adore it for the effects it gives, but, at that time, I did not have the same reaction at all. I found it almost irritating.

And as I was about to enter this house, I was made me to take off my shoes. Why not, wondered I ?

The ambiance was at least « exotic » and I felt on the defensive.

Moving into the entrance hall, I was assailed by puffs of incense, which put me even more on the defensive !

Love is the Key...

I was at the time so full of prejudices that I am almost ashamed to talk about it, but, oh well…, after all…, it was me!

Yes, but that « me » has since died,… to be replaced by the one which I am now!

I pushed open the door of the room where Amma was and, as I entered, several phenomena occurred almost simultaneously.

At the end of the room, which contained perhaps a hundred people, there was, sitting on a large armchair, an Indian woman with a dazzling smile. The majority of the people present were sitting on the ground, apart from some who were sitting on chairs set along the walls. Behind Amma were women in white saris and men clothed in orange. They were all singing things which I could not understand at all and some of the people sitting in front of Amma were singing in chorus, seeming to know this unknown language. Sometimes, a woman in white approached her to fan her or massage her shoulders. People sitting in front of Amma had formed a queue and, one by one, each one of them knelt before her, for a few moments, she took them in her arms.

This « highly exotic » show filled me somewhat with fear and incredulity.

Bad-mouther that I was, I said to myself :

-« So what? Yes,… she is sitting,… she smiles at these people,… she takes them in her arms,… Ok,… and so? … I'd be happy too, to sit and to take people in my arms, while I am being fanned, and so on… »

You can imagine the picture !

However, a surprising thing that I cannot deny had happened at the very moment I had entered the room.

I had had an impression that, I had experienced only <u>once</u> before : that of entering a kind of pink cloud of palpable peace.

And as I moved into the room, this state of peace invaded me.

And that surprised me !

One time, <u>one only time</u> had I already felt that in the past !

It was at the very beginning of my path, when I was about 25 years old. Jean-Marc, my therapist, had suggested I join his « *Chakra Group* »[1]. To prepare myself for this group, I had fasted with only water for the 3 previous days. Once this group was over, I went to a conference that Eileen Caddy gave in the Cirque d'Hiver in Paris.

Eileen is again one of these « wise-women » that have put me back on the path, which I will speak to you about in a moment. She is the author of several splendid books[2] and is the Co-founder of the FINDHORN community in Scotland, with Peter Caddy her husband, and a friend, Dorothy Mac Lean.

For those of you who do not know Findhorn, it is a non-religious spiritual community, about which the press spoke in the Seventies because of the giant vegetables that they grew, thanks to a particular relation with nature and what are sometimes called elementals[3], in very arid, sandy ground.

But for me, Findhorn, is something else than giant vegetables ! It is firstly the message of Eileen Caddy.

And the message of Eileen is simple :

-« Listen to your inner voice. »,

-« Do not search outside what you already have inside »,

-« Learn to make the calm within you and to search this still small voice that guides you… ».

It is a message at the same time very simple but also very deep.

---

[1] See Chapter 6

[2] Eileen Caddy is the author of several wonderful book, including : « *Flight into Freedom* », « *Opening Doors Within* » and « *Footprints on the Sand* » published by Findhorn Press.

[3] The elementals are beings, invisible to most of us, whose function is to look after nature. We refer to them sometimes as Elves, Gnomes, Fairies, Sylphs, Salamanders, etc...

Love is the Key...

When I met Eileen for the very first time, after her splendid conference where she had spoken about the power of Love, I had very much wanted to speak to her, to simply approach her and to THANK her for the so soft words she had pronounced.

And when I approached this charming old English woman with a radiant smile, I had the extremely strange, but strong and pleasant impression of walking into a pink cloud which literally « sparkled with love ». And I had been very troubled because of it. A kindness, a palpable love emanated from her and did me an immense amount of good. I remember having mumbled some words to her but, in fact, being in her presence was enough. Her simple presence gave me peace.

When I returned home that evening, I was floating on a cloud !

And here I am, more than 8 years later, having this same experience with Amma !

And that, in spite of everything, made a deep impression on me.

However, at first, my scepticism was very strong. I can still see myself, leaning against the wall, both arms crossed *(symbolically closed)*, watching and staring at either Amma, or these people that I saw as somewhat « crazy ».

I think that what shocked me most, like many Westerners filled with prejudices and not yet having made the effort to understand Hinduism, was the fact that all these people where kneeling or prostrating themselves in front of this woman.

Ok, she seemed pleasant and smiling, but she was only a woman, not more important than any other, as I saw it through my blind eyes !

Having taught in the past, for many years, that: « <u>we all are equals,</u> », and that : « *What one person has been able to do, anybody else , including YOU, can do.* », you can understand why I felt as if these people were « lowering » themselves, *(in my perception)* before her.

Although quite blind and hardened at the time, fortunately for me, I was not stuck completely.

A part of me was thinking at the same time :

-« Patrice, you wished to see a Master and the Universe answered you ! Here she is a front you ! Forget your stupid prejudices ! Go ahead ! Go for it ! Get in the queue and go see her ! At least you will have had the experience, and then, it is better to have remorse than regrets. If you don't go now, you will regret it, it's sure !»

Putting aside all of my prejudices, I got in the queue. I sat down in a tailor's position and moved slowly forward. One by one, the people in front of me passed in the arms of Amma and I approached her.

And as I approached her, an odd phenomenon occurred. I felt emotions being released, I had a sort of desire to cry, not knowing why…

Finally, my turn arrived.

In order to be taken in Amma's arms, we had to be kneeling, because she was sitting in her big armchair.

Nevertheless, I remember being upright, on my knees, facing Amma, looking at her straight in the eyes, while through my eyes, I was telling her :

-« Listen, Amma, I do not know you. I am willing to believe you are more evolved than me, but know that, for me, we are ALL equals ! You and Me, we are the same.»

And at the same time, Amma looked at me with an incredible expression.

A superb, magnificent smile.

And in that second, it was as if, through her tender look, she was saying :

-« My son, my dear son, here you are finally, Finally,…here are you coming back. How glad I am to see you again, to find you again,…for such a long time I have been waiting for you… »

She reached out her arm to put hand on my shoulder and hold me against her breast. And as she gave me the impression of cradling me, I felt I was melting, I was surrendering to her.

And in my ear, she murmured what seemed to be :

-« Amma, Amma, Amma, 'ma, 'ma, 'ma, 'ma, Amma, Amma, 'ma, 'ma, 'ma, 'ma Amma, Amma, Amma, 'ma, 'ma, 'ma, 'ma... ».

And as for me, I was feeling good, I was feeling so good, I was feeling really good.

After some « time » *(how much time, I do not know, I had the feeling of being out of the time...)* she stood me back up, and stared at me in the eyes with a wonderful smile.

And it is as if, through her smile, I felt recognized and totally accepted. In this « magical » moment, I knew that she knew. She knew. She knew everything about me and Loved me nevertheless. And it was good, it was good. It was really good to feel so totally accepted and Loved.

She placed her finger on my forehead and pressed between my eyebrows for… a moment, one second, one minute, I do not know… Anyway, for a moment during which I had the impression she was entering within me. Like a kind of a benevolent spiral that I felt in my head, she was entering within me,…and it was good, it was good…she entered within me then, opened a door, then descended again, deeper, always deeper in me, like a spiral transporting me and again, she opened another door and transported me again, deeper,…

deeper,….always deeper, transported as I was in this wonderful spiral

I do not know how many doors she opened…may be 5, may be 6, may be 7. I do not know, she went down,… down,… down in me while I was opening,…opening,…opening.

Finally, she took her finger away from my forehead, smiled at me again with her angelic look and put a sweet and some rose petals in my hand.

As I moved away to let the next person behind me pass, I stood up again, having the impression of staggering slightly, and, so I sat down again very quickly.

And once seated, without really understanding what was happening, I HAD to close my eyes. And as I closed them, I sank down into myself…I felt falling, falling, falling into my deepest depths,…like an endless well, while at the same time, a feeling of a Love, of an incredible Peace was rising, rising, rising in me. I was literally bathing into Love. And it was good ! So good !

Never, <u>never</u> in the past had I felt that. A feeling of extreme presence accompanied with that immense Love which I could not contain and which was overflowing from me, I knew it…

It was as if I was disappearing in that Love, and, again,… it was good…

I now understand why words are always inadequate to describe these transcendental experiences. In fact, words apply to the intellect and, by nature, they « define », they give a finite form to something.

However, I was then touching and experiencing the Infinite. I was experiencing Love. And no word could ever really describe it !

And as I was immersed in that Love, the music, which a few minutes ago I found irritating with its high notes, was transporting me with it.

It was taking me into it.

It was as if this music was a path…

A path like an automatic escalator.

A path on which I just had to stand and let myself be carried along.

I was going into the music,…in its rises,… its falls,…in its magnificent spirals which made me discover new landscapes…

I was going into its rhythm,… into its progressive splendid accelerations which were impelling me towards a new space.

I was going into its ralentendos, which, like a key, opened a door to a pure new free space which was filled by my consciousness …

The music was carrying me in its welcoming arms to the discovery of magnificent inner spaces.

Because all this was in me… It did not come from elsewhere,…from somewhere outside…

Yes, everything I was experiencing was in me.

And it had always been there… Waiting for me to return

I understood. I understood. I understood.

I just have to surrender...

To surrender ...

And trust...

It is so simple !

Surrender like a child in his mother's arms…

After a very long time, I felt I was gradually coming back down to my « normal » state.

When I opened my eyes again, I stared at Amma, my eyes wide open with admiration and filled with Love for her.

And I remained in that blessed state until the end of the ceremony.

After everyone present had passed into Amma's arms, everybody stood up, forming an aisle so that she could leave us.

Amma left this room joyously, and as she passed she sent her beautiful smile to the people saluting her, hands joined in front of the heart.

Little by little, people left the room and I hurried to inform myself when and how I could re-visit this being whom already I found seemed so exceptional.

I was told that, during the few days Amma was here, she would give her « *Darshan* »[1] twice a day.

After having bought one or two tapes of this beautiful *music (after all, only imbeciles never change their mind !)*, I took my car to drive towards St Denis, cradled by the sound of the « *Bhajans* »[2].

Needless to say, I managed to come back the next day.

As I arrived on the premises, I noticed that I was still full of resistances, and prejudices. And as I questioned myself, I realized that these tenacious prejudices had nothing to do with Amma, whom I perceived from the bottom of my heart to be completely pure.

---

[1] *Darshan* is a Sanskrit word signifying literally the « vision ». The *Darshan* is the moment when a Sage, a Saint, a Master gives us the Grace to watch him/her, to behold him/her... The belief tells us that this vision will bring to the observer some of the virtues attributed to the person or scene he is watching. According to the Masters, the « external » form of the *Darshan* is different. With Amma for example, she takes individually each person in her arms. With other Masters, the *Darshan* can take another form.

[2] *Bhajan* is a Sanskrit word. The *Bhajans* are devotional chants. Certain *Bhajans* are dedicated to the representations of God or of the Divinity, for example Shiva, Jesus, Krishna, Allah, Buddha, Zoroaster, and so on... Other *Bhajans* are dedicated to a Sage, a Saint, or a Master.

The prejudices which I had were more concerned with the external form. They concerned more the « container » than the « content ». I was not at the time <u>at all familiar</u> with Hindu ritual and I was a long way from understanding the symbolic importance and the beauty of these practices.

So I decided to inform myself, to learn the reason for such a ritual, such a gesture and so on… because I felt, beyond the form, something deeply right in all of that. Also, I knew that if I wanted to really discover the enigma that was Amma and be able to get a TRUE idea of it, I HAD to leave aside all my prejudices in order to have a direct experience, un-polluted by these beliefs.

Some people there had told me that, if I wanted to, I could ask questions of Amma

That really interested me. But being at the same time still very sceptical about all this, I thought to myself:

-« Since these people say to me that she is an awakened state of consciousness, that she is Realized, She must thus know everything ! And if She knows everything, I do not have to ask her a question, because, if all that is true, She should be able to say to me exactly what is important for me ! »

I decided therefore my question should be :

-«Does Amma have any advice to give me ? »

When I saw Amma the following day and my turn approached to receive her *Darshan*, I gave my question to the interpreter. Once he had translated my question to Amma, She looked me with an astonishing glance. Instantly, I had the impression of being pierced through by Her glance which seemed to read into me. It was as if I went through the scanner of Her eyes. As if a laser beam went through me from top to bottom then to top, and then from left to right, from right to left.

After Amma had scanned me this way, she said a few rapid words to the interpreter, who said to me :

-« Amma says : more spiritual practice... »

And, there I am, left alone with this sentence. *« More spiritual practice... »* What does THAT mean !

At the time, I did not really have a spiritual practice. I did small meditations, of course, visualizations from time to time, but rather irregularly. It is true on the other hand that, very often during the course of the day, I repeated certain positive sentences but, in fact, nothing really like an « assiduous and regular » practice.

I turned to one of the « women in white » around Amma and asked for some explanation.

She explained to me that the spiritual practices could vary according to the person. That it could be a question of meditating each day, of practising *Japa*[1], of making a *Puja*[2]...

When I asked her with what I should start, she explained to me the meaning of *Japa*, that repetition was very powerful and very effective to begin a practice. She explained to me that I could get a *Mala*[3] and request a *Mantra*[4] from Amma.

---

[1] *Japa* (pronounce Djapa) is a Sanskrit word meaning « repetition ». Doing *Japa* consists of repeating over and over a word, a name, a sentence... In the catholic religion, the faithful do *Japa* when they recite a Chapelet repeating their prayers.

[2] A *Puja* (pronounce POUJA) is a ritual of adoration of the Divinity where certain symbolic offerings are made to the Divinity of one's choice.

[3] Un *Mala* is in fact a sort of chapelet with 108 beads. 108 is considered to be the number of God. It is the number of times that theoretically one must repeat the word, the name, the sentence or the mantra.

[4] *Mantra* is a Sanskrit word. A *Mantra* is a word, a sentence, an idea, a prayer that we repeat over and over. For example, the *« Hail Mary »* can be considered as a Christian *Mantra*. In Hinduism, there are many different *Mantras*. For exemple, *« Om Namah Shivaya »* is a *Mantra*. This *Mantra*, considered by many as a *Mahamantra*, which means « a great *Mantra* » has many significations. *« Om »* is the original sound, *« Namah »* means « I bow before You » and *« Shivaya »* refers to the Hindu God the transformed Shiva. In Sanskrit Shiva means also *« The one that gives Joy »* and therefore refers to any form of Gods or God in general. It is said that this *Mantra* refers to God, whatever our religion is. So it also means: *« I surrender to God »* or *« I bow before the inner God »* or *« Lord, thy will be done »* or again *« I take refuge in God »*.

However, to receive my *Mantra*, I had to wait a few days because Amma gave *Mantras* only during one specific ritual.

As I spent hours in the presence of Amma, seeing her continuously welcoming each person with the <u>same</u> smile, the <u>same</u> presence, the <u>same</u> warmth, I realized more and more that she was **really** « special ».

I was very curious concerning what inhabited Amma. Obviously, she « was inhabited » by something. By something beautiful, big , soft…

And as I stayed hours observing her, I asked myself questions like :

-«But what can She be seeing when She looks at this woman like that ? Why such a smile when She welcomes this man? What can She see in him? What can She feel when She sings the way She sings ? When She looks the way She looks ? »

And of course, I was to receive answers.

Did not Jesus say:

-« Ask and it shall be given you … »[1]

The answers came to me in a strange way[2]. Suddenly, as I was asking these questions, I myself was also propelled into this experience. I saw as She saw for one fleeting moment. Suddenly, whereas the second before I looked at the people around me and simply saw « people », the second after, I found them beautiful, luminous or moving, as looking at them, I saw either their inner beauty or why they felt bad.

---

[1] Matthew 7:7

[2] In fact, I now know that it seemed « strange » at the time dimply because I had not yet understood the mechanism.

As I was analyzing what was happening to me, I understood that Amma's presence and my state of openness to her energy was enough to make me « ascend » in my *Chakras*.

Amma was actually an elevator !

An elevator to Divine consciousness... always ready to lift us up, **IF, AND ONLY IF**, we choose to get in !

And I understood why she was saying to use Her as a ladder ! Everything was becoming clear.

I understood also what I had read years before about the *Darshan*, the vision of a Saint or a Master. I had read at the time something that said the simple fact of **seeing** a saint was a benediction. I remember at the time, being extremely sceptical when I read that.

-« What ? ? ! !, The simple fact of looking at a Saint is a benediction ? ? ? I want to see ! »

Well , I SAW !

I saw and I felt !

I felt and I understood that it was true!

To be in the presence of a Saint is really a blessing ! It was only a few years later that I was to really « understand » the physical principle of resonance[1] underlying this phenomenon, but nevertheless, I was experiencing it. Without any possible doubt.

The Master or the Saint emanates such an energy of Peace and Love, that it is enough to be in his/her presence, to look at him/her or « to connect » with him/her so that this splendid energy flows into us and us thus allows to experience it.

---

[1] In a few words, the principle of resonance says that an object in resonance or in vibration which is close enough to an « inert » object will, by *resonance*, put it in motion... For example, if you bring up a vibrating tuning fork by a « dead » tuning fork, this second one will also start to vibrate, according to the law of resonance...

This only confirmed what I already knew intellectually. I was used to explaining that « all states of consciousness are contagious but particularly those considered as positive ».

For example, you have all, I suppose, already felt that the fact of being next to a sad or depressed person can undermine your morale. In the same way, when somebody very happy, joyous and positive approaches you, you can feel transported by his joy.

This principle is the same with Amma or any other being like Amma. In fact, these beings are numerous and often known by the name of Wise Ones, Saints, Masters, *Gurus*[1] or *Avatars*[2].

In their presence, if you are open, you are caught up by this energy that they literally radiate and you can then experience part of what they are experiencing.

This is how, In the presence of Amma, I was growing little by little.

Finally, the day of the *« Devi Bahva »*[3] arrived, the day when She was going to give me my *Mantra*.

I lined up in the queue with the other people who wanted to have one.

The « woman in white » who had so gently explained what a spiritual practice could be, asked me then if I had a Divinity of choice. She wanted to know if, for me, I felt close to a God « in a form » or a God « without form ». For me, it was clear that my image of God was associated to Jesus Christ, considering

---

[1] *Guru* is a Sanskrit word often misunderstood in Western society because of the number of negative connotations associated with it. In fact, the true literal meaning of *Guru* is the Spiritual Master who guides us towards Knowledge.

[2] An *Avatar* is a Divine Incarnation. We will talk about this later.

[3] The *« Devi Bahva »* is a magnificent ritual in which Amma manifests a deeper part of Herself. After a special *Puja* (a ritual of offerings), Amma goes into prayer and then manifests a particular aspect of Divinity. She radiates a much stronger, more powerful energy.

my initial education and the deep experiences which I had had with Him.

I received that evening from Amma a specific *Mantra* so that, thanks to my practice, I could become inwardly closer to Jesus.

This is how I started a new form of spiritual practice.

I returned to France, happy to have made this meeting that I felt was extremely important for me.

CHAPTER 26
Acceleration...

Once home again, I took up my rhythm of giving workshops, taking care to practice more and more « Japamala »[1] with my new *Mantra*...

I chimed out this *mala*, repeating 108 times in a row either my *mantra*, or a word... 108 is actually the number associated with divine principle, the 1 symbolizing Unity, the 0 symbolizing the void or nothingness « from whence everything emerges » and the 8 representing the Infinite.

In Hinduism, 108 or 1008 is a number which appears in many rituals. There are for example the 108 or the 1008 names of God which one can repeat. There are also the 108 or the 1008 names of the feet of God, each name corresponding to one of the divine characteristics.

Personally, I took much pleasure in chanting my *Mala*. I felt that it did me a lot of good.

Hervé having left me, I had all the time to devote myself to spiritual practice ! Moreover, his departure was so painful for me that I threw myself whole-heartedly into the practice as a compensation mechanism.

However, after some time of practice with my new *Mantra*, I directed myself towards another form of *Japa*. Somehow, either because I was neither Hindu nor Indian, or rather because I think it was not my path at the time, I lost interest in my Hindu *Mantra*. I had the impression that it did not really « speak » to me, although I knew the translation.

So I decided to get a rosary and to start repeating sometimes a series of *« Hail Mary»*, sometimes *« Our Father »*, sometimes, I followed the recommended ritual with however a few

---

[1] Doing *Japamala* consists of using a *Mala* (prayer beads) to practice *Japa* (repetition) therefore the name *Japamala*.

personal modifications, due to the fact that I really did not know *(and did not want to learn)* the *« I believe in God»*.

And as, regularly, I recited my little rosary, I started to notice surprising things !

First, <u>I liked it</u> !

Yes, I, Patrice, I liked it !

I couldn't get over it, I who had always looked at the « bigots » reciting their rosaries with such suspicion ! I was becoming one !

On the other hand, now, thanks to Hinduism, which seems to me much more precise than the catholic religion, and thanks to my understanding of consciousness, I understood better the principles in action and the interest in disciplining consciousness and always directing it towards God, by whatever name we call Him.

And so, not only did I like it, but sometimes, and in fact, more and more often, when I was at my 7th or 8th *« Hail Mary»*, a kind of excitement filled me because, soon, soon, I was going to be able to say one *« Our Father »*[1]. It was as if I was joyful inside to get to the *« Our Father »* who seemed to me so beautiful, so just, now that, understanding consciousness more, I had been able to « translate »[2] Him into term of *« Chakras »* and levels of consciousness, language which was now completely familiar to me.

---

[1] Here is an explanation fot those of you who are not familiar with the chapelet (prayer beads), or the rosary. For one chapelet, you recite 5 times 10 *« Hail Mary »* followed by one *« Our Father »*. A rosary represents the recital of 3 chapelets. It is thus a « triple » chapelet, with 150 beads representing *« hail Mary»* and 15 beads representing *« Our Father»*.

[2] I could understand thet the *« Our Father's »* referred to the different levels of consciousness symbolised by the *Chakras* and to the levels of perception pertaining to them. This prayer, like a mental purification, a positive mental reprogramming allows the devotee to give hinself auto-suggestions and to accustom himself progressively to the direct experience of God.

Sometimes, at other moments, I felt very bad as I recited my prayers. The more I moved forward, the more I felt bad. It was as if a deep feeling of suffering from the absence of God was filling me. I suddenly felt so alone, so « abandoned » by God. And I suffered terribly from it. Sometimes, the lack of God was so intense that I would cry. And inside, it was:

-« Why,… why,… why have you abandoned me,… why do I not feel Your presence,… why do you leave me so alone… I need You… »

And then, suddenly, as I was in tears, suffering from His absence, He filled me ! In a quarter of a second, I was literally filled with Him as His Peace filled me and comforted me. And I bathed, for who knows how long, in His Divine Presence.

While all this was going on, I obviously continued to teach my workshops at a furious pace. Sometimes here, sometimes there…

I noticed however a definite change in my way of teaching.

More and more, I heard myself speak of God and of the effects of prayer…

I noticed that the « magical » states of consciousnesses during which I was filled with this calming force would now happen much more frequently and would last longer as I accepted them more openly.

I was going through exactly the same process as my students did as they improved their eyesight.

I used to explain that a person who is improving his/her sight will go through periods during which he/she will see more clearly. These periods of clarity are sometimes called « flashes of clear vision ». At the beginning, they are short because very often, people consider them to be « extra-ordinary ».

Why ? Because, especially in the beginning, they do not yet believe that it is <u>normal</u> to see clearly without glasses. They are so « accustomed » to seeing blurred that it seems to them non-ordinary to see clearly now. Only, with time and determination, the person will start to accept clarity as being a natural and ordinary state. He/she will thus experience increasingly long periods of clarity, more and more frequently, until finally, he/she completely accepts clarity and because of that, he/she stabilizes there.

For my part, I was going through exactly the same process, except that I had not asked for a <u>physical clarity</u> but rather a <u>spiritual clarity</u>. I had asked to experience more and more what I perceived as being this Divine consciousness of which I had already tasted.

Only, and especially so at the beginning, this consciousness which filled me seemed so beautiful, so « extra-ordinary » that, somehow, I did not accept it.

I was telling myself things like :

> -« *This is too beautiful for you !... You do not deserve such a gift... »*

And, because of that, these experiences remained fleeting for me !

I too had to integrate this principle that I regularly transmitted to my students :

> «*If you want to experience something else, be it seeing clearly without glasses,... be it healing,... not feeling pain in the shoulder,... feeling Loved,... feeling abundance, anything in fact..., you <u>must totally accept</u> that this new state is natural so that it can become so. As long as you regard anything as « too beautiful » for you or « difficult to reach or maintain », you will remain prisoners of your beliefs. »*

It seemed obvious to me that my meeting with Amma had served as a catalyst which triggered what I perceived as a wonderful acceleration of my « spiritual evolution ».

One day when I was near Lyon, giving a Better Eye Sight workshop, I had an experience which I will NEVER forget.

It was Sunday morning and I was guiding the participants through a guided relaxation.

In this relaxation, I present positive sentences that each participant is supposed to repeat mentally, in order to see more clearly without glasses.

One of the sentence is :

-« *I am determined to see* ».

The following one is :

-« *I am determined to see more clearly* ».

Theses sentences are actually from a wonderful American book : « *A Course in Miracles* »[1].

And as I was saying out loud these sentences to the participants, mentally I was telling myself :

-« I am determined to see YOU... I am determined to see YOU more clearly... », calling the Divine principle to manifest to me.

And **THE VERY MOMENT** when I completed the second sentence, an incredible experience happened. Suddenly, I « saw » a form of bright light appearing in the central aisle, between the participants. And as I was sitting on my table *(it was my favourite position !)*, I felt instantaneously my Soul bow down at His feet as immediately, it recognized this

---

[1] « *A Course in Miracles* » is published by Penguin Books Ltd. It is actually a course in 365 lessons. Each day, you are supposed to repeat certain positive sentences which have the effect, through repetition, of reprogramming you inside and opening your consciousness to new levels of perceptions. This course allows you to understand the creative nature of your being. It is a wonderful tool of transformation. It is now available in French from Editions du Roseau.

presence as being the Christ. And while I went trough this incredible experiment of being sitted on my table whereas my Soul was bowing at His feet, I saw Him stand me upright and bow down at my feet !

And at the precise moment I experienced that, Bruno, one of the participants present. started to cry. But not from sadness. I knew that it was an opening of his Heart *Chakra* that was happening.

I knew that he was opening to a Love he could not contain.

I looked at him intensely, mentally sending this message :. - « Stay open..., Stay open..., all is well..., Accept this Love and open... ».

And as I continued to guide the relaxation, within, I was very emotional.

I was wondering :

-« Did you dream it or not ? ».

I was sure however I had not dreamed what had happened, considering the reality and the intensity of my experience, but..., nevertheless,... a doubt invaded me... I had not been taking drugs...

When the relaxation exercise was over, as usual, I asked each student to look around so that he/she could notice the progress in his/her sight.

When they had told me about their progress, I turned to Bruno, asking him :

-« Tell me, Bruno, I am curious... It seems you had a strong experience during the relaxation... What was it ?.... Would you like to talk about it ?.... »

And as he was explaining his experience as he lived it from within, I was astounded !

He was saying :

-« Well yes, it was weird... I was thinking about my grand mother when suddenly, I saw Jesus. He was there in front of me and He bowed down at my feet... and then I started to cry and cry »

I did not know what to say anymore...

I mumbled some words and freed the students to go to lunch.

Some moments later I joined Bruno, who, shaken by his experience, was walking alone.

I was feeling a bit uneasy and with almost a feeling of shame, I shared with him, what I had experienced at that same time...

I was extremely moved because now, I knew that what I had experienced was « real », because it was being reflected in the physical world.

My subjective experience was now objective because of this.

And this was some thing I often told my students :
-« You work here, with me, in a subjective way, in your consciousness, imagining that you see more clearly, but, do not be victim of an illusion... What you are doing in your consciousness will eventually and MUST be reflected in the physical world. If it does not, it is an illusion...... ».

Actually, many of my students told me that after a while their doctors noticed and rated their progress. It was not subjective anymore but objective.

I myself was at the very same point. My apparently « subjective » experience was being confirmed in the physical world by an outer person. It was therefore « real ».

As Bruno was listening to me, he started to talk in such a way that I knew that at that very instant, he was a « channel », he was « a medium » for an energy talking through him.

He told me amongst other things that : « Jesus was offering me His cup and inviting me to drink from it with Him... »

And as I heard these words so clear, so just, so « more than human » that Bruno was delivering, I burst into tears.

And I knew I should not resist this immense Love which wanted to enter me at that very moment. And still, I kept saying to myself :

-« *It's too beautiful,… too great,…no,…no,…no,… I don't deserve it… »*

And at the same time, I knew what I had to do. I had to open up,… open up,… open up,…even more and accept…and allow this Love to invade me.

After some moments, I became more « functional » again, and, both shaken, we went to lunch.

And as I ate, I again felt progressively caught up by « something » magnificent.

I was sitting on my chair and I felt this energy rising, rising in me. And to allow it to rise, I had to open to it. I felt that I was to physically open. I had to open up my legs wide, stand up and hold myself straight, open my arms and my hands, placed on my knees, and close my eyes.

Then this wave took me,… swept me away…

Sometimes, I opened my eyes and amazed at the beauty I was seeing, I « had to » close them again...

I remember looking at the portion of onion quiche before me and it seemed so beautiful… I felt filled with gratitude towards this quiche that was about to feed me. And as, slowly, I managed to taste a little bit, I felt that quiche like millions of particles of life sparkling in me. And I had to close my eyes again to try to contain, to contain in « me » this experience.

As if it was overflowing from « me ». This « Me » that no longer had the form I believed I had been…

I looked at the air, and saw it… as « me »… This air that I was breathing was « me », was pure Love… and I literally existed beyond « me ».

And again, I had to close my eyes. And I had just one wish, to go… To go with these waves of Love which were taking me away, one after the other...

When I opened my eyes again, I saw myself again,… in the air,… in the wall,… in the glasses,… in these people sitting beside me and who were all so beautiful, so beautiful… And I saw literally my aura of an incredible clarity radiating from me… And, dazzled by so much splendour, so much beauty, I closed my eyes again …

And as I fell within myself, I was growing. I was growing in an incredible way...

And when, after some time, I opened my eyes again, I beheld that « beautiful » onion quiche and I understood the principle of the Eucharist in Christian religion.

I knew that this quiche was like me, it was me, it was pure Love. And yet, as I looked at the people sitting at the table, I noticed that they were not aware of their own beauty and perfection that seemed so obvious to me beholding them.

They had not yet realized their divine nature.

And in that blessed instant, I understood why Jesus told us what I now <u>know</u> to be the truth.

   -*« Take, and eat, for this is my body. »*[1].

Through this symbolic ritual, those who believed in Him could, by « ingesting » Him and « assimilating » Him through this bread, expect to « become » what He was by this process of assimilation…

---

[1] Matthew 26:26

Because actually, when I myself ingested that onion quiche that was pure Love, this food which I knew as divine was regenerating me and becoming more of what it was, which means of what I was…

And as I looked at the beings sitting next to me and noticed their beauty, I saw how my regard, which in that sacred instant perceived only perfection was creating it simultaneously. It was as if my regard was « giving back » to things and to people their original perfection…

I now really understood that sentence I had so often pronounced :

« *Your perceptions create your reality.* »

With however an **ENORMOUS** difference...

I **SPONTANEOUSLY** perceived the beauty and the perfection of **EVERYTHING** my eyes were beholding and amazingly, it was as if **SIMULTANEOUSLY**, my glance of perfection **RETURNED** to them their beauty and their perfection. I gave them back to themselves. My glance, which saw beyond the external form and saw the immense Love which was everything, allowed these objects, these people to own again that part of themselves hidden deep within which they had forgotten.

And dazzled with so much love and of beauty, I became lost within myself…

And after some time, I was afraid...

Afraid of disappearing...

Afraid of dying.

And as I was again swept away by this energy in which I wanted to surrender, I had the impression that if I surrendered to it completely, I was going to disappear in it and die.

And yet, I really wanted to go even further into this unending Love...

But little by little, this fear of « disappearing » made me come out of my state and I slowly, gradually, became aware again of my body which had seemed so far away.

Slowly, I became « normal » again... But, in fact, what is « normal » ? ? ?

Slowly, very slowly, little by little, I left that Divine space and re-entered the « human » world.

And when I became more « functional », the day continued its course.

But for me, I had lived something True, something Pure, something Beautiful that moved me deeply.

Sure, I knew intellectually that that state where one is aware of existing simultaneously in various places was possible... but I had never lived it before !

And as I lived these experiences, a part of me wondered whether I were not becoming « insane ». And I knew very well that I was not, because what I lived was real. Actually, it was much more real than my other qualities of experiments were !

Of course, I had « learned » that the states of consciousness beyond the 3rd *Chakra* were considered in our society, as being either extra-ordinary or pathological...but I never had experienced them with such intensity.

And I realized how lucky I was to be able to understand what I was experiencing !

How lucky I was to have a mental structure that was able to integrate the experiences I was living.

When I think of the number of people living these experiences who end up in a psychiatric asylum, simply because they do not have the mental structure to understand what they are experiencing !

Simply because their doctors or their loved ones do not have the <u>mental structure</u> to understand such experiences… and to reassure them and explain to them that it is normal, at certain levels of consciousness, to hear voices, to see spirits, to see Auras, to hear the thoughts of people, to feel you exist elsewhere than in your body or that you are not this body which you thought you were. Because indeed, I am not this body. It is only one of my multiple aspects…

The problem which arises then is this : When these people start to experience these non-ordinary states of consciousnesses, they start to fear their experiences since in the West, nobody has ever explained to them that these states of consciousness were natural. Fear being a very powerful creative force, they start then, « thanks » to their fear of these states, or thanks to their incomprehension of these states, to live them again… Therefore more panic and so on… and so on… and they thus fall into an « infernal » spiral whereas a little awareness and comprehension of this could tilt them into a « divine » spiral.

Martin used to ask a question :

> -« *Do you know the difference between a fool and a genius ? ».*

Answer : functionality.

If you are a fool and non-functional, unable to function in your « madness », to go and get some bread in your bakery or to function in your society, and so on….people will place you in institutions, asylums.

On the other hand, if you are crazy AND functional, people will call you a « genius »…

And as in the following days, I was questioning the experience that I had undeniably lived, I received an answer to my question.

I had asked about that fear of dying I had experienced as I was feeling carried away by that Love.

That « damn » fear that had made me leave this wonderful experience.

The answer was given to me as a picture that appeared to me.

A child was shown to me. A child who was playing with blocks and who, as he grew up before me, abandoned them to play with more evolved, more complex toys.

And « they » explained :

> -« *Do not fear... You will not die... because you cannot die... You will simply leave your primitive « toys » to play with « bigger » more complex toys... »*

« They » explained that, actually, I was not going to die but, on the other hand, my experience of « Me », of « I am » would disappear and dissolve itself into the experience of « Being ». An experience of being, but without form, beyond the « I am »...

And I understood...

I understood I had to continue working, continue praying in trust... continue unendingly to open myself, or to die.

I understood I had to <u>die to a picture of myself</u> in order to let a new self emerge.

The cup had to be emptied of the old so the new could fill it !

CHAPTER 27
Something MUST change...

In the weeks which followed what I call now « the Lyon experience », I was to receive several messages which only confirmed the reality of what I had experienced.

Indeed, I met people whom I had not seen for a long time who, surprised, asked me :

-« *But what's happened to you ? You seem so different.* »

Fortunately, they said that I had changed for the better !

I was even to meet somebody who knew me before, who when he saw me said :

-« *Hey , Patrice, what's happened to you ? Did you have a rise in Kundalini[1] or what ?* »

And as he was speaking, suddenly I understood !

-« *But, of course!* »

That's what had happened without me realizing it ! I had not made the connection until now.

I had indeed already read about the « rise of *Kundalini* » in which the person is « obliged » to take up a certain physical position of opening up while this energy rises within.

That was exactly what I had felt when I « had to » open up my legs, stand up straight and open my arms… in order to let this energy take me where it wanted.

Everything was becoming clear.

---

[1] « *Kundalini* » is a very powerful energy which is said to coil in the first *Chakra*, at the base of the spine, at the level of the Coccyx. It is the source of all energies (*Shakti*) sexual et spiritual. Certain Yoga techniques offer some exercises so that this energy rises to other *Chakras*. As the *Kundalini* rises, the *Chakras* are opened and the person feels his/her consciousness expand, experiencing new perceptions. Nevertheless, some people say we have to be very careful as, in fact, as the person experiences new perceptions while this Kundalini rises, he/she could be frightened. Especially if the person has no comprehension of it or if no « guide » knowing these « territories » is present to reassure him/her about the intensity or apparent strangeness of his/her experience..

But what this experience mainly taught me was that actually, **there is no need of a particular technique to make one's consciousness evolve.**

The technique in itself has no importance. It is the <u>will</u>, the <u>desire to transform,</u> <u>the openness to transformation</u> which makes it happen.

Any technique, whatever it is, is actually only a « ritual » to make us feel safe !

But it is not the « technique » that makes the transformation happen, it is consciousness itself that does it.

And please understand, I am not saying here that techniques are useless.

Simply, do not be attached to a technique which, finally, is only one belief, one idea, one thought which has taken form.

But on the other hand, believe, believe, believe !...

Believe that whatever you are doing now, whatever it is, is actually, bringing you closer to your goal, whatever it might be...

As time passed by, I realized that I was adopting more and more in my workshop a devotional type of language. I encouraged people more and more « to let be » and « to trust ».

I continued my trips around the world at an intense pace.

And because of the fact that I wished to see Amma again, I arranged each year to fly to Reunion Island to give workshops while She was staying there.

Each time I would see Her and have the luck to be in Her arms, within, I was always asking her for more.

I remember a *Devi Bhava* in Reunion Island where, despite people looking *(I was still at the time rather concerned about how people would look at me),* I was standing up, for nearly one hour, awaiting my turn for my *Darshan*.

And standing, eyes closed, hands joined in front of my heart, completely ignoring the hundreds of people around me, I repeated over and over, without ending : .

> -« I want God,... I want God,... I want God,... I want God,... I want God,... I want God,... » again and again...

When finally my turn came, I was in such a state of concentration as I had never felt before. There was nothing in me but this thought :

> -« I want God... »

Then Amma took me in Her arms and I sank down while I surrendered completely to her incredible Love. I left Her after She had again laid Her finger on my forehead and had kissed me on the cheek.

And as I was about to return to sit down, one of the people accompanying Amma tapped me on the shoulder and said :

> -« Amma would like you to sit next to Her. »

Hearing that, I was exultant! She knew ! She knew ! She had heard my silent request and was answering this way !

She was according me the Grace of sitting in her pure energy. I could not believe it !

I spent the rest of the evening two feet away from Amma, bathing in Her Love and opening up as much as possible to the transforming power of Her energy, so beautiful and so pure.

During another of my trips to Reunion Island, where I again met Amma with much pleasure, I decided this time to speak to Her directly.

Until then, I had not dared speak to Amma during *Darshans*.

Inside, it is true that I asked Her always more, but outside, I remained dumb. I felt now too impressed by the beauty of Her Soul, which I had now recognized, to dare to speak to Her.

The very first time, it had been easy to me to talk to Her because, at that time, She was for me just a woman like any other !

But now that I realized the depth of Her Love and the importance of Her presence for each person there, I did not dare « delay » her by asking Her questions. After all, hundreds of people behind me awaited also the Grace of Her *Darshan*.

So I made the most of a *Darshan* in St Louis, as there were few people that morning, to speak to Amma. I was determined not to « miss » my chance ! I had thought for hours about how to formulate my request as clearly as possible, knowing the importance of clarity of expression, especially in the presence of such a being. I was also determined not to go through the interpreter. I thought that, although She spoke little English, Amma could better perceive my heart if I talked directly to Her.

Once my turn arrived, before Amma took me in her arms, I bowed down at Her feet.

Oh yes! Me, Patrice, who had been so reluctant about this ritual, I was doing it ! It is as if a small voice was telling me :

> -« *You see, Patrice, it is easy to judge when one does not make the effort to understand why people do what they do !* »

I had indeed understood that this bowing down was by no means a demeaning attitude of submission, as I had believed in the past, but rather a demonstration of trustful surrendering. By this attitude, I recognized Her greatness *(which in no way made me less or insignificant)*, I was showing Her my respect for what She was *(because, in fact, the Masters are neither more, nor less, that our elder Brothers and Sisters, only more advanced beings than us on the path)* and surrendered to Her wisdom that I knew could take me out my situation.

Once straightened up from my bow, I looked at Amma straight in the eyes as I said to Her in English, convinced that even if

She did not speak the language, She would understand the one of my Soul :

> -« *Amma, I want to be healed... I want to see the way you see... I want to hear the way you hear... I want to feel what you feel...I want to experience what you experience... and I want to raise my consciousness to the level of your consciousness.* »

It seemed to me that, with this formulation, I gave a good summary of what I wanted to live, since after all, everything is just an experience in our consciousness, isn't it ?

Once the interpreter had translated my request into Her native language, Malayalam[1], She looked at me intensely, smiled at me, caressed my cheek several times and took me in Her arms for a long time.

After having touched my forehead with Her finger for a few seconds, She signed me to stand on one side and wait.

And I waited, and waited, and waited...

And my knees hurt...

It was difficult for me to keep standing on them.

Humility is sometimes a difficult lesson to learn in the West
And I waited, and waited, and waited...

Sometimes, Amma would glance at me confidentially but she still made me wait.

And finally, after a long time, She looked at me, made a sign to Her interpreter and started to talk to him, at length, as She continued to take people in Her arms.

She would stop talking for a moment to take someone else against Her breast, and, looking at me, She spoke to Her interpreter.

---

[1] Malayalam is the dialect in the province of Kerala, in the south of India where Amma comes from.

Finally, he came to me and said :

> -« *This is what Amma said ... bla bla bla... bla bla bla... bla bla bla... »*

And as he went on talking to me, I had the impression I understood <u>nothing</u> of what he was telling me. Nothing except two things :

Amma was telling me :

> -« *You think you are doing something... but you are doing nothing... ! »*

And whack, take that on the head sweetie ! And there was I expecting encouragement !

But it was not all over yet ! This was only first helping ! She had even better to come...

She was saying :

> -« *You must let go of the arrogance of knowing ! »*

For me, it was as if She was saying :

> -« *You must let go of the arrogance of believing you know ! »*.

I now understood better why certain people said that Amma was also perceived as an incarnation, a manifestation of Kali !

Kali or the « black goddess », often represented with a great red tongue and wearing around her neck a collar of human skulls !

One of the characteristics of Kali is to « kill the ego ».

Indeed, Hinduism explains us that to realize God, it is necessary that the personality or the ego disappears and Kali is the Divinity that can help us there.

And with Her two sentences which pierced me like a knife, Amma in fact gave me a splendid gift. Obviously, I was only to become aware of it several weeks later !

And if I thought that a Master, who is all Love, always expressed it in the form of smiles or comforting sentences, I was largely mistaken !

My consequent experiences taught me that, while it is true that at the beginning, a Master expresses his Love to the Disciple in a reassuring and warm way, so afterwards, and <u>especially if the disciple shows real efforts to progress</u>, the Master can use hard external forms to allow the sincere devotee to realign himself/herself.

So that you can understand it better, I will use a metaphor. If a nail is twisted and I want to make it straight so that it can do what it was created for, it is not by caressing it with a finger that I will rectify it. I will have to give him some blows with a hammer, sometimes violent ones, in order to get it straight and to align it. And even if the process must be painful or unpleasant , once back in shape and straight, the nail will be « happy » because it can then take up the function for which it was created.

I thus returned to sit in order to think about Amma's message. fortunately for me, I knew already knew that a Master does not do or say **ANYTHING** by chance.

I was privately convinced that this stinging message from Amma was a gift. I had just not realized yet what sort. I just accepted that what she had said to me was for my own greatest good.

It is during the workshop that I presented a short time after that I was to notice how much Amma had transformed me, by those few words. I should even say metamorphosed.

During this workshop, as I heard myself explain the principles of Healing, I felt in myself a softness, a compassion, a patience which I had hitherto never experienced.

I remember one moment when, suddenly « filled » by this consciousness which was becoming now increasingly familiar,

I became a witness and an observer of a magnificent phenomenon.

There was I, in my own centre, and there was this energy radiating from me. An energy which I saw reach out to the students. And when this energy touched them, I could « see » zones of shadow disappear in their Auras. I was witnessing these changes happening « all by themselves ».

I understood in this blessed moment that these people did not even need « to believe » in me or in Healing in order for it to happen because I KNEW that there was sufficient trust in me to annihilate their doubts…

That energy was enough...

I KNEW that if they were « open », that if they were « like little children »[1], without any limiting beliefs, this energy emanating from me would heal them and would give them anything they wished.

And I understood Amma's words.

Of course, I was doing nothing ! « I » was doing nothing !

Each of us, we do nothing… We just believe we do…

And I realized that before, I had this sort of hard and arrogant attitude when I explained consciousness to people: .

> -«What ? You don't understand ? But all you have to do is change ! It is so simple ! »

And suddenly, in a few words, Amma had opened my eyes.

Yes, She opened my eyes,… to me who spent my weekends pretending to open the eyes of my students…

I realized that, even if it is true that you only have to change, it is not always so simple… Besides I saw it in my own life !

---

[1] On this subject, Jesus told us truly: « Suffer the little children to come unto me ; and forbid them not: for of such is the kingdom of God. [15]Verily I say unto you, Whosoever shall not receive the kingdom of God as a little child, he shall not enter therein.. »
Mark 10:14-15

I saw how I could have developed a form of unwitting pride having accumulated all of this metaphysical knowledge ... But after all, what use was it, since I realized that I did not have the <u>experience</u> of what I was talking about !

I realized also now that I could see « things » happening beyond myself.

Beautiful things...

And actually, I noticed these beautiful things happened **mostly** when I was doing nothing. They happened when I was simply open and let this energy flow from me and radiate towards the participants.

They happened when I opened my heart, stopped judging and started to really LOVE AND APPRECIATE the beings around me.

Yes, Amma was right !

It is not me, Patrice, that is doing !

It is this Love filling me that is doing it, it is Life, It is God! But not my « small » personality, not the part of me with which I had identified until then...

As time passed by, I felt much more soft, more simple, more natural, more tolerant, less directive, less arrogant in my way of sharing my experiences and my beliefs.

And paradoxally, as I was « doing » less and less, I noticed faster healings for my students.

Amma was right once again.

And I realized the extra gift she granted me while I was waiting such a long time before she would « gratify » me with these piercing truths.

She allowed me to understand that with a Master, with God, one **always** has to be patient...we have to be **PATIENT** and **CONFIDENT**...

If you ask sincerely, deeply, God will always answer… I am sure… Simply again, we have to be patient and confident.

As the proverb says :

-« *Everything comes to he who waits.* »

What happened finally to me was that, little by little, I was feeling more and more uneasy teaching « word for word » the method that Martin Brofman had put together. It was actually a method that appeared to me to function so much on notions of power and control, that I felt it did not suit me anymore.

I had to lead people elsewhere and especially, by an other path which I was starting to perceive in a vague fashion.

I had to explain things in another way, I had to integrate these spiritual truths which appeared to me so present and so obvious.

More and more, I talked openly about God.

At the very beginning, finding the word God on the tip of my tongue, I would slip it timidly into the conversation.

Nevertheless, as His reality appeared to me more and more obvious, I <u>could no longer</u> not name Him.

More and more, I would hear myself say to students:

-« *You want to talk about Eyes ?… well… let us talk about God…* »

I must say this is a typical French play on words… "about eyes" is pronounced "d'Yeux" and God is pronounced "Dieu"…. It sounds very much alike…and I am French… It is only recently that I felt ready to translate this book into English so that it could be spread more widely abroad …

On the other hand, as I was more and more caught up into transcendental experiences as I talked about consciousness, I no longer managed to have the time to do such or such an exercise that Martin absolutely wanted me to do.

I felt now « trapped » by a structure. A structure which was good, I must say, and one that was necessary for certain people still functioning at certain levels of consciousness, but which I felt now restricted me and prevented me from going where I wanted to go.

Where I NEEDED to go…

I was trapped in a structure that made me feel somewhat frustrated after a workshop.

Frustrated to have not taken time to explore those territories where I knew Healing was happening beyond me, beyond my own will.

Frustrated, because of lack of time, to have not let myself be invaded a much longer time by this consciousness of Love which, beyond me, had an obvious positive impact on the students.

On the other hand, I wanted to lower the price of the workshops because I found a more economic price would make it more affordable to many more people.

When I talked about it to Martin, he refused categorically.

He could not allow me to modify a single word in his relaxation exercise and even less that I, sometimes, because of lack of time, modify what he perceived as « HIS » structure.

As if he owned it !

I can obviously understand his power functioning, but one thing was clear, something had to change !

Change finally fell into place through an astonishing meeting *(one more you say !)* which I was to have..

It was once more in Lyon that this « magical » meeting happened.

During this workshop I was giving, a charming couple presented themselves. Their name were Claude-Annie and

Pierre. I was to find out later that only Claude-Annie originally had the intention to follow this course. Her friend, Pierre had only decided at the last minute *(Fortunately for me !... and for him too I hope !)*.

The workshop took place normally and I do not recall having had a particular interaction with Pierre during these two days.

Nevertheless, once the workshop was over, he approached me and started to talk to me.

He explained that he was physicist and, with a language I absolutely did not understand, he started to explain certain principles I had talked about in the light of his knowledge of physic. And as he talked…, and talked…, and talked…, I understood NOTHING ! Not a word… He was obviously living in a « model » I did not know and it seemed to me he was talking Hebrew !

But strangely, even though I understood NOTHING of what he was explaining with charts and drawings, a part of me was shouting in my head :

-*« HE IS RIGHT !... LISTEN TO HIM ! »*

And I listened… without understanding !

And then suddenly, he said in a voice that was powerful, determined, almost authoritarian, as if to wake me up :

-« Patrice,... you have to understand one thing... In any school,... there is an **ENTRANCE**...(and as he said that, he almost violently drew an arrow on the board with on one side the word Entrance) ... and ... an ... **EXIT**... (he wrote the word « Exit » at the point of the arrow) ».

-« You have to understand that you are getting close to the EXIT (as he underlined in a quick gesture the word on the board !) of the school of Martin Brofman ! »

-« It is obvious, when we listen to you, that you have much more to say than the structure allows you to. You are trapped in this rigid structure that prevents you to express what you are really feeling ... And you MUST go further... That you express what you have inside...! It is really important ! »

And I was listening blissfully !

It was as if Pierre *(Bless him !)* was clearly formulating, directly, what I felt inside without daring the admit it to myself clearly, probably for fear of « getting out » of a model that, even if it was suffocating me, reassured me.

He was right,... He was right,...that was sure !

Something had to change !

That evening I went back to my hotel room, overcome by the meeting with Pierre and touched by what I had felt as he was talking. I understood almost nothing of what he said, but I <u>KNEW</u> he was right, that he was speaking the Truth. <u>And that it was important to me to listen to him.</u>

I could not deny he had touched key points for me. He had put his finger exactly on the spot where « it hurt » !

But, now, that he had « confirmed » in a <u>very clear</u> way what I felt, what was I to do ?...

How could I change ?...

How could I <u>leave</u> Martin with whom I had been working for almost 9 years ! ?...

And how would he take it ?...

And mostly, what would I do next ?...

It was as if I had gone back to 8 years earlier, at the time were I started to stop my salaried activity...

Quickly, I recentered myself by repeating several times :

-« Don't worry Patrice, It is all right,... It is all right,...... and everything will be all right... Trust... »

It is with these questions that I went to bed that evening.

And during the night, I was to have a dream, a wonderful dream... or should I say a meeting...

A meeting with a wonderful being that was to have an extreme influence on my Life.

CHAPTER 28
The Dream...

In this dream, but,... was it really one ?... I was in India, a country where I had never been.

I found myself in India, with thousands of people, and we were all going to see Saï Baba[1] *(I had heard about Saï Baba years before)*.

We were in his « Ashram »[2]. (Astonishingly, at that time, I did not know what an Ashram was!).

And as these thousands of people were walking forward, I found myself amongst the last ones, being wounded or handicapped in my left leg, and unable to walk as fast as the others ! *(Again, in an astonishing way, when I was to go to India some months later, I was, just as in my dream, suffering in my left leg !).*

Nevertheless, even though I was amongst the last ones, strangely, I found myself in the first row, with all these Indians next to me.

Suddenly, all these people put their hands in front of their hearts as a murmur went through the crowd :

-*« Here comes Saï Baba ! »*

---

[1] Saï Baba (pronounced SA-I Baba) is a Sage, a Master living in India, near Bangalore. He is a Master of whom I had heard many years before and of whom I spoke frequently in my classes, even though I had never met him. I quoted him regularly when I spoke of the 7thChakra and of the states of consciousness, Omniscience and Omnipresence which are associated it. Saï Baba has, in fact, on many occasions, demonstrated these characteristics. It is said of Saï Baba that he is not only an *Avatar* but a *Mahavatar*, that is, a human manifestation of the Divine in its totality. In India, an *Avatar* is considered to be a divine being, manifesting certain divine characteristics, descended into flesh to aid humanity. A *Mahavatar* or a *Great Avatar* (*Maha* means Great) is said to manifest all the aspects of the Divine. **Rama, Krishna, Bouddha, Zoroastre, and Jesus** are condidered to be divine *Avatars*. There are many books about Saï Baba. When I began researching him and my attraction towards Jesus, I particularly enjoyed *« A Catholic Priest meets Saï Baba »* by Father Don Mario Mazzoleni, edited by Leela Press.

[2] An *Ashram* is a hermitage, the welcoming place and structure which is progressively built around a Sage, a Saint, a Spiritual Master or a Realised Being. It is there that he lives and where the devotees come to see him.

And as I turned my head in the direction where everybody was looking, I saw appear, in my dream, a little man in a long white robe and, really weird, wearing a red clown nose !

I remembered having exclaimed in my dream:

-« *But this is not Saï Baba !* ».

I had already seen him in a photo and I told myself :

-« *No, Saï Baba wears an orange robe and not white (I learned afterwards that for certain ceremonies, Christmas, for example, he really does wear white !), He has a lot of frizzy hair with type of afro hairdo like the Jackson Five and he is at least 6 feet tall!» (I must say that, for me, having seen pictures of his upper body, I though he was 6 feet tall minimum ! I actually discovered afterwards that he was only 5 foot one !).*

So in my dream, I was saying :

-« *This is not Saï Baba !* »

And at the moment I had this thought, an inner voice of great gentleness told me :

-« *Saï Baba can take many forms... If we tell you this is Saï Baba, it is Saï Baba !* »

Surprised by the power of the message, I accepted.

Saï Baba came towards me and took me by the hand. As he took my hand, his robe was now orange and his face more like the one I knew.

He led me to what seemed to be a small shop and took a present which he held out to me. It was a very beautiful plaque of gold or golden metal, rectangular, about 1 foot by 8 inches, on which seemed to float, *(because probably fixed on a small stem)*, a magnificent heart, made of the same metal.

And putting it in my hands, he looked at me with a magnificent smile while I thanked Him and, in a slow movement, he passed his hand over the gold plaque.

And as he took his hand away and I saw what I had in my hands, I started to panic. In an instant, the golden plaque had transformed into green marble and a magnificent red rose bud was in its centre. *(A <u>real</u> rose, and fresh as well !).*

And in my dream, I was panicking. A **real** panic ! It was not possible,… I thought I was going mad ! I had gold in my hands and, a second after, it was marble…

And I remember, in an effort to stabilize myself in my panic, I started to repeat, very quickly, a kind of *« I believe in God»* like this :

> - *«I believe in God, and in Jesus, his son, our saviour, creator of Heaven and Earth, I believe in God… I believe in God… »*

May those of you who know the « Real » Credo forgive me ! ! Ok, I was baptised a catholic but I did not really know the prayers...

And as I was totally « freaking out », Saï Baba, impassive, was looking at me with a smile of an incredible beauty… And I was totally panicking !

And as he was watching me with this beautiful smile, Saï Baba moved His hand again above the green marble plaque I was holding in my hands, and when He took it away, I was to panic even more !

It is true that with my height of 6 feet 7 inches, I have <u>big</u> hands, but then in my hands, I held mountains ! **REAL** mountains more than 1000 feet high, with snow and fir trees… I could even see skiers ! It was a **real world** that I had in my hands !

And I was completely panicking… I was telling myself :

> -*« But it's not possible… »*

And I wanted to close the eyes… but I could not… With my eyes closed, I continued to see these mountain in my hands !...

And I was repeating at a frenzied rate as if to reassure me :

-« *I believe in God, I believe in God, I believe in God...* »

as Saï Baba, impassive, looked at me « freaking out » with an expression of incredible gentleness in the eyes...

And suddenly, « He » swept me away.

I « knew » that He was taking me into the depth of that mountain I had between my hands... He took me into the core of matter... I knew He was taking me into the core of atoms...

And as I found myself in the core of the atoms, I could « see » 360 degrees around me. I had a global vision, total, simultaneous of everything there was, there, in the core of matter.

And I SAW in there, at the core of Atoms, there was **ONLY** Love, there was **ONLY** Light, there was **ONLY** God...

There was nothing else than that : Love, Light, God...

And at that very moment where I was realizing what I was seeing, He told me in a voice of power and extreme softness :

-« *You see, ... This ... , Is the nature of the Universe...It awaits only You to become what you want it to be....* »

And I knew it was true! This voice only confirmed what I had just experienced.

The whole Universe is only Love... It is one and the same « substance » taking for us the form we give it, for Love of us...

And it is with that certainty I woke up that morning, filled with a feeling of absolute trust.

Following that dream, *(which I am sure, was not a dream)*, that I decided to go and see this being, this Saï Baba who had appeared to me as if to call me to Him.

CHAPTER 29
First trip to Saï Baba...

Very soon, I decided I « had » to go to India. I <u>had</u> to see with my own eyes this being that had appeared in my dream...

All of a sudden, all the fears and prejudices I had towards India left me. All those things I had been told about poverty, filth, disease, suffering, the shock produced by a trip to such a country... all that disappeared in this imperious desire that took over me.

I <u>had</u> to get there.

While at that time, giving or translating about forty workshops a year, my agenda was generally filled a year ahead, I realized that I had two possible « spaces » to go to India. Either I could go there in May, that is, two months away, or between Christmas and New Year, in more than 10 months.

I decided to go as soon as possible because I felt it was urgent for me to meet this being.

As the date of my trip approached, I told myself I would profit from this first trip in India to see not only Saï Baba but also Amma who had helped me so much.

Astoundingly, once I had bought my plane ticket, a kind of voice in my head told me :

-« No , it is only Saï Baba you are going to see ! ».

And as I heard that, I realized it was true. I vaguely felt that going to see him was a great Grace and that I should not « waste » my time doing something else.

It was however a strange feeling for me because, actually, I did not know him, this Saï Baba ! It was Amma I knew, after all !

Well,... God moves in mysterious ways!

Anyway, as my departure got closer , I did some research on life in the *Ashram*.

At the time, I did not really know what an *Ashram* was, or the life in India next to a Master…Did people sleep on the ground ? in caves ? in trees ?...

I was told that I should not expect much comfort and I should not worry about bringing clothes, because on the premises, we could buy white clothing. It was customary, as a sign of respect, that the men wore white in presence of this Wise man

I was told that at that time of the year, we did not really know exactly where Saï Baba would be *(as I was told he had 3 main Ashrams and that he could be in one or the other)*. On the other hand, once in Bangalore, I was told I could find out and take a taxi to the *Ashram* where he was.

So I was to go, in the beginning of the month of May 1997, with my little travel bag, for a journey to the land of miracles.

I had with me several letters to give to Saï Baba. Friends who either knew this Wise man Sage from personally meeting him, or had heard of him, had given me their mail.

They had explained that unlike Amma which gave Her *Darshan* by individually taking each person in Her arms, Saï Baba, gave it in a completely different way. Indeed, he « simply » went out among the people present, among the devotees, walking among them, sometimes stopping to someone to speak with him, take letters, or sometimes even, I was told, to manifest some *Vibhuti*[1] by making it appear « miraculously » between his fingers…

It seemed indeed that this Wise man was constantly performing numerous miracles, one of the most current being to make this sacred ash appear in His hands!

Personally, I asked to see it ! And… obviously,… I DID SEE !

---

[1] *Vibhuti* is a sacred ash often used in many Hindus rituals. I will be talking about it later.

I had been told that, when He took the letters of the devotees, instantaneously, He knew what was inside and could then help and miraculously answer the request.

So I decided I too would write a letter to Him, listing one after the other my requests.

And I thus found myself for the first time in India, in Bangalore, in search of this Holy Man.

Very quickly, somebody explained that Saï Baba was at that time in Kodai Kanal[1] which was with more than 9 hours away by taxi, but that in three or four days, he would be in White Field, a small village approximately half an hour away from Bangalore.

I discovered that in India, one rarely speaks of distance in kilometres but rather in hours of travelling time.

I was a bit disappointed because I had only 14 days to spend in India, and it seemed to me that 4 of these precious days were going to be lost. In fact, these 4 days allowed me to better familiarize myself with this being that I did not know yet and to deeply prepare myself for his Presence.

I decided to go to and wait at White Field, and to take a room in a small hotel while waiting for him to arrive.

En route towards the *Ashram* of Brindavan[2], I discovered driving « the Indian way » who was for me somewhat alarming ! Imagine cars driving on the left *(we drive on the right in France)* on often narrow roads, battered, with masses of pedestrians going in all directions, overtaking when another vehicle approaches in the opposite direction and pulling in at the last second...

---

[1] Kodai Kanal is a small town in Tamil Nadu province about 200 miles south of Bangalore where Saï Baba has a small *Ashram*. It takes about 9 hours in a taxi from Bangalore to get there.

[2] Originally, Brindavan was the name of the place were Krishna lived. It is also the name given to the *Ashram* of Saï Baba in White Field.

Love is the Key...

I could only do one thing : decide that my driver must be the best in the world,... cross the fingers and pray to Saï Baba whom I did not yet know!

After all, if he had called me, « He » had to watch over me so that I got to Him safe and sound! I had indeed learned that only those whom He has called come to Saï Baba. It was a concept for which I had at the time a lot of resistance and which I was to understand only much later !

Once at White Field, I easily found a room in a small hotel.

The price seemed ridiculously cheap, since I paid, I think, 100 rupees the night, approximately 3 dollars. It is true that the standards of comfort were far from being those to which I was accustomed... I had a simple bed with a kind of « mattress » about an inch thick to isolate to me from the board which served as a base.

Well, after all, I had not come to be a tourist!

Very quickly, I got information about the *Ashram* which was just opposite my hotel.

It was confirmed that Baba would arrive here in a few days and I was told where to get my *Kurta* and my « *pyjamas* »[1].

As soon as I was settled in, I decided to go into the *Ashram* because, although Saï Baba was not there yet, the doors were open.

I passed under a very colourful archway and found myself in a large court made of concrete. On my left was a small Reception Office, then further, a long building that I was told were the

---

[1] The « *pyjama* » and the *Kurta* is the clothing that men wear inside the *Ashram*. It is a large pair of white trousers, (« *pyjama* ») and a long shirt with long sleeves (*Kurta*), also white, worn above the trouser, going almost halfway down the thighs. The ensemble is sometimes called *Dhoti*, as normally, the *Dhoti* is a piece of rectangular cloth men use to wrap around the waist to cover their legs. Within the *Ashram*, men generally wear white. On the other hand, women wear a lot of colours. Traditionally they wear the Sari, or the *Punjabi*. The *Punjabi* is an coloured ensemble consisting of wide trousers, a shirt much like the men's *Kurta* and a piece of cloth serving as a shawl.

kitchens and the restaurant. Further still, a shop where books were sold, then buildings to host the visitors. Opposite me was a large building, one of the free schools that Saï Baba had opened, with a splendid coloured fountain facing it. And on my right, was a large hall with a black stone floor and a roof of green plastic material. At the end of this large hall, a splendid life-size copper statue had pride of place and against the back wall, four large photographs of Saï Baba.

Intimidated by the size of the place, I went into this hall.

Very quickly, I learned that I was to stay on the « men's side », which meant on the right. As for the women, they had to remain on the « women's side », on the left.

Ok by me ! No problem.

I sat down on the ground, in a lotus position and looked around me.

Here and there, some people seemed to be meditating or were absorbed in their reading, others were telling their *Malas*. .

After a few moments spent to satisfy my curiosity, I closed my eyes and bathed in the ambience of the place. There was indeed something « special » about it. Outside, there was noise, dust, masses of people swarming in all directions, but here, in this temple open on the outside, although the noises of the outside reached me, they seemed as if they were muffled by the peace emanating from this place.

I suddenly felt I had settled in…

Here I am, finally !...

I had arrived !

And I was feeling good...

I was absorbed within, opening my eyes from time to time to look at the enigmatic glance of this Saï Baba who was evident in the photos laid out at the end of the hall.

After a long while, I rose and left the temple, feeling at the same time centered and peaceful.

I left the *Ashram* and found myself again in the tumult of the village, with its noises, its strong smells, its variegated crowd…

During the days that followed, I bought books on this Saï Baba who was to be seen everywhere in the village.

Sometimes, I could have felt like I was in Lourdes with the merchants of the temple stuck close to one another, with the difference being that it was not Mary who was here the cult object but rather this Saï Baba of whom one could buy hundreds of different photographs. It seemed that the very whole city revolved around this Wise man. Not a coffee shop, not a restaurant, not a hotel, not a shop which did not have somewhere a photograph of this being !

I spent my days in the calm of the temple, absorbed in my reading or the into the contemplation of the photographs of Baba.

I was to then meet somebody who had seen him,… for real.

I hastened to ask him :

-« So, it's true,… You <u>REALLY</u> saw him ? … You <u>REALLY</u> saw him manifesting Vibhuti? … And how was it...»

And the other told me :

-« *Oh yes, many times, he's doing it all the time…* »

And me, I looked at him as the man who had seen the Man ! Admiring and incredulous at the same time.

As the day of Saï Baba's arrival approached, the city filled up more and more. More and more « temple merchants » invaded the street with their small stands on wheels.

I had been told that once Saï Baba had arrived, it would be possible to take a room in the *Ashram*. However, I had to get organized, because they said that this Ashram was very small *(to me, it seemed already quite large[1]!)* and so it could not accommodate many people. It was first come, first served !

I was told that it needed a small group of at least 2 or 4 people to get a room more easily.

I had become acquainted with a young man from the States and had suggested we register together.

The following day, D-day, I was getting ready, accompanied by this friend, to line up in the queue. However, there was already a considerable crowd when we presented ourselves. It was impressive and I started to doubt whether we could get a room. There were so many people...

I was however on the point of experiencing one of these marvellous miracles, one of these « *Leelas* »[2] that Saï Baba excels in manifesting continuously..

I circumvented the crowd to see where this impressive queue started. And just as I saw that there was right at the head of the queue an enrolment desk, a young man whom I had briefly met the day before said to me, as he held out a ticket :

-« *Here,... take this ,... you need a numbered ticket.* »

I looked at the ticket which was marked number 4.

At the same time, I heard someone call :

-« *Number 6, ... Number 6...* »

I approached the table where the voice came from.

-« *Hello, I blurted, I have number 4* ».

I called the person with whom I was going to share my room and I gave our passports to the person handing out the rooms.

---

[1] I was to realize later, during my other trips to India that the *Ashram* of Brindavan was indeed « very small », lodging only 2000 people. The main *Ashram* of Saï Baba in Puttaparthi can lodge some tens of thousand people !

[2] *Leela* is a Sanskrit word meaning « Divine game ». These are little miracles, little « winks» that the Divinity can give us, these little signs through which it manifest to us.

And in a few minutes, he gave me a key with a ticket bearing our room number.

I could not believe how fast it happened ! There was such a crowd and I was practically served first ! And so easily!.

But Saï Baba had an other *Leela* for me.

When I looked at my room number, I had been allotted the room number B 3 in building 2. The number on my ticket was 2 B 3. The resemblance to « To Be Free » seemed only too obvious!

In France, we used to have a famous boys band called the « 2 Be 3 »…

I had however, by now already left in the past the spiritual blindness from which I used to suffer !

Of course,…

Why had I come to see Saï Baba ? : « To be free !...

To be released from my mental chains !...».

And it was thus exultant with joy, thanking God for this gift, that I went up to settle into the room.

It is amazing to see, when you start to open your eyes and to **really** see, to what extent there are always signs around us, little winks for us to indicate the road.

If you look closely, if you learn to look and to see, I am sure you will see them too !

Once checked into my room, or should I say the bare space that served for sleeping, I went into the village to buy a mattress and a mosquito net. For the price of 8 cents a night, beds were not included. But with the « mattress » costing about 6 US dollars, the expense was still more than reasonable.

I was then told that Saï Baba would give his *Darshan* next morning and that we would have to queue.

I was to discover that queuing was one of the most prized activities in India *(or at least in an Ashram !)*...

In fact, because of the number of people present and to give everyone a chance to be close to Saï Baba, I was told there was a kind of lottery, or draw.

Here is how it works : about twenty people sit next to each other and afterwards, all of the others *(hundreds of others !)* choose a line and sit behind each other. Each line can hold many tens of people. After a while, a Seva Dal[1] makes the first person in each line pull out a token from a purse. And according to the number pulled out by the first person, the whole line in which you were placed enters the temple as the first one, the fifth one or… why not… the last…

It is the Divine game.

I understood now why it had been possible, in my dream, to come last and to be nevertheless placed at the first row ! This is, by the way, an experience I was to live regularly afterwards !

Obviously, no need to say that the first who entered rushed to get a place on the first row so that they could have a chance of giving their letters to Baba or better, of talking to him or being able to touch his feet or simply his robe[2].

In the four days preceding the arrival of Baba, I had read <u>many</u> things about this astonishing being and I started to better understand why he was the object of such admiration.

---

[1] *Seva Dal* are volunteers who organize the devotees in the temples or work as volunteers in hospitals, schools, homes for the aged, and so on… *Seva* is a Sanskrit word which means Uninterested service.

[2] In India, beings like Amma or Saï Baba, are the object of such adoration that, by respect, a devotee should touch them only on the feet, or the hands and that, normally, only with the agreement of the Master. One also says that the energy is so intense that, when someone touches him/her, his/her energy, by simple differential of potential, flows to the person having touched him/her. (Remember the story of Jesus having felt *« a force »* leave him when the *« woman suffering from an issue of blood for twelve years »* had touched *« his mantle »*.

Matthew 9.20-22 ; Mark 5.25-34 ; Luke 8.43-48.

What I found magnificent in his message was its universality and its simplicity. He said amongst other things :

There is only one religion : The one of Love.

There is only one language : The one of the Heart.

There is only one caste : Humanity.

There is only one God, and He is Omnipresent.

And on this subject, he had chosen as a symbol of a kind of rosette with 5 petals, each one containing a symbol of a great religion. A cross for Christianity and Judaism, an Om sign for Hinduism, a Wheel for Buddhism, a Flame for Zoroastrian and the Crescent Moon and star for the Islam.

His extremely simple and universal language pleased me enormously.

And although using very simple words, his message was at the same time simple and complex, powerful and of an incredible breadth. Indeed, despite the extreme « simplicity » of his message, I could feel the colossal implications and the marvellous effects which it could have on the life of each one of us.

In addition, he strongly insisted that people not venerate him, as many tended to do. He insisted on the importance of venerating God.

He said that there was only ONE God who is Omnipresent.

Thus, he said, if you pray to him in the form of Rama, of Allah, of Krishna, of Jesus, of Buddha, of… whoever, you are always referring to the same energy.

Saï Baba thus said that we should not venerate HIM as a form.

But that we had to, on the other hand, <u>strengthen our faith in God</u>.

He said for example :

> -« *If you are catholic, be good Catholics and STRENGTHEN your faith in God. If you are Moslems, be good Moslems and STRENGTHEN your faith in God; if you are Jewish, be good Jews and STRENGTHEN your faith in God... »*

This universal and simple message pleased me tremendously.

I had also been surprised to see representations of Jesus on Hindu altars. When I asked about this, I was told that for the Hindus, Jesus, like Rama, like Krishna, like Buddha, was considered to be an *Avatar*, which means an incarnation of the Divine Principle and venerated as such.

Understanding Hinduism better, I deeply wished to see the Catholics develop such broadmindedness and tolerance !

By studying Hinduism a little more deeply, I realized that this religion which appeared to me at first polytheist was in fact monotheist. Indeed, each Divinity of the Hindu Pantheon represented and incarnated in a form suited for the veneration of the devotees, one of the multiple principles composing the Ultimate and Single Divinity. One also finds this concept in the Catholic religion with the notion of the Father, the Son, and the Holy Ghost.

I understood that Saï Baba was right and that all religions should be able to look at each other being aware that each one contains « a part » of the Divine message. That it is by integrating the various religions, like many parts of a puzzle, that one can better understand the total image that is this single God.

I now awaited impatiently my first *Darshan* with Saï Baba. During my readings I had read that he said, amongst other things :

> *«Do not underestimate the power of Darshan. All that my eyes see is transformed... And as you are seating here each day, you will be transformed and this*

> *transformation will appear in good time, when you return home… So, after Darshan, remain in silence, if not, this precious energy that I send to you returns to me unused… »*

The next morning, I presented myself to queue and, not having chosen the « good » line, I had to be satisfied with a place in the 4th or 5th row. We had to all sit on this black ground where white aisles delineated areas in which the *Seva Dal(s)* made us sit down as close as possible to each other, to fit in a maximum number of people. I understood that these white aisles delineating the areas where we sat were those where Saï Baba was going to walk during the *Darshan*.

After we had waited a long time, a music filled the air as Saï Baba appeared.

Surprisingly majestic in his orange robe, he walked slowly on the women's side, taking some of the letters which these women held out to him. Others, their hands joined in front of their hearts raised eyes filled with wonder towards him. And while I looked at him taking these letters, I noticed that apparently, he did not take all of them. Whereas several people held them out, he would advance to take those of a person in the 3rd row and not those of someone in the first row…

What was amazing, was to see the fascination he seemed to exert on all these people. All eyes seemed riveted on one point : Him.

And as I observed him, I also felt a kind of fascination fill me. From Him emanated…. Something… Something indefinable… but nevertheless very perceptible…

A kind of strength, of power, of kindness, of peace that I could feel simply by looking at him move around.

Finally, he arrived on the men's side. I carefully held the letters which had been entrusted to me and waited until he approached where I was to be able to give them to him.

My disappointment was great when I saw him approach where I was, walking a few blocks away and then return again « to the women » to finally, leave the temple towards his residence.

And he had not even condescended to throw me a slight glance, even from a distance!

When I saw everybody stand up, I had to me admit the evidence : It was already over...

It had lasted barely 10 minutes !

I had thought that he was going to pass around each block so that each one of us could see him closely, but I had been mistaken !

Some people « accustomed » to the *Ashram* explained that in fact, one never knew where *Swami*[1] was going to pass. According to them you had to « pray and trust *Swami*... ».

On that subject, Saï Baba himself would say :

-*« Love my uncertainty »*

When I asked what was going to happen next, I was told that in the afternoon, there would be *Bhajans*, devotional songs, and that Saï Baba would grant us the Grace to be present for this occasion.

I therefore returned a bit disappointed to my room.

As soon as it was 2 o'clock, I decided again to queue for the *Bhajans* planned for 4.30.

The « draw» found me in line number 9 and I was positioned a bit better than in the morning.

---

[1] *Swami* is a title of respect given to a Spiritual Master. It is also the affectionate « nick name» given to Saï Baba by his devotees.

Bad luck for me, when the time of the *Bhajans* arrived, I was given to understand that Saï Baba was not walking amongst us but was going directly to sit on the big red armchair that had pride of place on the stage in front of the statue which I knew now was that of Krishna playing the flute.

During *Bhajans*, Saï Baba, sitting on his red armchair, would beat the rhythm by clapping his hands, look from right to left, and sometimes do strange gestures with his pointed finger. At other times, he would absorb himself in the music, his eyes closed.

And while everybody seemed to know the lyrics, I was feeling very stupid. I had no idea of what was being sung,… although I found these chants very pleasant. With Amma, I had not really tried to sing the *Bhajans*, but here, I was feeling very interested in participating.

I quickly understood that they all had a very simple structure : One sentence was sung by one man or woman « soloist » then every one would sing it in chorus. One by one, each sentence was sung twice. Once arrived at the end of the chant, the rhythm accelerated and each sentence was then sung once by the soloist and then by everybody. The *Bhajans* always finished in the same way, with the first musical sentence being slowly sung as a reprise by everyone.

Once the *Bhajans* finished, after about half an hour, Saï Baba stood up as someone waved before him what seemed to be a kind of little saucepan from which flames emanated.

I was to learn later that this ritual, called *Aarathi*, during which some camphor is burned, was a ritual that the devotees traditionally performed after the *Bhajans* or after other rituals, even in their own homes, to thank the Divine principle for having been present with them during the ceremonies.

I learned in fact that, just as the Catholics say, the Hindus believe that God is present everywhere where you pray to him... The ritual called *Aarathi* is a way that the devotees express their gratitude to the Divine principle for its gift of Grace in being with them.

Before the ritual was even completed, Saï Baba left for his residence and the ceremony continued without him. After a moment the man who had waved the « flaming saucepan » in front of Baba turned round and presented this flame to us. And as if to attract the purification of this flame towards them, I then saw many people, lean towards this flame with their finger tips which was so far away from them and, turning around their hands, move it around their face, or over their heart, as if they were purifying themselves by doing so.

Although I did not understand everything that had happened, I felt that these rituals were extremely powerful and beneficial. I also realized that if I wanted to understand these rites, I would have to put aside the last of my prejudices and really learn about it.

The ceremony was to be completed by a very beautiful *Mantra* which I had already heard at *Amma*'s place which means, « May Peace reign in all worlds »[1].

When I returned to my room that evening, I started to write in a small journal which I had begun. In this journal, in fact, I was speaking to Baba.

I was telling him how disappointed I had been that he had not have even looked at me. Indeed, everything I had read concerning the effects of *Darshan* made me intensely wish that he would look at me in order to « transform me ».

I had indeed understood, years before, when I had my first direct experiences with Jesus, how He could heal us at the time He was on earth.

This was not through a particular technique but rather <u>by a particular consciousness</u>.

---

[1] « Loka Samastha Sukhino Bhavanthu »

Jesus was <u>so deeply aware</u> of His Divine Nature and of that of all around Him that by looking at us, He COULD NOT see in us anything else but perfection. And someone who is gazed at with such a certainty can only accept it *(if, of course, he really wants to become as the other sees him !)*

And I was persuaded that this Saï Baba had that ability. Not only because he said so but because of what I had experienced in my dream. Everything had been so <u>real</u> !

It had all been <u>real as an experience</u> but on top of that, everything I had now experienced fell into place with the intellectual knowledge I had gathered as years passed by.

And in my journal, I reproached Saï Baba for having ignored me when I longed so much for a glance he would make towards me...

The next morning, I was in a luckier line because it was number 3. Thank to that, I obtained a place in the 2nd row. I had chosen a block to sit in, hoping it would be one of those Saï Baba would deign to approach.

When He came at precisely 7 o'clock, majestic again in his orange robe, I closed my eyes to silently ask him to « pass » where I was.

He started to walk among the women, going much further today than the day before in the temple. Finally, he crossed over to the men's side and presented himself at the corner of the block I was in. I was at last only 5 or 6 people away from him.

And as my eyes were riveted on Him, Saï Baba looked at me straight in the eyes, with an expression that clearly said :

> -« You wanted me to look at you ?... Well there, my child,... I'm looking at you... ».

And he stared at me, not moving for a moment that seemed to me everlasting as his magnificent eyes were diving into me as I was opening to his incredible energy.

After a time that seemed very long but probably lasted 5 or 6 seconds, he keep on walking, and going right around the block I was in, passed again in front of me. There was only one person separating Him from me. I held out the letters it was my mission to give him and He took them immediately. I was now reassured because these people really wanted *Swami* to receive them. They had told me, and I had noticed myself, that even though you held out letters to him, He sometimes ignored them totally.

At the moment He took these letters, although there was no physical touch between his hand and mine, I instantly felt a « wave » of heat come up my hand holding the letters into my arm, then into my heart. It was like a kind of electric current at the same time very powerful and very gentle.

And as He moved away, I was looking at Him blissfully, feeling this gentle heat radiating in me.

As soon as he had left the temple, I closed my eyes to, as *Swami* so rightly said, « keep within his precious energy ». Astonishingly, I felt that by opening my eyes, I had the feeling of emptying out this softness that was inhabiting me, whereas if I closed them, it was as if I had closed the door through which it was leaking from me.

And as I remained seated, my eyes closed, I felt that gentleness, that energy beating in my heart… How good it was !....

As I opened inside more and more, little by little, like waves taking my whole body, I felt that Love grow,… grow,… grow…

And after a while, I felt something like « hands » hold me at the level of the shoulders and straighten my back as other « hands » were opening my arms. And as I straightened up, as I was opening, that energy flowed in more powerful waves that gave me the impression they were lifting me up,... transporting me ...

Then « something » straightened me up even more, pushing at the bottom of my spine to straighten it up, and then, another wave took over me...

I was literally bathing in pure Love !

After having spent some time like this « something » lifted my arms, both together, and the more they opened, the stronger, and gentler was the wave lifting me up.

And again, it was as if something opened even more my arms, always more... I now had my arms totally wide open and, to my great surprise, it was not a wave of softness that entered in me but a wave of sadness.

In a quarter of a second, I found myself in an infinite sadness that was filling me and I was crying, and crying, and crying... And as I felt I was physically closing, bowing my back, I had the impression that those « hands » that had opened me were straightening me up again,... and at that time an even stronger wave of distress filled me,... and I was crying, and crying, and crying,...

And suddenly, without understanding why (I had during these astonishing moments **no** reasoning faculty, I could only feel and experience !) a wave of sparkling Joy filled me instantly.

The previous second, I was in tears, overcome by infinite distress and now, I was laughing like a little child as I saw the beauty, the simplicity and the magic of the world...

And I was laughing, and laughing, and laughing at the beauty I was feeling. Life sparkled out of me with an enormous strength...

And as I was at the « crest of the wave », suddenly, without any warning, the wave of Joy was replaced by a wave of distress...

It was an incredible moment in which I would pass from magnificent ecstasy to the most dreadful distress....

And after having been taken several times to these extremes, in a second, as these « hands » again intimated me to straighten up, it was a wave of « NOTHING » that invaded me **instantly**.

Actually, it was not really like a wave.... It was more « like a point of nothingness » that was deep within the waves in which I was diving.

And as I was in that « nothingness », a peace that surpasses all understanding invaded me. A magnificent peace was inhabiting me and I was that peace simultaneously.

And in that « **NOTHING** » there was « **EVERYTHING** »...

« **EVERYTHING** » was present in that « **NOTHING** » that I was.

And I, I was like an observer of the beauty of that void, of the beauty of that « NOTHING » that allows « EVERYTHING »...

I had the impression that my physical body that seemed so far away, so far away, so far away... did not even breathe any more. It was my skin, it was my whole being that « breathed » by itself,... immersed in LIFE itself....

As I am now trying to rewrite this experience, I realize once more how small and limited words are to describe the Without a Name that was inviting me into His heart.

As I was bathing in that infinite consciousness, I KNEW that all I had to do, was to surrender to it... surrender in it... I knew that THROUGH IT, everything is possible and that it is enough !

And I realized why Jesus told us :

> -« *Seek ye first the Kingdom of God and his Righteousness, and all these things shall be added unto you* »[1]

Everything was true, of course !... It could not be otherwise !...

And as I was within that Infinite consciousness, I was telling it :

> -« *Here, I surrender to you, and, please, tell me who I am, Tell me what to do, Tell me where to do it, Tell me how to do it, because I am willing to surrender totally to You, that You take charge of my life because I know You know what is Good for me,... I lay my* **Whole** *life at Your feet... and surrender to You !* »

Curiously, it was as if at the time that I was abandoning my life to Him, He was giving it back to me... I felt carried by Him, more alive than I had ever been.

I do not know how long this experience lasted in the linear relativity that people call the physical world... May be half an hour, may be one hour...

After some time which really seemed to me out of time, one or two people came over to touch me, may be worrying because they could not see me breathing anymore....

And as they touched me and asked me with a worried look: « *Are you OK ?* », I, who felt pulled back by this physical touch into my body, I managed to move my mouth, that seemed itself to be so far away, enough to make it mumble a :

> -« *Oh yes, I feel fine,... thank you !... I feel* **VERY GOOD** *!...* »

It took me a long time, a very long time to reintegrate my body as I learned to make it move, part by part...

When I finally re-opened the eyes, I was deeply moved by what I saw outside. There were only a few people left in the

---

[1] Matthew 6:33

temple... but everything was so beautiful, everything was so alive !

And I was filled with gratitude towards this Saï Baba, towards this Holy Man whom I now recognized and whose Extreme Beauty and Transcendence I could not deny.

If, **by a simple glance**, without even touching me, he could allow me within seconds to attain this awareness of Awakening and of the Absolute, I had to listen to what He had to tell me and to follow the path He was showing me...

And I understood why the Master is necessary for the evolution of each of us.

This notion of Master, of *Guru,* is very often misunderstood in western societies. But, if you think about it, why did you become who you are ? Not by reading books..., not by accumulating an intellectual knowledge.

You became what you are because you **all** had your Gurus.

You all had two *Gurus*... *Guru* Dad et *Guru* Mum...And if one of them was missing, it was the same thing. If it was not *Guru* Dad and *Guru* Mum, it was *Guru* Grand-Pa and *Guru* Grand-Ma or *Guru* School teacher and *Guru* Professor, because somewhere, somehow, someone has been a source of inspiration for you and a model.

And how did your *Gurus* teach you ? Not necessarily through what they said... but rather through what they were !

By looking at them, by being close to them, you learned.

Before, as a baby, you were powerless, incapable of any autonomy and THEY, your Gods, your *Gurus,* your parents, showed you through their presence next to you a potential. They were demonstrating YOUR potential. And as you watched them, blissfully admiring, they gave you the desire to become more, because they were more than you... Actually, they gave you the impression of being more than you, but they, your Masters, your parents knew that, what they were, you too would become…

Well this reminds me of Jesus ! Didn't He say ? :

> -« *Verily, verily, I say unto you, He that believeth on me, the works that I do shall he do also; and greater works than these shall he do; because I go unto my Father.* »[1]

and again

> -« *Verily I say unto you, If ye have faith, and doubt not, ye shall not only do this which is done to the fig tree, but also if ye shall say unto this mountain, Be thou removed, and be thou cast into the sea; it shall be done. And all things, whatsoever ye shall ask in prayer, believing, ye shall receive.* »[2]

In that sense, your parents were not more powerful than you, they were simply older than you, more evolved.

And thanks to these models who were close to you and who demonstrated to you the potential existing within you, you could then manifest it.

And your parents, like Masters or *Gurus* sometimes encouraged you to go on walk when you fell or sometimes reprimanded you, out of Love, when they saw you stray onto a path that would not to lead you where you wanted to go or where it was good for you to go.

This is why I now know that, I, Patrice, as a « spiritual child », I NEED the presence of a « spiritual adult », of a « Master » so that I can, by being close to him/her see and become what I really am.

Thanks to Vicky, thanks to Martin, thanks to Lee and Michael, I had become aware of a potential I had manifested.

---

[1] John 14:12
[2] Matthew 21:21-22

And now, thanks to Amma, thanks to Baba, who were showing me by their simple presence, I could now SEE, UNDERSTAND and start to manifest another part of my potential.

With some teachers, you learn to walk. With others, you learn to fly….

Everything is so simple finally !

That morning, as I left the temple, feeling I was floating above the ground, I thought again of what I had just been through…

I thought again of that feeling, of that presence of Love that I had contacted…

I thought again about my life that I had just laid at His feet…

And as I thought again that I had laid **EVERYTHING** at the feet of God, feeling it was <u>absolutely right</u> that I **totally** surrendered to Him, I was suddenly filled by a thought that frightened me !

It was a bit as if a voice within was saying :

> -« *Hey… Patrice, Wake up, Yoo-hoo! You just laid your life at the feet of God, you just surrendered to Him…, OK !… Great !… But what would you do if God asked you for all of your money ! What would you do if the Universe asked you to sign a blank cheque ? Would you surrender EVERYTHING in trust ? Would you dare let go of EVERYTHING in confidence ?»*

And there, honestly, I was not that sure… I noticed that I still had fears, doubts…

Nevertheless, I quickly forgot that incident… but, future events were to soon remind me !…

As days passed by, I realized that the life in the *Ashram* was a great school of patience.

Everywhere, we had to wait… and luckily so !

In the bank, in the restaurant, before the *Darshan*, before the *Bhajans*, wait,... always wait...

And this waiting allowed me to centre myself, to remember my intentions, my desires, so that I could be even more receptive when the *Darshan* came.

When, some days later, I saw *Swami* manifest *Vibhuti*, I was dumb-founded. I actually have a brother who is a sleight-of-hand magician and I know the tricks he uses to make objects appear in his hands « like magic » out of thin air.

But here, with Swami, there could be no trick. He had no pocket,... He made no movement to attract our attention away as He went elsewhere to get His ashes, in some secret pocket... Nothing like that... Nothing...

Nothing, except the simplicity of the gesture.

A gesture that, after a while, seemed natural even to me.

> -« *Well yes, what else, He just manifested Vibhuti... Nothing to make such a fuss about...* »

After a few days, it had become almost « normal »...

He just stretched out his arm, the open palm facing down, and, after a little circular movement, « caught » this powder between his thumb and the tip of his fingers and crushed it as it ran from His hands and He gave it to the devotees.

To me, it was <u>certain</u> it could not be sleight of hand.

During the next ten days that I spent with *Swami*, I was to receive many graces and the list would be much too long to recount here.

And as I talked to many people who had all experienced sometimes incredible miracles, I realized little by little the greatness of this *avatar* and thus understood the truth of what John the apostle said about the *avatar* Jesus-Christ :

> -« *And there are also many other things which Jesus did, the which, if they should be written every one, I suppose that even the world itself could not contain the books that should be written*»[1]

... I understood also why the Master gives us only what we believe we will receive, or what we believe we deserve to receive.

In fact, <u>totally respecting</u> our free will, our choice, the Master can really do NOTHING for us, unless we give Him the power to.

And I understood why Amma said :

> -« *My Children, if you come to me to get a thimbleful of Love, as you leave, hold it preciously... but if you come to get a bucket of Love, keep it preciously when you leave...* »

I understood why Babaji[2], an other Master, said to a woman filled of doubts who came to see Him :

"If you come to me filled with suspicion, I will give you all the reasons to be suspicious... But if you come here to search for Love, I will give you more than you ever experienced ! »

And it was with my Heart and Soul filled with these marvellous experiences that I was to return to France.

Now, I KNEW !

And I was filled with gratitude towards this Holy Man, who, without even talking to me, without even touching me, had TAUGHT me, in the deepest, purest sense.

---

[1] John 21:25

[2] Babaji is an other spiritual master, considered by many as a *Mahavatar*, of whom it is said that he was the *guru* of the *guru* of the *guru* of Yogananda, author of « *Autobiography of a Yogi* ». It is also said He was the teacher of Jesus, when Jesus was in India. His last manifestation on Earth was between 1970 and 1984. They say that Babaji, known also as Haidakhan Babaji, according to the name of the place where he lived, when He manifest on Earth, does not go through the process of birth and manifests his body as an adult, by His simple will.

Thanks to Him, I had really SEEN and experienced this incredible strength, this incredible softness, this incredible kindness, this incredible power, this incredible joy, this incredible peace, this incredible Love some people call GOD…

CHAPTER 30
Integration et Assimilation...

To leave the Ashram was very difficult... There were such memories that connected me to it that as I was leaving, I had the impression of losing them...

Which was not the case... Far from it........

I knew it was just a beginning.... It was a new start... A new life that I was starting...

Yes, one more ! It is weird how many lives one can live in one life, isn't it ?

When I got back in France, I returned to my rhythm of work, sometimes presenting my own classes, sometimes translating for Martin here or there.

Some weeks after my return from Swami, I had to give a class in Reunion Island again. And I was going to have an astonishing experience there that would shake me to the core..

When the workshop was over, one the participant came to me and said :

> -« *Patrice, I have something to tell you... Do you mind ?...* »
>
> -« *Of course, go ahead !* »
>
> -« *I wanted to tell you..., Do you know why I signed up for your workshop ?...* »

And as I remained silent, knowing she would continue, she said :

-« Well , this is why,... when I saw you before your introductory conference before the workshop, I looked at you and said to myself : «This man saw God ..., He is Divine... » ... and that made me want to hear you... Now that you have explained us your path, I understand better... And really, Thank you, Thank you ! »

And as she was telling that, I was quite dumbstruck!

Of course, for me, there was no doubt that I had experienced what I had ... But here, again, I was having a « feedback »[1] from the universe that confirmed that my obviously subjective experience was in fact objective and real.

All of that could only encourage me to keep working and opening myself...

Since my return from Swami, I had decided to try to follow certain of the principles of life that he advised.

Since He was so obviously in a state of peace, of love, of joy and of serenity which I wanted to attain, I was determined to follow his advice. Who else than someone who had attained the heights of the Himalayas could be appropriate to guide me as I myself want to start the ascension.

I had already been a vegetarian for years and Saï Baba advised a nutritional approach a little more complex but which seemed very interesting. He explains that food determines the quality of thoughts which inhabit us and that, if we want to reach a greater peace and serenity, it is important to supervise our food. This idea was not new for me since I had already heard of it and it was what had motivated my choice for vegetarianism.

What was new, on the other hand, was this idea of various intrinsic qualities of food. That was really very interesting.

He explains, that in nature, in Man, in food, there are 3 principal characteristics, 3 *Gunas* :

These characteristics are called *Tamas*, *Rajas*, and *Sattva*.

The first one, *Tamas*, corresponds to the states of torpor, sleep, falling sleep, apathy, and heaviness...

The second one, *Rajas*, corresponds to the states of excitement, speed, and intense activity.

---

[1] A « feedback » is a return signal to indicate your position.

The third one, *Sattva*, corresponds to the states of peace, silence, truth, and serenity.

These three principles made me think of the three « elements » present in an atom: the proton, the electron and the neutron, each one having a different intrinsic *characteristic (positive, negative or neutral)*.

Saï Baba explained that, during a day, there is a period that is *Tamasic*, an other that is *Rajasic* and an other one that is *Sattvic*.

Thus, the hours of the night (between 8pm and 4am) where the body has a tendency to sleep is a *Tamasic* period.

The period between 8am and 4 pm is *Rajasic*, which means favourable for activity, speed, work.

The periods of 4 hours from 4am to 8am, and from 4pm to 8pm are favourable for peace, prayer, and meditation, that is, *Sattvic*.

And in the same way, he was explaining that all foods have characteristics which are either *Tamasic*, *Rajasic* or *Sattvic*.

And so, if you want to develop *Sattvic* characteristics, it is preferable to avoid *Tamasic* food, which is heavy or sleepy *(like meat, fish, eggs)* or *Rajasic* food, which is exiting or stimulating... *(like coffee, tea, alcohol, sugar...)* in favour of a more *Sattvic* food *(like milk, bananas, coconut, raw vegetables and so on...)*.

In general, he explained that food was more Sattvic when it is either raw or freshly cooked. A reheated food becomes much more *Tamasic*.

In the same way, he encouraged to eat with moderation, saying that even with a *Sattvic* food, a stomach too full became *Tamasic*...

These principles seeming very logical and coherent, I thus decided not to have any more coffee, tea or alcohol, which I still used to consume occasionally.

I also decided to avoid eggs, although I sometimes happens to eat some.

Having already noted in the past the benefits of a different food, I wanted to try out from the inside the principles suggested by Saï Baba.

I think indeed that if such a being gives me some advice and says that it is important, I must believe him, listen to him and do what he advises me.

<u>Attention</u>, I am not saying that it is a question of following an advice blindly. I can obviously, with my free will and my discernment, analyze this « path » which he proposes and, if it seems right to me, I can then <u>choose</u> to follow it.

And I was not to regret it in any way.

I am of course aware that there are other paths, other ways to arrive where I want to arrive but, having chosen to trust him, I decided to follow his advice.

Just as if I am lost and ask a policeman the way to take to arrive safe and sound, I must have the will « to surrender » to his advice and to follow the way that he indicates, I must have the will « to surrender in confidence» to the « Master » whom I have recognized as being able to guide me and follow his advice, since, *a priori*, He knows better than I the territory I am entering..

What I am talking about here is <u>one of the aspects</u> of the sentence « *Thy will be done...* » that one finds in the « *Our Father* ».

I am aware that this concept of « trustful surrender » can be very difficult to admit for a Westerner who is filled with prejudices about what one calls a « Master » or a « *Guru* » and who would not make the effort to understand these principles.

On the other hand, if you recognize that somebody is able to help you, it can be interesting to <u>really</u> trust him and not to reject an advice he gives you , simply because you do not understand it.

Indeed, because this being has explored territories which you do not know, he knows the dangers and the traps therein, and it can be <u>JUDICIOUS</u> to listen to his advice.

To illustrate this matter, I will use another metaphor.

Imagine that you want to go to the Mount St Michel and that I know it very well, since I live there.

In Paris, of course you heard about this splendid place but you wonder :

-« Where is it ?... How could I get there ?... »

Then, you look for a Guide *(for the moment, a roadmap will do the trick !)* and you see that you have to leave Paris by the west.

So you start to drive towards the west. But, if you really think about it, what <u>proves</u> to you that it <u>really</u> is in this direction? Simply a guide ! A map in which you <u>chose</u> to trust !

The road is long and you would like to have evidence that you are getting closer.

Fortunately, the road is marked out and from time to time, some signposts inform you.

Obviously, from Paris, the Mount St Michel is not sign posted, but you know that there are « step » cities to pass by.

When finally, after hours of driving, you see the Mount St Michel in the distance, in your state of excitement to see it AT LAST, you want to drive straight towards it.

But this is where the guide intervenes, and as it happens, that's me, who knows the area so well.

I will guide you and help you to go the few yards which separate you. But as you can see it so close to you, you could well say to me :

-« But look, it is right in front of me, I will walk straight ahead on the sand because the tide is low and I will be there in a few minutes… ».

Obviously, I who know the territory well because I live there, I will say to you :

-« Don't do that, because there are dangers which you cannot see… You have to go around the Mount to reach it. If you go there in a straight line, you risk serious dangers… The sea can come up very quickly here… and moreover, there are quick sands… »

But of course, <u>you could choose</u> to ignore my advice and to say to me :

-« I don't see any « quick » sands. I see only sand… And then the sea is so far away right now, there's no risk, I don't believe you Patrice. I'm going straight ahead ! … »

And what do you want me to say to you under these conditions ? Should I force you to go another way ? …

I could, of course… and I will try…

But, you are free and I must recognize your freedom to do whatever you want.

So, what I will do, it is you to tell you over and over,

> -« *Beware, do not pass by that way, it is dangerous ! Go this way.»*

But if, really, you DO NOT WANT to listen to me, what can I do ?...

Whatever, you will do what you decided to do !

Love is the Key...

I can only look at you make your choices with compassion ... and see you assume the consequences!

And once you are sinking in the quick sands or are caught with the rising tide which could drown you in a few minutes, do not worry, because I will be there to get you out of that dead end in which you have stuck yourself!

And then, you will realize that you <u>should really have</u> trusted me and surrendered to me!

Do you understand better now?

The path towards God is just the same! As it is on Earth so it is in Heaven!

It is up to you to see!

This is why, when this *Avatar* gives me some advice, I am willing to listen to Him, because I have already fallen and gotten stuck in the quick sands of the mind that surround Mount St Michel... and He saved me from them!

And if he tells me something that I do not understand, I avoid rejecting it outright simply because I do not understand it.

Which does not mean that I follow his advice blindly!

In this case, I use my intelligence, my faculty of understanding, my free will and also, I ask him for explanations. Once He has explained for example that, the reason why the tide comes up so quickly near the Mount St Michel is because of the extremely low gradation, having understood the good basis of His advice, I then choose to follow it... or to not follow it... and to assume the consequences of these choices...

And sometimes, I also recognize that <u>on my level of consciousness,</u> I do not <u>master</u> the concepts which he <u>knows,</u> and in this case, I can choose to follow him serenely while simply trusting him.

Why ? Because my <u>experience shows me that he is a good guide</u>, because now, from where I am, I can see Mount St Michel in front of me, much nearer than before, when years ago, I was still in Paris.

And if you have ever gone to Mount St Michel, you have seen that there are a lot of different guides, and each one proposes to get there by a different path.

And why do you choose one guide in preference to another? Because his path seems to you more pleasant,… or more rapid,… or simpler,… or riskier because perhaps, you like to take risks,… or longer because you like to take your time to stroll on the path,… or more rational because you are a logical person,… or more crazy, because you like madness…

It is true that among these guides, some are more honest than others. Some really want to make you discover the splendours of Mount St Michel and others are more interested in the price of the visit.

And how can you know if your Guide is honest ?

Well, do some research before choosing your guide, ask for the prices !

And do not be satisfied only by what they tell you about him…Go and see him… Test him… and have your <u>own</u> experience of him…

But above all, choose to approach him without prejudice because, often, people who slander a guide have not even bothered to test him or to visit him. Sometimes, if they approached him, they did so while clinging so strongly to their values, their beliefs, their prejudices that they gave themselves no chance to really try out or experience the paths proposed by this guide.

You could even choose to take several guides simultaneously, but there, you could find yourselves in a serious state of confusion whereas one tells you to the right while the other tells you on the contrary to go to the left.

You could, why not, choose to take several guides alternatively and to change guides each time just before reaching Mount St Michel, simply to have the pleasure of approaching it from another side, from another perspective. But in this case, what do you really want ?

To explore Mount St Michel or the various paths which lead you to it ?

Obviously, there is nothing wrong with that, it is simply about another choice, another goal quite as worthy.

I think in any case that one day or another, after having approached it on all the sides possible, you will want to go inside to discover his splendour !

Now, is one Guide better than another ?

<u>Not at all</u>, they simply propose different paths.

Is one path better than another ?

<u>Not at all</u>, it is simply different… and adapted to he who travels on it…

But on the other hand, **always** remember one thing :

As good he is, a guide is only « A Guide ».

He is not « Mount St Michel ».

CHAPTER 31
An American Dream...

Little by little, time passed by and the summer approached.

That year, I had planned to give workshops in Noumea, then in Tahiti and finally to stop over during 7 weeks in the USA before returning to Paris. In fact, I wanted to give workshops there. I had already in the past proposed some classes in Los Angeles and San Francisco but without much success. This 7 weeks' period there was to enable me to meet organizers there and to set up these classes.

I had another project: I wanted to buy a laptop computer.

I had formulated my request « up there » in this manner :

-« Here is what I would like. I would like the classes in Noumea and in Papeete bring me, once all the organization expenses have been paid, (you recall, you must be precise !) enough money to stay 7 weeks in an hotel in the USA and treat myself to a laptop computer with a powerful database and word processing programme !»

As usual, I bought my plane ticket using my credit card and trusting that the day when the sum would be debited, the money would be there !!!

Up till now, no problems ! Once my workshops in Noumea were completed, I transferred the money to my company account and, once more, all went well.

Once my workshops in Papeete were over, I once more gave thanks to the Universe for having once again granted my wish..

Indeed, I now had 18 000 francs (about 2 700 €) to go and spend my 7 weeks in the USA and to buy myself a computer !

I thus arrived to Los Angeles, rented a car and went to look for a small hotel on Sunset Boulevard.

I began my search for the computer and realized quickly that, considering the price of the one I wanted to buy, I had to find another cheaper lodging.

In one of the local gay newspapers, I quickly found a room at a very reasonable price, right in the heart of West Hollywood, the gay district of Los Angeles.

Los Angeles is a very rough city and often, unsafe. In very many districts you <u>really do not want</u> to walk in the evening ! On the other hand, West Hollywood is one of the « safe » districts of the city, because of the often high rents and a very present police force, which makes it a district reserved for the relatively wealthy. It is a district where you can walk at night, without too much fear.

I was lodging with a man about fifty years old, very nice, who rented one of his rooms on a weekly rate.

Two or three days later, as I was on one of the motorways of the city, I had what people usually call « an accident ».

A car that I had not seen was to brake abruptly in front of me and I hit it violently. Luckily for me *(fortunately, I do not lack luck!)*, the passenger was OK, and his car too! Hardly a scratch ! It was in fact one of these gigantic black solid limousines.

But whereas the other vehicle was unscathed, mine was in a terrible state, with the grill, the hood, the headlights, and the indicators completely battered !

Having filled in the report, I arranged to turn over the car to the hiring agency to have it changed.

Arriving on the spot, a huge surprise was waiting for me !

The hirer explained that, considering the basic insurance that I had chosen in renting my vehicle, there was an excess of 1 500 dollars, which was more than 9 000 francs (about 1 370 €) at the time !

It was **half** of the sum which I had for my stay **AND** the computer !

And moreover, I had already bought my computer !

After several phone calls to France with my bank, I succeeded in convincing my banker to unblock my credit card *(which could not obviously debit such a large amount in one day !)*

I had dealt with the most urgent matters and paid my debts ! I now waited for the rest of the saying to come true, that is, to get rich !

Actually, I felt very down, because I had barely 40 dollars left in cash and 60 dollars in travellers cheques. Why would I have taken more, since I had more than 18 000 francs (about 2 700 € on my account and an international credit card ? !

When I rang my travel company, they explained that in view of the special « *World Tour* » fare that I had obtained, I could not change the date of my return !

And my bank had completely blocked my card, once my debt was paid !

I was in a fine mess !

I had just one thing left to do, to understand why and how I had created this circumstance in my life.

But especially, once I had understood, or even without understanding… I had to change this situation !

I searched, and searched, and searched but could not find anything…

Then when I returned that evening to my landlord and explained my situation to him, he kindly offered a solution.

He was a masseur and explained to me that sometimes, he had too many customers or simply did not want to work.

He then offered to let me take some of his clients.. He said that his only requirement was that I would pay him 15 Dollars per customer since I would be using the room, the massage oils as well as the sheets laid out for hygiene on the massage table. The deal was very honest, the price being 40 or 50 dollars for one hour of massage.

He knew in fact that I had learned certain techniques when I lived with Myriam *(who herself gave courses in massage !)*. And moreover, he said that certain customers could be very interested by the energy re-balancing which I proposed.

The idea seemed excellent !

And although I had *a priori* agreed to the idea to start to do massages, nothing happened ! Not a client in sight…

The days passed by and no client came and I had almost no money left !

And I had to pay my rent each day !

And I continued to wonder :

-« *But why, why, did I create this situation ?* »

It took me in fact nearly two or three days to find the solution, whereas obviously, at times, I went through periods of depression.

If nothing happens by chance and everything has a raison for being, what could be the reason for this and what could the « gift » of this experience be?

I realized several things :

- - <u>Firstly</u>, I totally <u>refused</u> this situation which however did exist. I would have to accept it completely as I had understood some years before[1].

---

[1] See Chapter 12 « An instructive trip… »

- Secondly, I realized that in India, I had « surrendered » all of my life to the feet of God, somehow wanting Him to be my Only Security.

And I realized suddenly that somehow, I had put my safety, not in God, but in these 18 000 francs (about 2 740 €) ! I was counting on these 18000 francs to live on for 7 weeks in the USA and to buy my computer…

And I understood why God, to test me, was taking away my « little security cushion ». He wanted to see if I trusted money or if, REALLY, I trusted HIM !

Money is indeed for some a « God » that they venerate, that they want to reach, and in which they place their security…

Money can thus become an enemy to our spiritual growth. On this subject, Jesus said extremely precisely :

-« No man can serve two Masters: for either he will hate the one and love the other or else he will hold to the one and despise the other. Ye cannot serve God and Mammon. »[1]

It is indeed easy to say « I trust in God » when one has all the security in the physical world. It is another thing to say it and to live it when one has NOTHING.

And, by withdrawing all my physical security, He enabled me to experience it…

I understood what I had to do…

Determined that it change, I sat down in front of my altar, in my room, in front of the photographs of Saï Baba and Jesus…

I closed my eyes and, after taking some deep breaths, I addressed myself to God, speaking to Him like this:

-« Hello, I am calling upon you for the following reason : Yes, I realize that I was resisting the situation that you presented to me… and I apologize… I really believe that EVERYTHING

---

[1] Matthew 6:24

that you make me live is good for me, so, I am not resisting anymore… I accept this situation… I also recognize that I had placed my safety in those 18000 francs instead of putting it in You, as I had expressed the desire for it… I ask for your forgiveness, for this lack of confidence… but, now, you have taken away my « little security cushion » ... so… OK… I accept that… and I am willing to really put my confidence in YOU… but, NOW,… YOU HAVE TO DO SOMETHING… I have only 5 dollars left in my pocket, I cannot return to France for another 6 full weeks and TOMORROW, I must pay 15 dollars rent to my landlord ! **YOU HAVE TO do something NOW…»**

And while I was finishing my prayer/meditation with a series of mantras and one « Our Father », at the MOMENT I finished **the last sentence of my prayer**, the telephone rang !

It was my first client ringing who was to arrive in the next half hour !

What's more, he was very cute ! Which made my « work » even more pleasant…

And this is how, each passing day, for more than 6 weeks, whereas apparently, I had no money at all, I could always pay my rent and stay in the USA without EVER lacking ANYTHING….

I was experiencing Abundance...

Each day, day by day, I had what I needed. I ate my fill every day, I sometimes went to the pictures or went out in the evening… I could do what I felt like doing.

And if, one day, I did not have any clients *(because I « needed » at least one each day to pay the rent and to eat or go out at night)* somehow my landlord would be away. …

And often, if I had not had any client during his absence, the day that he returned, I had three or four and I could pay my rent !

Love is the Key...

It was magical ! Marvellously magical... and I KNOW now that if I put my confidence into God,... He will NEVER disappoint me.

One evening, as I was going out in a bar, I was to have a disturbing experience. In this bar were a troupe of transvestites. You know,... those men who dress as women.

And as I looked at this show with a certain judgement about these men, I suddenly thought about myself and of certain aspects of my life. And I realized that what I was could also be judged or condemned by certain people with narrow minds.

And while these ideas ran through my head, I thought with a kind of sad sigh :

-«Well, Patrice, you are now a long way away from what you lived in India... and you are far away from Saï Baba in such a place... ».

And believe it or not, but, **at this very moment**, a transvestite went up on stage to sing a song of Gloria Gaynor. He was dressed in a long orange robe and obviously with the imposing hairdo she has... just like *Swami* !

And in that precise second, I really believed I was seeing Saï Baba in front of me and I was immediately swept up in a feeling of gratitude which filled my heart as I was realizing his Divine Presence.

I realized that by this *Leela*, through this sign, He made me understand that EVERYTHING is GOD and that God is really present everywhere, including in this place which I had had a tendency to judge !

I realized even more the Omnipresence of God.

I realized that, even if it had seemed to me for a moment that God could not be present in such a place, this was false... because : **THERE IS NO PLACE WHERE GOD IS NOT !**

These experiences which I went through could only reinforce my faith in this marvellous energy of Love... and I seriously thought of returning to India to see again this dear *Swami* who had so clearly shown me the path.

My initial plan when I had arrived in the USA was to look for organizers to promote my workshops there.

However, my tricky experience with the car had forced me to reconsider many things...

Indeed, as I sought for the reason why I had attracted to me what others would call an « accident », I had become aware of a **very sensitive** point.

When in India, I had been transported by this Love which I knew to be God, I had surrendered my entire life to him... I had said to him **very deeply** in my heart :

> -« *Tell me who I am, what to do, how to do it, where to do it...* »

And as I made my inner « inventory », I had suddenly realized that although I was willing to leave to God the reins of my life, I, Patrice, was continuing to manage it. I continued to decide what I would do in one month, two months, six months or even more, because at that time, my agenda was always filled nearly a year in advance.

I realized that I had a contradictory behaviour where God was concerned. A behaviour which I <u>had</u> to change !

Please understand. It is a bit as if I was asking him :

-« Please, tell me what I am, what I must do, where and how... **BUT**, I am a teacher of Eye Sight Improvement and in five weeks, I will be in Paris,... in six weeks, I will be in Lyon,... in seven weeks, I will be in Noumea,... in nine weeks, I will be in Sydney,... then in Papeete... and so on... and so on... ».

How did I expect God to guide me if I had months ahead already decided for him what I was or what I was going to be !

We were in August 1997 and I already « knew » where I would be in April or May 1998 !

I had to **totally** surrender to him...

So that the mechanism which led me to this reflection appears clear to you, I will explain here certain dimensions which we have not explored yet.

Each of us have three principal aspects : the body, the mind and the spirit.

The body refers obviously to our physical body but also to the physical world with what people perceive as being the laws of physics *(a cause out there produces an effect out there)*

The mind and the spirit represent the non-physical aspects of our being and also realities which we could call Metaphysical since « beyond » physical.

Indeed, you do realize that you are not your body, since you say « *It is MY body* ». You are therefore the consciousness which is in this body and this consciousness has two principal aspects that I call the Mind and the Spirit.

The Spirit represents the consciousness of existing as an individual, the consciousness of being... It is the one and only point common to all of us, we are all aware of existing in the form of a consciousness having experiences. Each of us can say « I Am ». This consciousness of being « I Am » is what I call « the spirit ».

And when we were each of us babies, that is all that we were... We were simply being what we were, which is, a consciousness of being « I Am ». And we were then fully ourselves and, if we were happy, the whole world knew about it and if we were unhappy, the whole world was also informed ! You understand ?...

And when we were simply this « I Am », thanks to the mind, thanks to the intellect, this other part of us, this tool which we all have in the « I am », we LEARNED. And little by little, we learned how to define ourselves in terms of what we learned either by our own experiences, or by the beliefs that our parents or our society reflected on us. And thus I, who in the beginning was only this « I Am », which means a consciousness being aware of existing, I learned that this « I am » is « Patrice, who is boy,… who can do that… but not that ! because it is « difficult » and so on… and so on…» Thus I « was formed » with the image that I believed I was… And in this way, each one of us developed what is called a « personality » around what we really are, that is, the consciousness of being « I am ». This « personality » is in fact an image of ourselves which has been constructed according to beliefs or past experiences.

Sometimes, this personality is in accord with the spirit and in that case, everything is well,… The person is happy…

Sometimes and I must unfortunately say often,… the personality is **not in accord** with the spirit… and that is where illnesses start, to « wake us up » and attract our attention.

Thus, with the problems of eyesight for example, any person with an eyesight problem has developed a way of being, a personality which is not in accord with his/her spirit. The type of sight that he/she has developed *(nearsightedness, farsightedness, astigmatism, and so on…)* shows how that person « has lost sight » of what he/she was… and therefore what is necessary for him/her to restore balance.

For my part, I had been clearly aware that my personality was not in harmony with my spirit and I therefore learned more and more to be really myself.

But, thereafter, on my path, I had DECIDED what I was. I started TO CREATE myself such as I wanted to be and… fortunately for me !

I had wanted to become a teacher of Healing… And I became one !

I had wanted to travel the word…and I did it !

Love is the Key...

And that was great ! And that was right for me at the time…

However, my realizations made me more and more aware of this part of me deep within : my spirit. This spirit which, is naturally aware of its divine creative nature…

And I knew that this « spirit » which is what I am in the deepest part of me was a consciousness quite different from my personality. A consciousness much more beautiful, much more limitless … and of which I could obviously not have any « idea » because an « idea of me » would instantaneously be limited to this form, you understand… And I was determined to experience that part of me.

That divine part of which Jesus Himself said it is within ourselves[1].

And if I wanted to really experience it, I WAS TO STOP DEFINING MYSELF and TO STOP DECIDING IN ADVANCE WHO « I AM ».

It was the only way of letting the Universe show me who « I am », if that « I am » does not decide in advance what it is *(because if it does, it will be it !).*

I hope you are still following me !

And this was the reason why I decided to stop giving workshops. And although I took great pleasure in them, I realized that, perhaps, I was meant to do something else on earth. I had to be willing to release this aspect of me… and all others besides…

Anyway, I was approaching my 35th year and I felt that I had to question my whole life again ! Something had to change ! It is true that at the age of 28, I had retired from the world of work and dramatically changed my life but, now, after nearly 7

---

[1] In Luke 17:20-21, Jesus tells us : « The kingdom of God cometh not with observation: Neither shall they say, Lo here! or, lo there! for, behold, the kingdom of God is within you . »

years of teaching week after week, I realized that I had got into a kind of « routine », pleasant it is true, but nevertheless a routine which I MUST end.

I took a firm decision to stop giving workshops, unless I was specifically asked.

It was my way of saying to God :

-« You see, I believed that my role on Earth was to give courses in personal transformation… but I was perhaps mistaken… so, I am willing to stop it all… and if it is really my path, you will make it happen that people will call me to give classes… and if this is not my path,… well, I will do something else… I will follow the signs which you put in my path… »

I thus decided that I would give all the classes which I had programmed until May or June 1998 *(because they were planned… and many people expected my services)* but to plan no other workshop afterwards…

Therefore I decided not to « force » things anymore concerning classes in the USA.

So I freed my diary of the 3 weeks in October which had been « reserved » for these classes and I decided to use them to instead to return to India.

Obviously, I had at that time no idea of how I could get there, having no financial means, but I had learned to trust…

I had also learned that the best way to obtain something is not to need it. Indeed, if we think that we need to see clearly or to have this or that to be happy, we are proving by this declaration our limited nature… Indeed, by this declaration, we affirm that our happiness depends on something and that, if we do not have it, we are unhappy… However, being by nature unlimited beings, it is important, if we want something, that we realize that we do not **really** need it … In fact, we must simply say that it is a desire… That it would be good if we could do this or have that… BUT THAT WE CAN BE HAPPY WITHOUT IT, **SINCE** OUR HAPPINESS DOES NOT DEPEND ON ANY EXTERNAL CIRCUMSTANCES !

I had therefore formulated my request to God like this:

-« Listen, I would really like to be able to go to India for my 35th birthday and to see Saï Baba again, and I know that, for You, everything is possible (even if I really do not know how it would be at this moment !). And if it does not happen, never mind ! But I would REALLY like to go there and I would be very happy to be there…».

Once my request formulated, I was therefore to act as if it was to happen…

Remember in fact :

-« What things soever ye desire, when ye pray, believe that ye receive them, and ye shall have them. »[1]

And in order to prepare myself the best possible for my meeting with Saï Baba, I decided to prepare myself both physically and spiritually. I decided that, from September 9 to October 9, the date of my birthday, I was going to change my food so that my body would be as « pure » as possible. I decided to eat exclusively for one month raw vegetables and fruits, and in order to channel my sexual energy for my transformation, I decided to practise total abstinence during this preparatory month.

Considering the district where I lived in and the quantity of attractive young men that I came across each day, it was quite an interesting experience which enabled me to test my determination…

You can imagine a pastry cook going on a hunger strike for one month inside his pastry shop !

---

[1] Mark 11:24

However, my spiritual evolution being my first priority… I held out.

When I arrived in France at the end of September, I was however to realize bitterly that I had no means to go to India. My financial situation was pretty catastrophic and although two training courses were planned in the weeks preceding my birthday, they could in no way cover my bank overdraft and the plane ticket for India.

Thinking that my trip would be impossible, for lack of money, I felt bad. Really bad. I told myself:

-« But what that is the use of depriving yourself for « Him »… Finally, all of that, is bullshit… Look,… you don't have enough money to pay for your plane ticket,… Go ahead, … break out…Get laid, eat what you want... »

However, I was aware that this voice spoke to me was wrong… I knew that it was a « temptation » testing my faith.

And each time this voice of doubt spoke to me, I centred myself and prayed as follows :

-« Listen, I <u>still</u> believe that with You, everything is possible… Please, I would really like to be in India for my 35th birthday ! Help me…».

Somewhere, I had accepted the idea that I could not go to India and it is probably all that was needed to resolve the situation. It was again just like my instructive trip to London[1]…

And as I went to Lyon to give a workshop there, I went to visit Pierre and Claude-Annie with whom I had become friendly. Pierre had explained me that he had developed a revolutionary process for treating sound and that he was looking for funds to finance his research. At the time, I had helped him to contact various people who, in my opinion, might be interested by such a project.

---

[1] See Chapter 12

I had quite a surprise when I asked for the latest news :

-« Your contacts were interested by my products and it seems that we are going to work together. Here, here is a commission to thank you for your help... »

And he gave me a cheque for 10 000 francs (about 1 500 €) !

Immediately, I realized that I could go to India... It was Friday 3rd October, 1997 and my birthday was 6 days away... Everything was still possible...

So I bought my ticket Friday afternoon in Lyon. At the travel agency, they explained that there were only three available seats left on this aircraft... Once more, I had what many perceive as « luck »...

Monday morning, after my class in Lyon, I was in Paris at the Indian Embassy to request my visa, which I picked up Tuesday afternoon.

On Wednesday morning, I was on the plane to India... and on Thursday October 9 at 12 noon, on my 35th birthday, just as I had wished, I was in the *Ashram* of Saï Baba in Puttaparthi...

Once more, I realized everything was really possible...

But I now realized that everything is possible, <u>through the Grace of God...</u>

Indeed, by myself, I would never have imagined that such a thing was possible.

And I realized more and more that by surrendering in trust to the principles of my dear *Swami*, I was surrendering to God, who was fulfilling me beyond my dreams...

And He had still many gifts for me !

CHAPTER 32
My second stay with *Swami*...

When I arrived at *Prashanti Nilayam*, which is the name of *Ashram* of Puttaparthi and means « Residence of Supreme Peace », I was immediately impressed by its size... It was like a city within the city...

And as I noticed the size of the place, I understood better who Saï Baba was, or rather what He was.

If it is by observing its fruits that one can judge a tree[1], I realized more and more the beauty of the Tree called Saï Baba.

I was told that He had created many free schools, that He had supplied drinking water to hundreds of poor villages by building wells, that He built many hospitals, schools and clinics... The list was long... and all the centres which He set up were <u>totally</u> free... Clearly, the fruits of Saï Baba were very beautiful fruits.

During this stay, I was to find that *Swami* was closer to me ... and although there were more than 10,000 people present each day, I was given the Grace to see him get closer to me every day, which only encouraged me to seek in my heart to be always closer to God.

I had read the story of a man who had experienced a radical transformation[2] thanks to *Swami*. He explained in his book, That as he got closer and closer to God, in his heart, he clearly noticed a greater physical proximity with Baba.

And this is exactly what I was experiencing

The more I became close to God in my heart and in my consciousness..., the more Saï Baba gave me the Grace to come closer to me.

---

[1] Matthew 7:16-18 « Ye shall know them by their fruits.... » Matthew 12:33 « for the tree is known by his fruit. ... ». Luke 6:44 « For every tree is known by his own fruit. ».

[2] « *Saï Baba: The Holy Man and Psychiatrist* » is a book by Samuel Sandweiss published by Vedic Books.

And I understood how the Master or the *Guru*, who is, by his purified consciousness., nearer to God, serves Him as an intermediary so that He speaks to us and transforms us through the Master who is a bit like his messenger... However, with Saï Baba, the process is different again, since He is a Divine *Avatar*.

I understood by observing *Swami* each day that He really represented my potential and everything I was becoming !

One day as He was very far away from me, on the women's side, I remember looking at Him approaching and feeling this certainty :

-« Actually, it is You who are my Real Father... ».

And a few minutes later, He passed in front of me, and graced me with some *Vibhuti*[1] which He was manifesting.

I swallowed this blessed ash which had a slight taste of condensed milk and again, I was transported into this transcendental consciousness which was now becoming almost familiar to me.

And while I was transported by these waves of indescribable love, I imagined and I knew that, through this *Vibhuti*, I was being healed and transformed...

It was in the afternoon of that day that I realized, amazing synchronicity, it was in fact October 23rd , my « true » father's birthday...

---

[1] The *Vibhuti* is the sacred ash used in Hinduist rituals... It is traditionally made from cow bouse mixed with *Ghee* (clarified butter) and sweet-smelling plants and slowly burned in a ritual in which *Mantras* are sung. It symbolises the fact that we are made from ash and will return to ash. Il also symbolizes what is left of us when our ego is burned in the fire of « devotion ». It also represents that part of us which is eternal and unchangeable, which is what the Indians call the *Atma* or the unique Soul, sometimes called God... It is used symbolically daubed on the forehead (as Catholics do on Ash Wednesday) or swallowed. Saï Baba manifests a great quantity each day. When He chooses to give some to someone, it is always symbolic. It is either for that person to ponder on his true nature, or to encourage him/her in his/her practice or for his/her physical or spiritual healing. Indeed, many people have undergone spectacular physical or spiritual healings thanks to this *Vibhuti*...

Again one of *Swami*'s *Leelas* ...

Obviously, for someone who has been close to and knows Saï Baba and his way of « talking » to us by signs, these synchronicities quickly seem natural.

When two days later, *Swami* gave me some *Vibhuti* again, some people who saw this came to tell me :
-« Say, did you have something in you that needs healing? ... because if it was the case, do not worry anymore, by giving you some Vibhuti twice, Swami is taking care of you... »

And whereas during my first stay at *Swami's* feet, I had had no physical contact with him, except the « indirect contact » when He took the letters, during this second voyage, *Swami* was much more close to me...

Already, from the second day, when He again took the letters I had to give Him, I had the good fortune that He lightly brushed my right ring finger, and a sublime energy instantly filled and transported me as I closed my eyes.

I realize that it could be difficult for some to understand how such a light contact,... so subtle... and so fast, could trigger such effects... I can only wish from all my heart that one day you have the grace to experience it too...

Over the next days, as I was in the *Ashram*, I was able to touch his robe, then His feet, which was a splendid experience[1]..., until He manifested twice more some *Vibhuti*...

Each day, *Swami* chose from the crowd some people who had the Grace of being received by Him in private for half an hour to one hour.

All the people whom I had seen who had been received in this « interview » said how much it had changed their lives...

---

[1] When you touch a Master's feet, (*Padanamaskar*), automatically, his energy flows through you via potential differential...

And as each day, I prayed to *Swami* in my heart to grant me an interview, the day before my departure I had the Grace of a almost-verbal interaction with Him.

As He passed close to me, I said to him in English:

-« *Swami, can you grant us an interview ?... »*

And as He moved away, He looked at me and made a sign with his hand and a glance which clearly meant: « Yes... but wait... ».

I exalted with Joy since I had his promise...

I just did not know when it was going to manifest !...

For those of you who have never been to see Saï Baba, it can seem exaggerated to have such a reaction to a sign from Him apparently so « small ».

However, when you find yourself with tens of thousands of people who, like you, are each one awaiting a sign from Swami... a simple glance is already perceived as an immense good fortune...

Then imagine what it is like if He can gives you the Grace of : (and here, I will « classify » the Graces in order of importance...)

- Giving you what is called a « personal Darshan» as He looks at you for a few seconds.

- Coming so close to you that you can touch His Robe.

- Coming so close that you can touch His feet.

- Talking to you straight through His Eyes.

- Hearing him say something to someone... (Oh, yes, this too, is considered a Grace, because tradition says a Master never does anything by chance and whatever He says or does has a great symbolic importance for the one who sees it or hears it !)

- Talking to you or even better, touching you...

In fact, the closer the Master is to you, the more it is considered a « great » Grace.

I can obviously understand that this concept can seem very strange for a Westerner who is not familiar with Hinduism and with <u>the reality of the extraordinary energy which emanates from a Master, a Saint or an *Avatar*</u> !

This is unfortunately the problem of transcendental experiences which are by their very nature subjective, so that only the one who has experienced them can really understand them.

However, no need to go as far as India, those amongst you who know Marthe Robin[1] have , I think, heard of the effects that her simple presence caused for the people going to see Her.

After three blessed weeks spent in the presence of Baba, I finally returned to France, reinforced in my faith, transformed again and ready to move to another step in my life.

---

[1] Marthe Robin is a woman who bore the stigmata of the Christ and who lived for years fed only by a sacramental wafer and a teaspoon of water... Some books tell about her extraordinary path...

CHAPTER 33
A new Departure...

Once back in France, I met Martin again to translate one of the classes he was giving.

He had offered to me, years before, when I became a teacher of his method, a very beautiful Tibetan ring bearing a large lapis lazuli. It was his custom to offer it to each new instructor.

But I was feeling more and more resistance to teaching according to the structure which he had developed, feeling trapped inside it, unable to express the truths which seemed now obvious to me. So I had decided, months before, to take it off, and no longer wore this ring which now symbolized for me the « mental prison » in which I had let myself be locked.

And as with great pleasure I saw Martin again, whom I had not seen for months, he invited me to follow him.

Once in his room, he went to his suitcase and took out a small packet that he handed to me. I opened it, and discovered ... a ring !

I asked him :

-«But why are you giving me this ring ? »

He answered :

-« Well I was sorting out my things and when I found it, I immediately thought that it was for you ! »

When I asked him whether he knew that some months ago I had symbolically removed the ring he had initially offered me, he admitted that he didn't.

I personally found this synchronicity quite amusing.

At the time when I was detaching myself from Martin's method, it was somehow as if he had felt it and this new ring he was offering me was symbolic of taking me under his wing again.

At that time and still to this date, I have nothing against Martin and the man he is. Quite to the contrary, he is a being whom I love, deeply admire and respect for what is as well as what he has achieved. I think that his method is and remains a wonderful tool of self-knowledge and of transformation.

What was happening was simply that, thanks to him, I « had grown » and that I was no longer able to teach according to his model.

And as Martin himself had done years before, when he « left » the post of teacher of the « Silva Method », I too had to fly with my own wings, thanks to what I had learned from him. Like him at the time, I had to feel free to teach according to what my heart was telling me.

Having expressed this to Martin, I explained that I would keep my commitment and give the classes which were planned until the end of December 97 « according to his structure », and that from January 1998, I would start to fly with my own wings.

It is thus in December 1997 that my professional collaboration with Martin came to a close.

Surprisingly, I had spent 9 years exactly working with and for Martin.

For those of you who know numerology or the study of the numbers, it is said that each year is under the influence of a particular figure. So, for example, when you are in a « 1 » year, you begin a new cycle, and it is often a period of significant upheavals in your life. This cycle lasts 9 years and is completed obviously with the year « 9 ».

By another of these astonishing synchronicities, I had met Martin exactly 9 years before and had started to work with him as I began one year 1, a new cycle. And it is true that it really marked the beginning of a new life for me !

And as if, 9 years later, the cycle was being completed *(and it was clear that for me, it was)*, I left him, ready to begin another cycle…

Leaving the structure of Martin enabled me to make modifications to the classes, to lower the price and to explore with the participants some of the fields which I could not broach in the past.

I had, since the month of July, drastically slowed down my activities and I was determined to not work any more at my old pace. Obviously, very quickly, I was to face a sudden drop in income.

However, I was determined not to make compromises for money.

I was determined to surrender in confidence to God and to voluntarily cut off from « earning a crust »…

It seems to me easy to say *« I trust in God… »* when one has all that one wants… And it is true that this was my case…

In the past I had made certain decisions about myself, deciding that I was a teacher of healing, deciding that my diary would be blocked a year in advance, deciding that I would teach in the Dom-Tom, and so on… and all that…, I had done that …

Somehow it was as if it wasn't fun anymore !

If God gives me all that I want, I started to ask me a question which seemed much more interesting to me :

-« What would God give me, if I did not ask him ANYTHING ?».

In addition, I was REALLY aware I was where I was by my own will and I was rather proud of it… It is after all, thanks to that that I could have this credibility with my students. I was really aware of what I had been in the past and I fully realized that if I had become what I was, it was because, bit by bit, I had created myself like that… And this obviously gave me a very strong conviction which enabled me to encourage the participants in my classes to do the same.

I could tell them in all sincerity :

-« Decide what you want to be or what you want to experience and… do it… become it !... »

But now that I had reached 35, I knew that I had to radically change my life again.

I wanted to let God reveal to me who I really was and I decided to stop claiming I knew who I was.

Indeed, I had arbitrarily defined myself as a teacher of healing, whereas my path was perhaps elsewhere…

By deciding to stop organizing my classes myself, I allowed God to reveal myself to myself. I was working from the principle that if healing was really my path and it was right for it to be my activity, that would be shown to me.

From January 1998, there « remained » 5 or 6 classes for me to give and I was determined not to program any others. I was determined to simply « answer » the Universe and to give classes only if people organized themselves to invite me over to share my ideas and my experiences with them.

I wanted to put my back to the wall, to cut myself off from my revenues and to see what would happen if I stopped putting my security in a well-filled diary, and transferred it to what seemed more and more to be the true absolute reality : God.

Very soon, the drop in my income obliged me to leave the apartment where I had lived alone in since Hervé was no longer there. I felt that it was a good thing because this place was so charged with memories that it could only be good to leave it. However, where was I to go ?

For several months, I lived here and there, camping in my brother and my sister-in-law's place between my trips.

This is where Pierre and Claude-Annie, whom I had met a few months before, started to come into my life.

Having made friends with Pierre, I had helped him to meet people who could allow him to develop the technologies that he had invented. This way, I had learned to know him better and to appreciated the astonishing being that he was. He explained me how, thanks to his particular attitude towards Life, ideas,… inventions… would spontaneously come into his head as he meditated and made an empty space within him… I felt that what he did was profoundly right and that he was right… That there was really nothing to do except « to allow things to happen ».

And as I opened up to Pierre about my changes, he explained me that he had a house that he used exclusively to produce the prototypes of his inventions and to present them to the public, and that he would be happy to put me up there.

I had at first a huge resistance to accepting his offer for reasons of pride. However, I had made a choice… and I must assume the consequences of it…

I had decided to stop giving classes and I had to assume the financial consequences of it and to trust God.

And after all, perhaps Pierre's invitation was a sign from Him!

After a few months, I decided to accept Pierre's proposal and to move to the Lyon area.

Today, I think that it is one of the best decisions than I ever made.

Once arrived, I discovered a charming house perched on a small hill. Although it was more of a workshop and a « show-room » for Pierre to present his products, I had on the first floor a bedroom, an office and a bathroom.

Living each day near Pierre and Claude Annie, I started to better understand the products that he had developed and to comprehend the commercial value of what he had invented.

As time passed by, I contributed more and more to designing prototypes, researching materials, imagining evolutions of his concepts… and this work was very pleasant. Moreover, I did not give any classes anymore and I had plenty of time at my disposal.

One day, Pierre explained me that his researches were expensive and asked me whether I would like to join his group to finance him. He said that if I could finance him, he would include me in his group with his other sponsors.

I found his project fascinating and his products brilliant but, I did not really have funds. And especially, the saving which I had were used to compensate for my lack of income now that I did not give my classes any more …

In addition, Pierre did not tell me at all how I would be included nor did he provide any of the recognized « guarantees » in this world such as a contract or a document attesting to my « concrete » participation in his project.

However, I was aware that through Pierre, an opportunity was being offered to me to really completely surrender to the Universe.

I had recognized in Pierre a being filled of Love, fundamentally good and in whom I could trust. It just remained to DEMONSTRATE this to him through my actions…

I felt that I should show him my confidence by some physical action.

I reconsidered the deep fear that had seized me after I had my first « contact by letter » with *Swami*.

When I left the *Ashram* that day, having consciously and conscientiously surrendered my life at the feet of God, I had thought :

-« And if God asked you all of your money… If He asked you to sign a blank check ? What you would do… ? Would you trust… ? »

Somewhere, I felt that this opportunity that Pierre was presenting me was a test from the Universe… That thanks to Pierre, I was going to be able to « demonstrate » into the physical world my real willingness to surrender everything to God.

When I asked him how much he needed for his research, he announced that initially, 50.000 francs (about 7 600 €) would do the deal…

Within, I thought, without daring to say it:

-« *Initially ! ?... Does that mean you will need more ! ?* »

However, feeling the opportunity provided by this « spiritual exercise », I decided to give it to him.

I remember the day when I wrote him the cheque. We were in the INPI[1] applying for the patent. And although I felt that the technologies he had developed were very good, I also knew a patent is worth nothing until it is exploited… On the other hand, a patent costs a lot of money before being exploited… And I was panicking about giving him this amount that represented a lot for me, and also about thus becoming the owner of a patent that was may be going to cost me even more…

Finally, I let go by saying, once more :

-«*Trust…* ».

---

[1] INPI NIIP (National Institute of Industrial Property). It is the body, in France, that deals with the registering of trade marks and/or patents.

As time went by, getting more and more involved in Pierre's project, I had to personally pay some of the bills which arrived regularly…

Then, little by little, I « broke into » the savings accounts which I had and transferred these sums to Pierre's profit.

Finally, research being quite expensive, my house went into it.

I had remained owner with Myriam of the small house which we had bought together but, the expenses related to the patents and research were such that I had to help Pierre. It seemed now obvious to me that at the stage where we were, we could not turn back.

I was more and more convinced of the beauty of our products and we had to hold on !

I thus decided to sell my share of the house to Myriam. However, the transaction not going quickly enough, I obtained from my bank an overdraft, which seemed to me colossal now that I did not have any more income… and again, I financed Pierre…

And little by little, everything went into it ! At times, I was really frightened !

However, each day, everything was going well… And if I decided to travel, in one way or another, it all went well !

I remember one day when I wanted to « pop up » to Paris. I however had only 30 francs (about 5 €) in my pocket ! And in a completely crazy way, the Universe organized itself so that my trip became possible…

And every day it was like that !

Mind you, I am not saying that it was easy !…

But what was undeniable, is that it worked !

Obviously, I spent A LOT of time in front of my altar calling upon Saï Baba or Jesus or whoever wanted to hear me up there ! But it worked !

I REALLY realized, CONCRETELY, that everything I had came from God… and this realization filled with gratitude…

And as I was very often with Pierre and Claude-Annie, I also learned to let myself receive… Indeed, when I was with them in a restaurant, it was always them who paid, which made me feel very uncomfortable as time went by. There was however no sign in them of false or power in inviting me, just the pleasure of sharing a meal with me… And I was very touched each time.

I remember the last « official » class, that is, arbitrarily organized, that I gave in Lyon. Pierre had come to join me once the workshop was completed.

And as I had just earned some money, I was proud to invite Pierre to dinner, since for once, it was possible for me to do it.

We had a small salad and a drink. And as, very proudly, I was going to pay the bill, the waiter handed me a bill for the amount of 108 francs !

Immediately recognizing the number associated with the Divine principle, I instantly understood the message that *Swami* was sending me !

-« Who are you to believe that it is YOU inviting Pierre ?... (And there, it was as if I heard Amma again when she said some years before : You believe that you do but you do nothing…) It is I, the divine principle inviting Pierre… It is Me who give you what you need… so that you can live what you want to live. !... »

Once again I learned a lesson of humility and I was again filled with gratitude towards God who indeed, had just given me the money so that I could now invite Pierre.

And I had to recognize that this voice that spoke to me was right !

It was true because my experience was showing me more and more that I really was supported by God who provided for my needs, sometimes in completely astounding ways …

But I had still a lot to learn.

Some time later, I was returning from Paris where I had given my last workshop. There had been a lot of participants and I was filled with gratitude towards God because, for the first time in months, I would have some money « to put aside ». I was up to date with the bills for the patents and the last products ordered for our prototypes had been paid. At last, I had 12 000 francs (about 1 800 €) which would be « MINE »...

Indeed, in the past, even the money that I gained from the classes was immediately swallowed up in the research, the costs of the patents and the prototypes…

And while I was driving, happy to « possess » this amount, the telephone rang :

-« Patrice, hello, this is Pierre… Listen, there is a very important transfer to make to a certain person… Would you be able to make a funds transfer? »

When I asked him for the amount, he announced that it was 12 000 francs !

Again, one of those marvellous synchronicities… and a marvellous lesson…

As I was clinging again to a material security, God called me to order and immediately withdrew my « little security cushion ».

Despite a small pinch when I made the transfer, again finding me with my entire savings being what I had in my pocket, some forty or fifty francs, I realized that it was right… It was necessary for me to go through this experience of TOTAL surrender so that, now, I KNOW, not like before, in a intellectual way, but now <u>through my direct experience, THAT GOD WILL **NEVER** ABANDON ME !</u>

Indeed, it was all very fine knowing something, but what use is it as an intellectual knowledge if I do not live it !

And I had accumulated a lot of knowledge !

But what was the use of it ?

NOTHING !

Except to flatter my ego as I poured it onto my students…

And I had learned, thanks to *Swami,* that the mind was a tool which could either free me, or chain me.

It is, moreover, one of the reasons for which I had decided to stop teaching. Indeed, following my trips in India, I had realized that for years, I had taught people to leave the mental prison in which they were locked up and, it is true that I had been able to help many of them to get out. However, thanks to the help of *Swami*, I now started to see the bars of my own prison !

Who was I to <u>dare</u> pretend to free them when I was myself in prison ?

I realized obviously more and more that Amma had been right when she said that I did not do anything.

I noticed it when I saw this love filling me and radiating from me as it permanently transformed the people it touched.

I realized that my feeling of « I » had to disappear so that I function more and more as an open channel through which the Great Being could flow and express its splendour.

Another reason which meant that I was uneasy teaching was this:

I had taught like Martin according to the concept of bubbles.

I used to explain that each of us lives in a bubble which is the filter of our perceptions. This bubble is a paradigm,… a reality… It is formed by the sum of the beliefs which we hold about ourselves or the world, and it determines our experiences.

I would then explain that if I am not happy in my bubble, I can change bubbles…

For example, if I am in a bubble in which I see blurred, I can change the image which I have of myself and change my perceptions, and thus change my bubble for one in which I see clearly.

And while I thought about this concept of bubbles such as Martin presented it, I thought about Champagne and its bubbles….

And I wondered :

-« *But why are there bubbles in Champagne ?* »

And the answer was obviously given to me. There are bubbles **because there is a substance** in which they can exist ! A substance which exists **before** the bubble can take shape in it… Without the Champagne, there would be no bubbles….

And in Champagne, they are many bubbles !

Bubbles in which for example I see blurred,… bubbles in which I see clearly without glasses… Bubbles in which I have good luck,… bubbles of which I do not have any… Bubbles in which I am in « bad » health,… bubbles in which I am in « good » health… Bubbles in which I am « sad », bubbles in which I am « happy »…

However, what is the nature of a bubble ?

It is ephemeral, it lasts only a moment and bursts at the surface… It is finally only an « illusion » within the « reality » which is Champagne.

And I wanted to taste Champagne !

I realized that I had amused myself for years moving from one bubble to another but that now, I wanted more... Much more....

I also realized that during these years, I had also encouraged other people to move from one bubble to another.

To move from a bubble in which they saw blurred into a bubble in which they saw more clearly without glasses...

But what did I **really** do ?

I helped them move from one « illusion » into an other « illusion ».

And to this day, as more and more former participants contact me to give classes again and share my experiences with them, I have much pleasure in doing it... However, I prefer more and more to speak about the reality of God than of the illusion of His bubbles... Even if they are fascinating...

However, I realize that there are around me people who, like you perhaps, really want to change their bubble... or experience another reality...

I also know that there are people who prefer to explore the bubbles rather than the Champagne...

And, after all, why not ?... If they want to ?...

But I am sure that there are also other people out there who **really** want to experience the taste of Champagne in which the bubbles can exist....

And after all, since God gives me the possibility of experiencing what I want... as I want it... everything is possible... and everything is good !..

And on the other hand : « What would Champagne be without its bubbles ? ? ? ! »

They are what makes Champagne interesting. Without them, it would just be a flat little wine !...

The bubbles are in fact just one of the multiple aspects of Champagne,… Just as the plus and minus sign, Yang and Yin, hot and cold, man and woman, « good » and « evil » are just some of the multiple aspects of God...

I feel filled with gratitude as I realize more and more the perfection of the Universe, of God and of everything He does…

I realize more and more that if He placed me in a particular bubble, there is a reason for that and that I do not have to want to change it. Because if I WANT to change my bubble, I am refusing the perfection of the Universe… I am « believing » that what I live is not perfect…

Now, if God made me in His image, He made me perfect.

And if the creation is made in the image of its creator, the creation and the whole world must also be perfect !

So, where is the problem ?

Once again in my perception ! In my point of view!

The world is by nature dual.

We need « cold » in order to experience « hot ». We need « hot » in order to experience « cold ».

We need « bad » in order to experience « good ». We need « good » in order to experience « bad ».

We need « sickness » in order to experience « health ». We need « health » in order to experience « sickness ».

We need « sadness » in order to experience « happiness ». We need « happiness » in order to experience « sadness »….

The one cannot exist without the other…

The « problem » is that if I decide that something is « good », I am at the same time deciding that something else is « bad ».

God is neither good, nor evil, neither heat, nor cold, neither disease, nor health, neither the top, nor the bottom, neither man, nor woman... He is the sum of all of that... and much more still... Each polarity represents only One aspect of God. The whole Universe is the demonstration of God but no part of this Universe can be regarded as being Divine or not Divine. All is God. Nothing exists without its opposite...

I must therefore accept everything, assimilate everything, integrate everything, unify everything if I want to experience this consciousness called God.

And this is something we find hard to accept...

Why ?

Because we all have a certain picture of happiness...

And yet, when the Universe manifests it for us and allows us to live this happiness, very quickly, we become dissatisfied, we want more...

Again, why ?

Well, because **NOTHING** in the physical Universe can satisfy us in a lasting way except our relation with what we really are, that is, this creative consciousness, this consciousness of love that some call God...

Which does not mean that I must separate myself arbitrarily from the physical world and its pleasures because, in doing so, I would be separating from an aspect of God.

I must live into this world while remaining aware of its True illusory nature.

And somehow, the fact of accepting my Divine nature makes me « not of the world ». It is not that I do not live in the world, but in fact, it is that I am no longer subject to the same laws as the rest of the world. My acceptance of God means that it is now divine laws which apply to me, and not the laws of the physical world.

Jesus talked about it very aptly when He said :

> *-« I have given them thy word; and the world hath hated them, because they are not of the world, even as I am not of the world.*
>
> *I pray not that thou shouldest take them out of the world, but that thou shouldest keep them from the evil. They are not of the world, even as I am not of the world. »*[1]

He explained that he who accepts the word of God is then « released » from the world and seems to become « different » from the rest of the world... This difference explains moreover why those who « integrate » the Divine word are often misunderstood and rejected by this same world. It is again what Jesus explains us when he says to his disciples :

> *-« If ye were of the world, the world would love his own: but because ye are not of the world, but I have chosen you out of the world, therefore the world hateth you.. »*[2]

Thus, once I have realized the nature of the world, I must continue to live in it, <u>but without</u> world « deciding » my state of consciousness. The world was created by God, out of Love for me, **but** it does not have to be my Master and I should not then be <u>the slave</u> of the world and its circumstances.

And as Saï Baba so rightly said :

-« A boat is designed to go on water but water should not get into it. In the same way, we are designed to live in the world, but the world should not invade us. »

Moreover, if the world were created in the image of its creator, it is thus perfect, in any time and any place...

The only thing which I lack then is the perception of the perfection of my world.

---

[1] John 17:14-16
[2] John 15:19

And I am sure that if I accept my « world », my reality, my bubble, as being perfect *(even if I notice that this perfection is not always harmonious)*, the fact that I release my perception of the imperfection will allow another form of more harmonious perfection to manifest for me <u>without me having to do anything</u> !

Actually, as it begins its ephemeral life, and emerges in the Champagne, the bubble is small, « tight », confined and it might even feel « unhappy » like that…

But if it lets go,… if it surrenders to its TRUE bubble nature,… if it trusts,… it will see that as it rises in the glass, it expands naturally and grows bigger… until bursting naturally onto the surface and becoming absorbed into the air which covers the whole planet.

And becoming again a particle of air making up the totality of air, it may then find itself, one day, will be ingested by bacteria at the bottom of a Champagne bottle so that again, it can feel it exists, « separated » again from the air of the planet, separating in the form of a bubble, an individualized consciousness of an ephemeral nature…

Little by little, I understood more and more things…

Thanks to *Swami*, thanks to Pierre and Claude Annie, I could see myself evolving greatly.

Pierre had, and still has, an exceptional consciousness of service.

Many times, he had to take me in hand when he saw me acting motivated by fear. And like a Master requiring of me <u>absolute</u> precision of my internal processes, he trained me to open myself more and more to God.

Sometimes, he reproached me in a manner that I perceived as extremely hurtful, as I came out of almost an hour of meditation and rituals of worship:

-« But what is the use of spending an hour praying if, for the rest of your day, you do any old thing with your thoughts !».

And in doing so, he was right !

I can today only thank him and give thanks to God to have placed him on my path !

Indeed, I came out of my prayers filled with joy and as soon as I lit the computer on, or looked at the bills piling up, I « freaked out » completely, filled with fear about the future of the patents…

The twisted nail that I had been needed some good hammer blows in order to be straightened up again so that it could rediscover its lost beauty.

One day, Pierre had to give me a particularly violent « hammer blow ».

It was as I was giving one of my last workshops in Lyon area, several months after I had moved there.

Coming back on Saturday evening, I found on my desk a terrible letter…

In it, Pierre reproached me for my lack of balance and told me that such « energy » was intolerable for the products and the projects we had for them…

I was in tears as I read this letter and I must say I had trouble getting to sleep that night !

When I woke up on Sunday morning, I felt really bad !

Nevertheless, I had to present a day of class..

Now, Sunday was an extremely important day as I would then start talking about more spiritual realities. I absolutely <u>had</u> to be in good shape for my students.

It is true that as a teacher, I am a bit like a locomotive carrying each participant into my reality so that they « visit it ».

Love is the Key...

And that Sunday morning, I can tell you that the engine which I was supposed to be was not beautiful to see !

And while I was driving towards Givors where the class was taking place, I wondered how I was going to present this day, feeling so bad, with this letter which turned over and over in my thoughts...

This is when I thought of *Swami* and of the way he told us to surrender our problems at His feet.

And as I was driving, I imagined Swami before me and I told him :

-« Here, Swami, I have received this letter from Pierre, I cannot deal with it anymore, I lay it before your feet, take it please ! »

And AT THE MOMENT I abandoned this letter to Him, I « heard » him say :

> -« *But why do you return it to me ?, it is I who sent it to you !* »

And at that very second, suddenly understanding, I was exultant with joy, a marvellous happiness filled me up and overflowed from me...

But of course, all this, was the Divine plan...

And I must say that in a second, I had **COMPLETELY** forgotten the state of distress in which I had been.

This is the MAGIC of the Grace of God....

There is no distress, no sorrow, no sadness that God cannot comfort,... if you give it to Him...

There is no disease which He cannot heal, no burden that He cannot reduce, no problem that he cannot solve... **IF** you give them to Him... .

Swami sometimes explained this mechanism in an amusing way. He would say :

> -« *I tell people to surrender all their problems to me... therefore they do it... and as they leave their problems at my feet, I take them... Yes, but afterwards, they take them back again...*
>
> *So... I give them back... »*

Learn also to surrender everything and to abandon everything to God...

And he will give you EVERYTHING !

And I was to spend a wonderful day with my students that day.

When I rang Pierre that evening, I told him in a amused tone :

> -« *Good evening Swami (thus recognizing the role that he had played !) and* <u>thank you</u> *for your letter... »*

And he instantly said :

> -« *Ah,... good,... you passed... you understood the message... and your energy is now different... »*

I must explain that Pierre is an acoustics expert of a very high level who can, simply by listening to somebody speak, « feel » the blockages or the tensions that person has... In fact, our voice frequency is for him like a barometer of our psychic state...

My stay with Pierre and Claude Annie was both instructive and fascinating.

It was undeniable that in this burning crucible in which I was « worked » and « put through the mill » each day, I was transforming.

The impurities that polluted the Gold present deep inside my heart were little by little separated one by one, highlighted, and eliminated in the permanent melting pot which I experienced thanks to Pierre.

And I understood this process and accepted it, aware that everything that I was experiencing was the result of <u>my</u> deep decisions for transformation.

It is what sometimes makes me say to my students that, what is super about the process of transformation, it is that the more you feel good,… the more you feel bad…

Please understand me : the more I feel good… and the more I become aware of my potential… the more I experience at the same time all <u>these little details</u> which show that I am not yet at my optimum ! … And so I have the impression of feeling bad… But it is only an impression and this process is in fact marvellous. We must <u>see and experience</u> our impurities so we can then choose consciously to release them and not to manifest them anymore…

It is true that sometimes, it was very hard and I was at the verge of cracking up, dropping it all and leaving Pierre to manage it all alone…

But fortunately, in these times there, I had *Swami* with me. I had in me the memory of the experiments lived by Him and the certainty that beyond my perception of appearances, all was well. I was certain that, via Pierre, *(that I sometimes also put at hard test)*, *Swami* tested me and formed me. And this certainty enabled me to hold on.

I was not to regret it because, when afterwards , I returned to India, I noticed each time the progress I had made by seeing Saï Baba come increasingly close to me and granting me more and more Graces.

I had started a journey with no return, and I could not go back again…

And even if it is true that in fact, we can always go back, because God in his immense Love for us, authorizes everything we desire, including going away from Him, you understand that for my part, I certainly did not want to !

It would now be impossible for me *(and I give thanks here to God)* to function « as I did before »… As unfortunately the majority of the people on Earth still do…

Swami had taught me to give all of my problems to God, which I was doing more and more.

And because of that I had less and less problems.

And even if my circumstances of life could appear astonishing or difficult to people functioning with other values that mine, they were not for me. They simply resulted from a choice that I had made and that I assumed…

After more than a year spent with Pierre, we started to have interesting contacts for the future of our products. I say « our products » now since Pierre informed me one day that I was completely integrated into his team. Obviously, all of that had never been put onto paper… I never had any the safety measures which « normal » people could expect when they do business. But that was enough for me…

I trusted…

I trusted Pierre, who somehow was a catalyst of my first dream of *Swami*, the day we met… It is in fact that night that Saï Baba appeared to me in a dream[1].

And I trusted in *Swami*… and in God…

Thereafter, since it seemed that we were going to have to move, Pierre decided to let go the house where I was lodging.

Which made I found myself again without a place to stay….

I am aware that my life style could surprise many of you but I accepted in trust what I perceived again as a « test » that God was giving me.

And although some, not knowing the process I was going through, could see me as an SDF (**S**ans **D**omicile **F**ixe),

---

[1] See Chapter 28

(homeless person…) I preferred to see myself as an ELU…(Être Libre de l'Univers) (Free Being in the Universe…).

As the months passed by and that I was put up, sometimes here, sometimes there, I became aware more and more that I had everything within.

I had had professional security,… I had left it… and I was happy…

I had had financial security,… I had left it… and I was happy…

I had had an apartment,… I had left it… and I was happy…

I had had what people call a « life style » and I left it…and was happy…

I had had a house, left it and…I was happy…

I was travelling with my two suit cases in my car….sometimes here sometimes there, and I was happy…

As time went by, I realized that if one <u>of my two bags</u> was taken away, I would still be happy…

And some time later, I realized that actually, if <u>my two bags were taken away from me</u>, I would still be happy…

And as more time passed by, I realized THROUGH MY DIRECT EXPERIENCE that I could be happy without anything… except something that no-one will **ever** be able to take from me : **My relationship with God**.

Now, I really understand, and, not through an intellectual process, <u>but through my body</u>, why Jesus said :

-«*Destroy this temple and in three days, I will raise it up.*»[1]

I know now that if everything was taken away from me, I could rebuild EVERYTHING with what I have within.

---

[1] John 2:19

Because I have Love and Love can accomplish everything..

I have God and through Him everything is possible…

During my last trip to India, thanks to the presence of *Swami*, I was to live a magnificent experience during which I felt totally taken over by and taken care of by God.

The first time this experience was granted me, *Swami* had come much nearer than He had ever been during my previous visits since he took my left hand in his for many very long seconds…

And during this blessed moment, I <u>knew</u> that I was <u>really</u> and <u>totally</u> carried by God.

When He released my hand, it was impregnated with a really extraordinary odour. An indescribable aroma,… strong and soft at the same time…. A odour I had never smelled before… An « Odour of Holiness ». A Divine odour….

I was afterwards to have occasion to often smell this odour, because I was able many times either to touch Him, or be touched by *Swami* during this stay. And each time, this same Odour accompanied me for hours afterwards, whereas often, I had only touched *Swami* for a split second….

And I still remember the day when, as I was inhaling this divine perfume, I <u>KNEW</u> in that sacred second that this odour,… was God in His totality.

I <u>KNEW</u> that this odour was *Sat, Chit* and *Ananda*. That it was what one calls in India the three aspects of God : which in Sanskrit is Truth (*Sat*), Knowledge (*Chit*) and Bliss (*Ananda*).

And I knew that the only thing that I had to do, was to allow myself be filled by this « information », by this experience… And that it was enough… Indeed, I felt inside that all of my cells which, before, were orientated, or rather disorientated in any direction, were now re-orientating « around » this uniting « energy ». This odour brought me peace, knowledge and wisdom …

In addition, it was as if all my cells were waking up into the « frequency » that was this odour. Because this odour was also a « frequency », a « rhythm » that taught me,... that invited me too to function at this « frequency », at this rhythm...

I knew that the only thing that I had to do, was to allow myself to be carried into this consciousness to become it... this by the law of resonance about which we have already spoken.

And I knew that around this blessed consciousness, the whole Universe was orientating and was taking form for me, out of Love for me...

I knew then that that « frequency », that rhythm was in fact the cause of the Universe...

That marvellous « frequency » was what people called « GOD ».

But *Swami* had and still has many other things to show me, to show us...

At other times, as I was walking slowly, peacefully in the *Ashram*, I had the impression of being like a source of love. Each step that I took seemed to bring me closer to my Ultimate Goal, trusting that everything was perfect. And I felt Love radiating from my heart and from my hands, knowing deeply that all was well and that all will <u>always</u> be well, <u>as long</u> as I kept the vision and the thought of God and his incredible Love for me...

When some months later, having returned to France, I heard « *Ouverture* », the first song in the new album of Etienne Daho[1] I was staggered by the precision with which he described this state so simple and so beautiful that I had experienced in the *Ashram*...

---

[1] From the album « Corps et Armes »

He said :
> *Go towards your destiny*
> *Love within your hands*
> *Walking peacefully.*
> *Carry deep within,*
> *The torch of intuition,*
> *Adventure pure and beautiful.*
> *The one that reveals us,*
> *Superb and Childlike,*
> *In the depths of the Soul...*

These words described so perfectly and so precisely the state that Saï Baba had enabled me to contact that I wept with joy.

This state in which <u>I know</u> that, everything being already achieved, we do not have to worry about anything...

We have only to move forward, peaceful and trusting, and to keep in us this image of God who reveals us to ourselves, superb and childlike, as this inspired singer says so well.

And during this last visit where *Swami* had been again even nearer to me, He gave me a Grace which, although subtle, may be the greatest that He ever given me.

I was walking alone, that morning, in the streets of the <u>Ashram</u>. It was 4 in the morning and the birds were starting to wake up in the trees. I was wrapped up in my unbleached wool blanket...

I had just passed beside the residence of *Swami*, when suddenly, a thought came forcefully upon me:
> -« *Patrice, you really are a good person. Fundamentally you are beautiful... You are a beautiful Soul... You are « Loveable »...* »

And I think that, for the first time, I knew it was true!

And yet I had repeated this kind of sentence over and over hundreds of times...

However, for the first time, thanks to the incredible love that Saï Baba gave me and thanks to my trustful surrender to this Divine Incarnation, I <u>knew</u> at the bottom of my heart that it was the truth !

« Yes, I am a good person... I am fundamentally someone good and Lovable... »

And in a this subtle way, *Swami* again gave me a marvellous gift.

An **inestimable** gift...

And Life goes on...

And as it fulfils me unceasingly with its miracles which I perceive more and more each day, it seems to me more and more that the message of God **really** deserves to be heard, integrated and transmitted...

And my experience shows me each day that once more, Jesus was right when he said :

-« Verily I say unto you, There is no man that hath left house, or brethren, or sisters, or father, or mother, or wife, or children, or lands, for my sake, and the gospel's, But he shall receive an hundredfold now in this time, houses, and brethren, and sisters, and mothers, and children, and lands, with persecutions; and in the world to come eternal life..»[1]

This notion of « persecutions » could frighten you, but remember what Jesus told his disciples[2], the <u>integration</u> of the Divine word « takes us » out of the world and expose us to the disapproval of the « rest of the world ». Nevertheless, by doing so, you do not submit to the laws of the world but to the law of

---

[1] Mark 10:29-30
[2] John 15:19 « If ye were of the world, the world would love his own: but because ye are not of the world, but I have chosen you out of the world, therefore the world hateth you.»

God… And I think that this option is by far the best and the only one worth considering…

To this day, having lived all of these experiences, I know that actually, I have NOTHING to worry about.

But why would I worry ?

Since I have God !

When one NEEDS nothing, one can have EVERYTHING !

And as Saï Baba so rightly says:

 « *Why fear when I am here… , Be happy, very happy… *»

FINAL
Love is the key...

So there you are, I think I have now shared with you of all that seemed necessary to tell you... for the moment...

May be later, in the future, I will again feel this pressing need to take up my pen to entertain you with other subjects, other dimensions...

I do not claim to offer all the solutions.

It is clear for me that my path has brought a great amount to me.

It is clear also that I did not develop all these experiences from one day to the next.

I followed steps, a process... And I know that this process is natural and that many people go through it.

I just hope that my experiences, my achievements will also guide you to the discovery of this marvellous being that might be still asleep into you...

The path is not always easy, but the Light which it illuminates it is marvellous...

And even if it is not easy, it really seems to me that this path is worth travelling..

I hope that this book will make you want to mobilize ALL of your being so that you too discover this splendid part of YOU which is present in everyone one of US.

I hope that you too will want to go further on this splendid path ... because it has no end...

However, remember that until have realized **your UNITY with God**, you are **Co-creators with Him** of your reality. And as *Swami* demonstrated so well, the Universe, or rather « Your universe », becomes for you what you believe it is. And through your thoughts, your words and your actions, you define

It and you define **You yourself**. So do not forget that there are no neutral thoughts and see bigger, see ever larger, more beautiful, softer... and allow yourself to become what you really are.

For my part, the path is not completed yet, far from it...

And I am not yet perfect ...(or rather, I should say that I am not yet totally aware of my perfection)... And if my path seems surprising to you, « Let he who is without sin cast the first stone... »

To this day, I am still sometimes filled with doubts.

And that is good, because each doubt that comes to my mind gives me the opportunity to make a choice. Each doubt gives me the opportunity to decide what I want to experience and to decide what I want to be true for me. It gives me the opportunity to decide what I want to be and to experience it.

And through my choices, I define myself and discover myself continuously...

And if God presents me with a difficult experience, I can understand that it is a gift of Grace so I can make a different choice than what I have always made in the past.... Indeed, how can I know if I have escaped from a pattern if God does give me the chance to « fall back » into it....

And if God presents me with an experience which I do not understand, I choose to trust Him and not to resist it... Because **knowing** that God loves me, I **know** that if He presents it to me, it is for my greater good *(even if I am not always able to understand why it is so !)* and also so that I can grow still closer to Him.

In these cases, I try to remind me that in any tunnel, there is an entrance... and an exit... And I wait for it in trust...

And if sometimes the experiences seem really painful, very quickly, I decide to do something about the situation. I sit down somewhere, wherever I may be, and I close my eyes. And then, within, I conscientiously prepare a small gift package for Him. I wrap up all these problems which He has put in my path… and I give them back to him… :

-« Here, look, this is for You! This problem is not my problem any more … I return it to you… Take it back and deal with it please…»

And the moment I return my problems to him, I KNOW that He has taken them… because, **INSTANTLY**, I feel lighter and happier…

I just try not to take them back again afterwards !...

And remember: If you could not resolve your problems by yourselves, what do you have to lose by trying to have them resolved by this energy ? Nothing… You really have **NOTHING** to lose…

In fact, you have **EVERYTHING** to gain!...

So, ask Him for help and… know that you already have received it !

For my part, each day, I give thanks to Him for the good fortune I have to be alive, for the luck I have to be living everything that I live and for all the small and great « miracles » that He perpetually manifests in my life…

And to remain aware of His Divine Presence, I try to recall that each event of my life is a gift from God… That each food that I eat, that each meal that I have is like a Sacrament …

Each day, I learn more and more to see Him and to recognize Him in any thing and in every one.

And also, I try more and more not to define, not to set hard anything by my thoughts, not to « know » anything.

And I know this is the right way, because somehow, if I say « *I know* », I am, by my words or my thoughts « limiting » and restricting the Universe.

And this is something I don't wish to do anymore. I did it too much in the past even though, there again, it was good and perfect.

A truth that I hold about the Universe prevents it from being what It really is.

A truth that I hold about a person prevents him from being what he really is.

A truth that I hold about myself prevents me from being what I really am.

Because He and I are ONE, even if up till now I have not had the chance to experience it yet as a permanent state...

The Universe is the possible of all the possibilities.

And if I really want to get closer to Him and experience Him, I must leave Him free, totally free... just as He leaves me free in His immense love for me...

Today, I just know where I am.

And when I consider where I was nearly 21 years ago, it is clear that I have come a very long way,... even if I still have a long way to go...

As far as the H.I.V, I also think that up to now, because of the criteria they use, no doctor will want to recognize that I am healed... So, what must I do?

Wait until I am 80 years old to start to talk about my experiences?

Be sorry for my lot and resign myself?

I don't think so. I would not help myself at all like this, and in any case, I have no desire to!

I know now <u>with certainty</u> that if I am still alive today, it is thanks to my « work » on myself, thanks to Love and especially Thanks to God...

And I hope that my experience will be able to help you and to inspire you for your healing or your transformation.

God has proved to me His Love, his power, his gentleness, and if by chance I were to die tomorrow *(just as you could, too !)*, I know where I will go once my path on Earth is accomplished.

I know that like a Champagne bubble bursting to the surface, I will melt into Him, my beginning and my end.

But for the moment, I think that I have still something to do here.

May be only to be there to hold out a hand and to welcome you into the light when, dazzled and blinded by such Splendour, you feel lost in this new world which is opening up for you. This world which has rules that perhaps you do not recognize yet.

And so if it happens that, like the majority of people on Earth, I will leave one day, I know that it will be <u>at the right time</u> for me and those around me, even if they do not realise it, at least not straight away ! They will simply have to deal with their attachments to the transitory illusion which was the body that I lived in… The vehicle that God gave me so that he could experience Himself through Me and express through Me, his/her beloved son, his Love, his Power and his Glory…

However, I made, many years ago, the choice of Life, the choice of Love, the choice of God *(and in fact, all that is the same thing…)* and I will <u>NEVER</u> regret it.

So you too, make the choice of Life.

Make the choice of Love.

Make the choice of God.

Put your faith in what is TRUE and REAL. Not in the illusion of the physical world. Not in what is temporary and illusory.

And you will live happy..., beyond the circumstances which the world presents.

Learn also to love always more, always better...

Love is the key which opens all doors... Only, we have locked it up inside of us, by distancing ourselves from our true nature, by distancing ourselves from each other and by maintaining thoughts or envy, desire, lack, jealousy, judgement, doubt, guilt, lies, fear...

However, since nothing can exist without the grace of God, know that all is well and do not feel guilty for what you were... Simply decide to change and... do it !

All our experiences are given to us by Him to enable us to learn. So, let us learn how to eliminate our doubts, our fears, our perceptions of lack, our jealousies, our guilt feelings, our judgments, by giving them to God and let our hearts unfold always more.

Let us learn to develop gratitude for everything that we have.

Let us learn how to find this Love within us which will open all doors for us...

Let us immerse ourselves in it and let us again become Love.

Let us become instruments of Love, instruments of God, allowing Him to express through us His Splendour and His Glory.

Let us learn how to become increasingly more gentle, more patient, more tolerant, simpler, truer, more loving and let us again become what we always were.

The happiness we will feel then will fill us all to the highest degree.

Let us learn to align our thoughts, our words and our actions. Indeed, we often think one thing, say another and with our actions show still another... Let us simply recognize this process and learn how to transform it.

Let us choose to transform ourselves right now and to watch our thoughts, words and actions....

Love is the base of Life... Love is life itself

And if sometimes, it seems difficult for you, because of your external circumstances, to connect yourself to love, remember there exists in the deepest part of us all a source of inexhaustible love always available... a source that some name... God.

Saï Baba says it marvellously :
-« You become what you think...
Think dust...and dust you will be.
Think God...and God you will be. »

I think you know now what remains for you to do...

God is Love and God loves us...

Whoever we are,.... Wherever we are,... whatever we do...

So, surrender to Him and BE HAPPY !...

May his Love enlighten and accompany you as It has always done...

I wish you all, each and every one of you, a wonderful life in the realization of your Divine nature and I thank you for giving me the opportunity to share with you.

May the Great Being bless you and fill you with His Grace...

And may you <u>always</u> have the perception and the experience of being Loved.

Sincerely.
Patrice

And Since...

To reassure you, as I often say to some of my readers, I am « still alive » and more and more aware that I am not, as is the case with you too, this physical form with which I used to identify myself.

The small group of inventors metamorphosed itself into a company which deals with improving the quality of sound and is growing little by little, although still in the beginning stages.

In this respect, a « baby » will become, sooner or later, an « adult ». It is in the order of things...

And in the same way, a being that was « asleep and unaware of his creative nature » will also certainly become a being « Awakened or aware of his Essential Nature »

I must also recognize that I am **extremely** grateful towards « God » or « Life » for being able to present and share my experiences, by means of, amongst other things, classes and workshops in more and more countries round the world !

In this respect, a wonderful lady, Lise, contacted me one day from Quebec to tell me my book had meant a lot to her and told me over the phone *« What a shame we do not have people like you over here ! »*

Actually, the « Great Being », who created us all « in his image » has placed within us **ALL** the same spiritual essence, even though the « fragrance » of that essence is each time « different » and adapted to those who search to perceive it. Therefore, we **ALL** have something to offer to the world in a different « form » ...

This is how I offered to come to Quebec. I did it « joyfully » as I had, for many years, wished to visit this superb country.

This first contact with Quebec finally turned out to be a « tour » of lectures round all of French Quebec in 2005 !

In another situation, I received during one of my many visits to Tahiti a very beautiful Tahitian name « *Manu Tahi Ori* »

An « *Orero* », the equivalent of a « baptiser » in the Tahitian society, told me, when he came to my lecture : « *You, you are Manu Tahi Ori* ».

I told him that the name seemed beautiful but that I wanted to know what it meant.

He explained to me that « *Manu* » meant « *Bird* » in Tahitian, as it seems my arms were moving a lot during that lecture !

Then, he explained that « *Tahi* » meant « *Tall* » (I am 6'7½") or « *First* » and that « *Ori* » meant « *Traveller* » !

This superb Tahitian surname is in fact, quite a good synopsis of myself, as I had, at the time, already taught in French Polynesia, in New Caledonia, in Guadeloupe, in Reunion island, in Martinique, in Australia, in Quebec, and in the United States.

And as they say so beautifully in the dialect language of Reunion Island and as I often quote in my lectures and classes : « Semin Grand-Bois *(a local village),* ça lé long. Ti pas, ti pas, nous va river... » which means : « The path to our goals might be long, but each step taken get us closer to it »

It is obvious that I have not yet become what I know I can be, but as I look back at the path I have taken for 20 years, I see that I already have achieved « a part of the road » and that, as you **ALL** are, I am on my way towards something beautiful, simple and sweet...

I still have, of course, many desires that I know I will fulfil when the time is ripe and I feel ready to travel to transmit this message...wherever people wish, if it is also my own wish at the time.

Remember that, to be « HAPPY », it is finally quite « SIMPLE ».

Do what makes you « HAPPY » and stop doing what makes you « UNHAPPY »...

It is finally very « SIMPLE ».

Even though it is not always « EASY », I recognise that !

And I am also starting to realize that « HE » might have even more to give me if I stopped defining myself arbitrarily ahead of time !

I have in fact realized that if I ask « HIM » for something I want, « HE » gives it to me.

So now, I wonder:

« But what would « HE » give me if I did not ask for anything ? »

Wait and SEE !

I therefore allow myself more and more to be surprised by life !

So, be happy, if you choose to be !

I wish you all the wonderful things that you desire, that you can CONCEIVE OF, and **mostly**, that you know you DESERVE !

There is, I believe, a **PERFECTION**. It exists sometimes beyond my **PERCEPTION,** in what ever form it might take !

> *May the Great Being bless you all and shower you with his grace...*
>
> *And may you always have the perception and the experience of being loved and of being lovable.*

Sincerely.
Patrice-Manu Tahi Ori

If you wish to receive information to take part
in a workshop given by Patrice MORCHAIN
or to organize a workshop or a conference
in your area, contact :

HELYOGOS
21 Rue Jean Jaurès
59980 BERTRY
Téléphone : + 33 327 76 13 12/ +336 10 02 87 30
Or www.helyogos.com

**And to know more about Lee Pascoe
and her wonderful workshops :**
www.leepascoe.com

www.ingramcontent.com/pod-product-compliance
Lightning Source LLC
Chambersburg PA
CBHW070716160426
43192CB00009B/1203